THE ARMS TRADE
with the THIRD WORLD

The Arms Trade
with the Third World
revised and abridged edition

**Stockholm International
Peace Research Institute**

Holmes & Meier Publishers, Inc.

New York

Published in the United States of America 1975 by
Holmes & Meier Publishers, Inc.
101 Fifth Avenue, New York, New York 10003

First published by Penguin Books Ltd.
Harmondsworth, Middlesex, England

Library of Congress Cataloging in Publication Data

Stockholm International Peace Research Institute.
  The arms trade with the Third World.

  Abridged version of the 1971 work with the addition
of more recent material. This ed. prepared and edited
by J. Stares.
  Bibliography: p.
  Includes index.
  1. Munitions. 2. Firearms industry and trade.
I. Title.
HD9743.A2S76 1975b   327'.174   75-15746
ISBN 0-8419-0213-5

Printed in the United States of America

Contents

Preface

The geographical spread of the arms race is one important issue in the global search for peace and self-determination. Increasing quantities of resources in developing countries are devoted to the procurement of weapons from abroad and nearly all the wars which have taken place over the past twenty-five years have been fought in the poorer parts of the world. The weapons used in these wars have come almost entirely from the industrialized nations of the Northern Hemisphere. Moreover, in contrast to the interwar period, when the build-up of armaments was often attributed to the greed of private arms manufacturers, today the export of weapons is controlled by governments. So a study of the arms trade is crucial not merely because it is the route by which stocks of weapons in the Third World are built up, but also because it is one means by which the competition between rich countries is extended throughout the world and absorbs local disputes and wars.

The present book is an abridged version of a major study – *The Arms Trade with the Third World* – published by the Stockholm International Peace Research Institute in November 1971. Since the completion of the original study, SIPRI has continued its work on the arms trade, and the results of this work are published each year in the SIPRI Yearbooks. This present book has drawn extensively on this more recent material, and thus covers the period 1950 to 1972.

The book is organized in four parts. Part One presents the main conclusions and summarizes some of the more detailed material presented in the rest of the book. Part Two is an account of the factors governing the arms supply policies of the main supplying countries – the United States, the Soviet Union, the United Kingdom, France and China – which account for more than 90 per cent of major weapons exports to the Third World. (Minor arms suppliers such as Italy, Canada, the Federal Republic of Germany, Japan, Sweden and Switzerland are not discussed in detail.) The third part is a study of the factors governing the arms import policies of Third World countries in the Far East, South Asia, the Middle East, Africa and Latin America. This part also includes an account of indigenous defence production in Third World countries. Part Four is an assessment of possible proposals for regulating the trade in arms.

The original SIPRI study, *The Arms Trade with the Third World*, was prepared by Frank Blackaby, Prvoslav Davinić, Eva Grenbäck, Mary Kaldor and Signe Landgren-Bäckström. The present book was prepared and edited by John Stares, a member of the SIPRI research staff, with the cooperation of the authors of the original study.

March 1973   *Frank Barnaby*
                                                    Director of SIPRI

Part One

General Features of the Arms Trade

1 General Survey

The arms trade with Third World countries is only one strand in the multiple web of international relationships which connect rich or more powerful with poor and less powerful countries. Other strands include economic aid, industrial investment, trade in strategic and other materials and, indeed, direct military intervention. The trade in arms functions as one part of the whole international system and can be understood only within this general context.

As the structure of world power has changed, so, too, has the pattern of the arms trade. The two major systems to arise since the Second World War, dominated by the United States and the Soviet Union, have both competed and avoided collisions. Within the Western system itself lesser powers have also competed with one another: for instance, the old colonial powers, France especially, have followed policies which are partly complementary and partly in conflict with those of the United States. Similarly, the conflict between the Soviet Union and China has had its effect on the relationships of both with the Third World. On the margins of the two systems, small industrialized nations have tried to minimize their involvement in the competition between the two dominant great powers.

As the colonial empires disappeared and new countries came into being, so the pattern of arms trading has changed. In the years immediately after the Second World War these new countries were largely dependent on the West, but the new controlling groups which came to power in these countries have often found that their interests were best served by reducing this dependence. This has led some of them to turn to the socialist countries for support. Competition between the two major systems has thus been extended to the Third World and the individual and particular problems of the new nations have often been absorbed into, and become part of, the confrontation between them.

The role of the arms trade in this changing international system has been determined by three main factors. First, as the cost of developing and producing more complex weapon systems has increased, production has become concentrated in a few rich countries. Of the supply of major weapons – naval vessels, aircraft, missiles and armoured fighting vehicles – to Third World countries during the period 1950–72, an average of 86 per cent came from just four countries – the United States, the Soviet Union, Britain and France.

Secondly, the supply of weapons is largely controlled by governments. All military exports require government permission, and governments generally exert control over the defence industries and bear a large share of the responsibility for organizing and promoting the export of weapons. Less than 5 per cent of the arms trade is in the hands of private dealers and only a minute proportion of these dealers operate without government approval.

Thirdly, the two great powers, the United States and the Soviet Union, generally supply weapons free of charge or at subsidized prices and low interest rates.

In consequence, Third World countries wishing to buy or even produce weapons more sophisticated than rifles, machine-guns or mortars are dependent on the goodwill of the governments of a few industrialized countries. In particular, countries with scarce foreign-exchange resources are dependent on the goodwill of the two great powers.

THE FLOW OF WEAPONS

It is useful to start the discussion of the arms trade with the Third World with some orders of magnitude in mind – the size of the total trade and its rate of growth and geographical pattern – and for this some statistical framework is necessary. The published trade figures are inadequate: only a few countries include arms transactions in their statistics, and these are rarely comprehensive.

Official government estimates of the sale or gift of weapons are incomplete or non-existent.

The approach in this study has been to construct estimates of arms-trade flows from a register of individual transactions, each transaction being given a monetary value. These values, however, do not necessarily correspond to the actual prices paid, which can vary considerably according to differing pricing methods, the lengths of production series and the terms of each transaction. In order to provide some measures of the quantity of resources transferred, comparable values for comparable items of equipment were estimated, based on actual prices as well as such criteria as weight, speed, role and date of production. The final values are roughly comparable to 1968 prices paid for Western weapons in purely commercial transactions. As a consequence, the values of Soviet weapons are generally higher than their quoted prices. This system of valuation also allows for product improvement to be taken into account – the fact that an F-4 Phantom fighter, for example, incorporates a more advanced technology than an F-86 Sabre fighter – and also allows for the depreciation of second-hand items.

The figures given cover only the flows of *major weapons*, that is, aircraft, naval vessels, armoured fighting vehicles and missiles. The term 'weapon' is used to cover any type of military equipment. *Small arms* – rifles, sub-machine-guns or pistols – as well as the heavier weapons such as mortars, artillery pieces and anti-aircraft guns, are, however, not included because information about the transfers of these weapons is fragmentary and unreliable. The figures further include spares and equipment for aircraft and launching and other related equipment for missiles, but not the entire range of support equipment necessary to operate a particular weapons system. As shown in Table 1, the figures for major weapons cover just under half the total trade in military equipment.

The area covered, and referred to in this study as the Third World, consists of Africa (including South Africa), Latin America and Asia excluding the Soviet Union, China and Japan. The inclusion and exclusion of some of these countries is de-

Table 1 Total arms exports, exports to Third World countries and exports of major weapons
US $ mn

	A To all destinations	B To Third World countries	B as a percentage of A[b]	C Major weapon exports to Third World countries	C as a percentage of B[b]
USA average 1962–8	2,500	930	35	285	30
USSR average 1962–8	[2,000]	[800]	40	370	45
UK average 1964–8	400	[200]	50	115	60
France average 1965–8	470	[200]	40	70	35
Italy 1967	[75]	40	50	10	25
FR Germany 1967	75	20	25	10	50
Sweden average 1965–9	30	5	15	–	0
Switzerland average 1967–8	30	5	15	–	0
Canada average 1965–8	[80][a]	[30]	40	20	70
Other	[180]	[110]	60	55	50
Total	5,840	2,340	40	935	40

[a] This figure does not include Canadian defence exports to the USA, which average $300 million a year.
[b] Figures rounded to nearest 5.
Source: SIPRI worksheets and official government estimates.

batable, but China is excluded because it no longer imports weapons and now plays a more significant role as a supplier of weapons. South Africa and Portugal are included since the story of arms supplies to these countries is an important part of the story of arms supplies to Africa as a whole, as well as being of intrinsic interest. Greece and Turkey are included because of their importance in the US military-aid programme. Apart from these last two countries, the flow of weapons within the two major blocs – NATO and the Warsaw Pact – and between developed countries in general is not included in this study, as the problems raised by the trade in weapons between industrialized countries are rather different – for example, co-production, or specialization and standardization within the blocs.

The figures cover all transfers of weapons – whether as part of a military-aid programme or on the basis of a commercial transaction – to armed forces under independent control. Where a supplying country has forces in another country, the weapons supplies to those forces are not included. This is an important point to bear in mind when considering, for example, the relative importance of the United States and the Soviet Union as suppliers. In Viet-Nam, the United States has been intervening directly, and the cost of its intervention – which was of the order of $ 25 billion a year in 1968 and 1969 – is still very much in excess of the total value of arms supplies to all Third World countries together. The Soviet Union, on the other hand, has merely been supplying arms to North Viet-Nam. Estimates of the value of these Soviet supplies are included in the arms trade figures, while the cost of the US intervention is not included. It would thus be misleading to take arms supplies as in any way a total measure of the involvement of supplying countries in military affairs outside their borders.

Main trends

The increase in the flow of major weapons in the past fifteen to twenty years has been substantial: in volume, it was more than three times greater in the second half of the 1960s than in the first half of the 1950s. The rate of growth from 1950 to 1972 has been about 10 per cent per year with Viet-Nam included, and about 8 per cent per year excluding Viet-Nam. But it has not been a steady rate. There was a peak, mainly in Western supplies, in 1958, when the United States was consolidating the Western military alliances in the Middle East and in the Far East through the provision of extensive military aid, and when certain countries, such as India, were reacting to the arming of their neighbours. In addition, the Soviet Union had entered the market and was becoming an important supplier. In the early 1960s, the total fell somewhat, but it began to rise again from 1964 onwards.

Behind this rise lies an increase in the sophistication of the weapons supplied to Third World countries. The term *sophisticated weapons* is used to refer to those which incorporate a relatively advanced technology. Because fewer units may be required to fulfil a particular military role, technical advance has made for an increase in military efficiency, but it has also, obviously, meant an enormous increase in manufacturing costs. So it is that, for example, there has been a levelling-off in the crude numbers of combat aircraft supplied, but at the same time there has been a steady increase in their value. Combat aircraft account for a major share of the total flow of arms.

There has also been an increase in the quantity of less expensive major weapons supplied to Third World countries. Mounting guerilla warfare has led to a corresponding increase in the supply of appropriate weapons, armed trainers, patrol boats, helicopters, hovercraft and so on. These are called *counter-insurgency* (*COIN*) *weapons*. Because they are less expensive, and because many of them are small arms, they do not make a significant impact on the total flow.

THE MAIN SUPPLIERS OF ARMS

Over the past twenty years, the United States has been the dominant supplier of major weapons to Third World countries, followed by the Soviet Union. Together these two countries have accounted for about two thirds of total arms deliveries. The two next most important suppliers, Britain and France, have together been responsible for more than 20 per cent of total deliveries.

Chart 1. Exports of major weapons to Third World areas (Viet-Nam excluded): four main suppliers

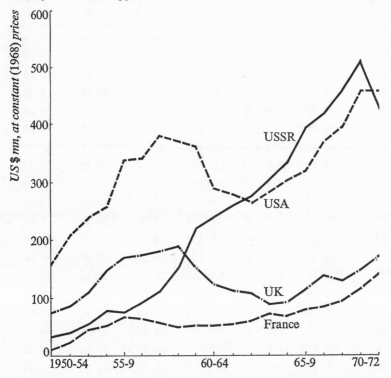

five-year moving averages

The pattern of arms supplies has changed considerably over this period. The most important change has been the decline of the United States', and an increase in the Soviet Union's, share of the major weapons market. In the first half of the fifties, the United States alone was supplying half the total, while the Soviet Union did not supply arms at all to countries outside the socialist camp. Even in the second half of the fifties, the United States still

Table 2 Values of imports of major weapons by Third World countries: by region, 1950–72[a]

	Far East, excl. Viet-Nam		South Asia		Middle East		North Africa[b]		Sub-Saharan Africa		South Africa	
	A	B	A	B	A	B	A	B	A	B	A	B
1950	100	–	30	–	30	–	–	–	*	–	5	–
1951	160	–	20	–	20	–	–	–	5	–	*	–
1952	60	120	10	40	10	40	–	–	5	10	10	10
1953	170	140	70	50	60	60	–	–	10	10	10	10
1954	120	130	80	70	70	110	–	–	10	10	10	20
1955	180	150	80	100	130	150	–	–	10	5	10	20
1956	140	190	90	150	270	180	20	–	*	5	40	20
1957	160	220	180	160	230	200	*	–	*	10	10	20
1958	330	250	330	170	190	190	*	5	5	10	10	20
1959	300	250	110	190	180	160	5	5	30	20	10	10
1960	320	260	160	180	90	170	5	10	20	20	*	10
1961	130	230	190	140	130	170	10	10	30	30	5	20
1962	220	220	120	130	250	180	20	10	30	30	10	20
1963	190	190	130	120	230	210	20	20	30	40	80	50
1964	240	210	60	140	200	230	10	30	40	50	20	60
1965	170	190	80	140	260	300	40	40	60	50	120	60
1966	250	170	280	190	210	380	60	40	80	50	50	50
1967	120	160	170	200	590	460	60	50	40	50	40	50
1968	70	150	350	210	610	560	30	50	20	40	20	40
1969	160	150	140	200	640	730	40	50	30	40	40	40
1970	140	130	110	200	710	680	60	60	50	40	50	30
1971	210		280		910		80		70		50	
1972	60		130		550		110		40		5	
Total	**4,020**		**3,200**		**6,550**		**580**		**630**		**610**	

[a] Figures rounded to nearest 10, except for figures under 10 which are rounded to nearest 5. Items may not add to totals because of rounding.

[b] Five-year moving averages are calculated from the year arms imports began.

* = less than $2·5 million.

US $ mn, at constant (1968) prices. A = yearly figures, B = five-year moving averages

Central America		South America		Greece and Turkey		Total (excl. Viet-Nam)		Viet-Nam, North and South		Total	
A	B	A	B	A	B	A	B	A	B	A	B
5	–	40	–	10	–	220	–	–	–	220	–
*	–	50	–	20	–	270	–	–	–	270	–
20	10	20	60	70	70	210	350	–	–	210	350
10	10	60	80	140	80	520	420	–	–	520	430
10	10	110	80	110	90	510	520	10	–	520	530
10	10	140	100	50	100	610	630	10	–	620	640
10	10	90	110	110	130	770	790	10	10	780	800
5	10	90	90	70	130	760	840	5	10	760	860
10	10	110	90	330	140	1,310	890	40	20	1,350	910
10	30	30	100	90	130	770	890	5	30	770	920
30	60	120	90	110	120	860	920	20	50	880	970
90	60	140	80	30	70	760	820	90	50	850	870
150	60	50	70	20	70	890	810	100	60	980	870
20	60	40	60	100	70	840	820	40	70	870	890
20	40	20	50	70	90	690	890	50	30	740	970
10	10	50	50	150	100	930	950	50	120	980	1,070
10	10	70	60	80	90	1,100	1,030	160	170	1,260	1,200
10	5	60	80	80	100	1,180	1,150	300	190	1,480	1,350
*	5	90	80	70	80	1,250	1,220	280	230	1,530	1,450
*	10	100	100	130	80	1,300	1,360	170	250	1,470	1,610
5	10	90	110	20	90	1,240	1,360	250	330	1,500	1,700
30		130		90		1,830		260		2,090	
20		140		130		1,180		710		1,890	
480		1,870		2,070		20,020		2,540		22,450	

Source: SIPRI worksheets of arms transfers 1950–72.

accounted for 40 per cent of the total. But from then on, its share in the total fell, and the actual volume of US supplies, excluding Viet-Nam, was only marginally higher in the second' half of the sixties than in the second half of the fifties. The main reason for this was the increased emphasis on guerilla warfare. While there was a levelling-off of supplies of sophisticated weapons, there was an increase in the quantity of COIN weapons supplied, and there was a big increase in supplies to countries involved in guerilla warfare, such as Thailand, Laos and Viet-Nam. A new rise in US supplies, which occurred around 1970, is largely explained by the delivery of sophisticated weapons to Israel.

Until 1970, the Soviet Union's major weapon supplies were rising very fast. The main increase occurred after 1955, when it began to supply arms to the Middle East, and since then the number of Third World countries which have received major weapons from the Soviet Union has reached a total of thirty-one. By the second half of the sixties, the Soviet Union was supplying more major weapons to Third World countries than was the United States. The peak came in 1967, when the Soviet Union replaced the very heavy Arab losses of the June War, but during 1968 and 1969 Soviet major weapon supplies declined, mainly because of the reduced requirement in North Viet-Nam after the United States ceased the bombing of that country in 1968. From 1970 onwards, there has been a new rise, but Soviet major weapons supplies have not since reached the 1967 level.

Britain was still an important supplier of major weapons in the 1950s, but was much less important in the sixties, by which time the United States and the Soviet Union had replaced it as the main supplier to many of its traditional markets in the previously dependent territories in Asia and the Middle East. In particular, there was a rapid decline in the export of military aircraft in the late fifties and early sixties, which was at least in part the result of difficulties in the aircraft industry. Britain was, however, much more successful in selling naval vessels, which have always accounted for a larger share of arms exports in Britain than in other countries.

France, on the other hand, although also an ex-colonial power, has increased its share of the market throughout the period. From an average of $17 million during 1950–54, major arms supplies rose to an average of $145 million in the five-year period 1968–72. France has taken advantage of opportunities created by reluctance on the part of the other supplying countries: a large proportion of its arms supplies went to South Africa after the British embargo of 1964; it made its entry into the Latin American market when the United States was discouraging Latin American purchases of sophisticated weapons; and it sold weapons to Pakistan after the US embargo of 1965.

Since the mid-fifties, there has been an increasing number of suppliers as more developed countries, for example the Federal Republic of Germany, Italy and Japan, have established arms industries. But the share of these countries in the total is small, because their exports consist mainly of inexpensive or second-hand items, while exports from the four main suppliers have a more sophisticated content.

Factors influencing the supply

Since the Second World War, the trade in weapons has been supervised by governments. All exports of military equipment require a licence issued by the government and, in most countries, licences have to be vetted by several ministries or departments. Important deals are often considered at the highest levels of administration. Although there are a few gaps in the system of national control – for example, some countries do not insist on end-use certificates to prevent the sale or gift of weapons to third countries, and only a few countries require government permission for the sale of production licences overseas – such gaps could easily be filled, if desired. It is therefore reasonable to assume that each arms transaction reflects a decision on the part of the government of the supplying country, and that the overall pattern of arms supplies reflects a government policy towards the arms trade.

Broadly speaking, it is possible to distinguish three main patterns of supply, here called *hegemonic, industrial* and *restrictive.*

Table 3 Values of exports of major weapons to regions listed in Table 2: by supplier, 1950–72[a]

	USA		USSR		UK		France		Canada		China	
	A	B	A	B	A	B	A	B	A	B	A	B
1950	50	–	20	–	70	–	*	–	20	–	40	–
1951	130	–	30	–	30	–	*	–	5	–	40	–
1952	130	160	20	40	40	80	*	20	*	10	–	20
1953	210	200	120	40	120	90	30	20	*	10	10	10
1954	290	230	*	50	120	110	50	50	20	20	–	*
1955	250	260	50	80	130	140	40	60	20	30	–	5
1956	270	340	80	80	140	170	120	70	80	30	–	20
1957	240	340	160	100	190	170	50	70	30	40	40	30
1958	630	380	120	110	260	180	100	70	5	30	80	30
1959	300	370	80	150	140	190	40	50	50	20	60	30
1960	470	370	110	220	170	160	20	50	10	10	10	30
1961	230	300	280	240	180	120	30	50	10	30	–	10
1962	200	280	510	260	50	110	70	60	–	30	–	*
1963	280	270	210	280	80	110	110	70	100	40	–	*
1964	250	290	180	300	80	90	90	80	30	40	*	5
1965	420	300	200	340	140	100	50	70	40	40	5	10
1966	310	310	400	400	120	120	70	80	5	20	30	10
1967	270	370	680	420	60	140	50	80	5	20	10	10
1968	320	390	510	460	180	130	140	100	20	10	5	10
1969	570	450	300	500	200	150	110	110	10	20	–	10
1970	510	460	420	430	100	170	120	150	20	20	5	20
1971	610	*	620		210		160		40		40	
1972	270		300		180		200		20		60	
Total	7,220		5,390		2,980		1,640		540		430	

[a] Figures rounded to nearest 10, except for figures under 10 which are rounded to nearest 5. Items may not add to totals because of rounding.

[b] Five-year moving averages are calculated from the year arms exports began.

* = less than $2·5 million.

US $ mn, at constant (1968) prices. A = yearly figures, B = five-year moving averages

FR Germany[b]		Italy		Czecho-slovakia[b]		Nether-lands		Japan		Sweden		All other[b]		Total (excl. Viet-Nam)	
A	B	A	B	A	B	A	B	A	B	A	B	A	B	A	B
–	–	5	–	–	–	20	–	–	–	*	–	–	–	220	–
–	–	30	–	–	–	10	–	–	–	*	–	–	–	270	–
–	–	–	10	–	–	5	10	–	–	10	5	–	–	210	350
*	–	*	5	–	–	*	20	*	–	5	5	20	–	520	420
5	–	*	5	–	–	*	10	20	–	5	5	*	–	510	520
10	5	*	10	30	–	60	10	–	5	5	5	5	5	610	630
5	5	20	10	40	–	*	10	5	10	5	10	5	10	770	790
*	10	20	10	5	30	*	10	5	5	–	10	5	10	760	840
10	10	20	20	20	30	–	*	10	5	30	5	30	10	1,310	890
20	10	*	10	40	20	5	*	*	5	*	5	30	10	770	890
20	20	10	5	30	20	*	5	*	10	*	5	5	20	860	920
20	20	–	5	5	20	*	5	10	10	*	*	*	10	760	820
5	20	*	5	5	10	10	5	20	10	–	*	10	5	890	810
10	10	10	5	10	5	10	10	20	10	–	*	*	10	840	820
30	30	10	5	5	5	5	10	10	10	–	*	*	20	690	890
10	30	5	10	*	5	10	5	10	20	–	*	20	30	930	950
100	30	10	10	5	5	–	5	10	10	*	*	60	30	1,100	1,030
20	30	10	20	5	5	–	5	30	10	–	*	40	40	1,180	1,150
10	30	30	20	5	5	–	5	10	10	–	*	10	30	1,250	1,220
10	20	40	30	*	5	20	10	*	10	*	*	60	30	1,300	1,360
20	30	30	40	*	5	5	10	–	5	–	*	10	30	1,240	1,360
40		50		5		20		*		–		50		1,830	
60		40		10		10		–		5		20		1,180	
420		350		230		210		170		60		385		20,020	

Source: SIPRI worksheets of arms transfers 1950–72.

Clearly, different countries have different policies, but each of them tends to be a mix of these patterns – a mix which, in turn, is reflected in the international position of the supplying country.

An international hegemonic system is one in which some countries dominate other, dependent, countries. The word describes a relationship rather than a policy objective. Used in this widest sense, hegemony covers both these cases and also those in which a larger country has the means to influence a smaller country in minor matters.

The supply of weapons from industrial to developing countries can be an element in a relationship of this kind. Arms supplies can be used to support a particular group in power or to prevent the emergence of an alternative group which might lead to dominance from elsewhere. Soviet supplies have been used to support anti-Western groups in power, and US arms supplies to support anti-communist governments. Further, arms supplies can be used to induce, or to try to prevent, particular actions. For example, the United States supplied weapons to South Korea in exchange for troops in South Viet-Nam, and the Federal Republic of Germany, at one time, supplied arms or military assistance only to countries which refused to recognize the German Democratic Republic.

The industrial pattern of supply occurs when it is important to maintain, in the supplying country, an advanced domestic defence industry and where this is made possible through the export of arms. If this is the *only* function of the arms trade then arms are supplied indiscriminately to any buyer who can afford them.

The characteristic feature of a restrictive supply is that arms are not supplied to countries where this may directly or indirectly involve the supplier in a local or international conflict. In contrast with an industrial pattern, it is one of restraint and may often operate by working against an industrial or hegemonic pattern.

Although to some extent they conflict, these patterns are not mutually exclusive. Any policy is the product of a number of decisions taken, perhaps, by different departments or individuals, or of a compromise between competing pressure groups. In attributing a policy to particular supplying countries, the pressures which exercise a predominant influence are described. This policy may not be explicit. Indeed, it may never have been formulated. It is inferred from the country's pattern of behaviour. The policies of the United States and the Soviet Union primarily represent hegemonic patterns of supply. This stems from their leading positions in the two major systems. Both countries can maintain very advanced defence industries without reliance on exports. Their mutual competition, which is extended to Third World conflicts, undermines the possibilities for restrictiveness. The Chinese pattern of arms supply might also be described as hegemonic or, perhaps more accurately, as anti-hegemonic. This arises from China's position outside the international hierarchy: its entry into the system can be facilitated by providing a viable alternative to the two great powers. Nevertheless, China's arms exports are small; its manufacturing capacity is barely sufficient to meet domestic requirements.

The arms supply policies of Britain and France are dominated by the industrial pattern. For such medium-range countries, an advanced domestic armaments base is considered necessary to ensure their independence both within and outside the major systems, and in maintaining such a base the export of arms often plays an essential role. There are elements of hegemony in the international positions of these countries, especially with respect to their former colonies, but the needs of the defence industry, particularly for Britain, have often impaired the function of the arms trade in maintaining hegemony.

Sweden and Switzerland have restrictive patterns of behaviour; their policies are based on the principle that no arms should be supplied to countries in conflict. This pattern arises from their position outside the East–West struggle, which could be compromised by involvement in local conflict.

The Federal Republic of Germany, Japan, Canada and Italy have, at least in part, restrictive policies towards the Third World. But as part of the Western defence system these policies do not apply to the major power blocs; they all prohibit the supply of arms to communist countries, whether engaged in conflict or not, and they all supply arms to the United States, despite the war in Viet-Nam. They recognize, however, that given the limitations on their resources, involvement in Third World conflicts could harm their commercial and political interests. In addition, together with Sweden and Switzerland, these countries tend to emphasize their independent international role by taking an active part in peace-making initiatives. The Federal Republic of Germany and Japan are also anxious to erase their historical image as 'warmongers'. These restrictive attitudes are reinforced by public opinion, which in many Western countries has tended to push in a restrictive direction.

A major determinant of policy is the size and structure of the defence industry and the planning of procurement. Of particular importance are the methods adopted to ensure full and stable employment. In almost all countries, productive capacity tends to exceed immediate defence requirements. That is to say, the plant, machinery and labour available for the production of weapons is, in any one period, greater than the government's demand during that period. This has traditionally been put down to the need to maintain, as a matter of public policy, considerable excess capacity in the defence industries so as to be able to expand supplies quickly in case of emergency. This is still true for certain types of equipment, chiefly ammunition. But with the rapid change in military technology, the increasing implausibility of a long conventional war in Europe and the fact that most armed forces, in industrialized countries, are kept in a state of readiness, the argument has lost some of its force.

However, other factors come into play with much the same effect. The most important of these is the rapid change in technology which has led to a lumpiness in government purchases. On the one hand, governments are anxious to replace obsolescent equipment as quickly as possible, on the other, continuous replacement has often proved too expensive because each new type of equipment incorporates a more complex and costly technology. Thus, governments tend to procure such items as aircraft, missiles and tanks in a two- or three-year period every ten years or so. This problem is exacerbated by the fact that the resources required to manufacture a complex weapon system vary from activity to activity throughout the long development and production cycle, so that it is virtually impossible to ensure that all the differing resources are employed all the time. In addition surplus capacity cannot be left idle. Income is insufficient to maintain skilled labour and other resources for use on future contracts. Skilled labour, temporarily released, may be lost forever. Thus the defence industry – labour management and their parliamentary spokesmen – represents an important political pressure group.

For most European countries exports are the ideal solution to this problem. For the United States and the Soviet Union, exports are too small in relation to total defence production to fill surplus capacity, but these countries can afford more expensive alternatives. They can increase defence spending when necessary. They can also devote sufficient research and development (R & D) resources and order weapons in sufficient numbers to reduce the generation gap. And they can also afford to employ surplus capacity on prestige items, such as space programmes.

For European countries, the main alternatives to exporting are international collaboration in weapons production and the production of related goods for the civilian market. In practice, international collaboration has not lessened the need to export. Although it has slowed down the growth of national development capacity, it has led to an overall increase in production capacity both because it has involved an increase in costs, through duplication and administrative inefficiency, and because each nation demands delivery priority. That is to say, each nation constructs its own assembly line which may become idle after national orders are completed.

Civil production also involves difficulties. Civil aircraft and advanced electronic equipment are similar to prestige items, such as space programmes, in that they are expensive and require government subsidies. In other fields, it is difficult to build up a competitive scale of operations. For one thing, it is often expensive to produce civilian goods with facilities intended for military purposes. For another, the types of related civilian goods which can be produced by a particular defence firm are often unrelated to each other and involve a conglomeration of small-scale industries. Defence firms also complain that they lack marketing skills. Indeed, it is only where military production is a spin-off from civilian production, as in the vehicle industry, rather than the other way round, that civil production represents a viable alternative to exports.

The importance of exports in maintaining full employment in defence industries is suggested by the striking inverse relationship between exports and domestic procurement in countries where exports account for an important share of total production. In Britain and France, exports account for more than 30 per cent of total defence production. In both countries, rises and falls in exports have closely compensated for falls and rises in domestic procurement.

In these countries, exports can also make another contribution, through lengthening production runs. The benefits of long production runs are two-fold. First of all, the cost of R & D and the special installations required for the production of particular types can be spread over a larger number of units. Secondly, productive efficiency increases over long runs as a result of the 'learning' process; that is to say, labour and material costs fall as experience is gained.

These benefits are probably not as important as governments claim. The vast bulk of R & D expenditure is financed by governments, who can recover it through levies on exports. However, they are often prepared to waive or reduce levies for important sales. Further, 'learning' advantages are concentrated in the early stages of production, which are normally intended for domestic consumption. The gains from 'learning' as a result of exporting are generally outweighed by the extra risks and costs involved.

There is a potential conflict between the needs of industry and a position of hegemony. The provision of arms often alternates with the provision of troops: it is part of an overall military strategy designed to maintain hegemony. A broad armaments base is required to meet many different military contingencies –

an armaments base relates to the requirements of other nations. But for countries where exports are necessary to maintain the domestic defence industry, the choice of weapons for the domestic armed forces is made with an eye to their export potential. Both the British and French governments have issued directives that foreign requirements should be taken into account when drawing up weapons specifications.

An industrial policy also implies a willingness to sell and a readiness to guarantee follow-up supplies. If arms supply is used to reinforce hegemony, then this requires close government control over all transactions and the willingness to interrupt or ban supplies. Otherwise no sanctions can be applied against actions taken by a recipient country which are contrary to the interests of the suppliers. An industrial policy dictates the sale of weapons, generally on commercial terms, while hegemony requires the provision of military aid and, in particular, the free gift of weapons as well.

Britain provides an excellent example of a country forced to undergo a transition from an arms-supply policy which served to reinforce its position of hegemony, to one dictated by the requirements of the domestic defence industry. First, Britain was unable to offer military aid to its traditional recipients, mainly former dependencies, and thus could not compete with the Soviet Union and the United States. Secondly, Britain's attempt to maintain an advanced defence industry without reference to export potential proved too expensive. Military exports fell drastically from 1958 and, to compensate, domestic procurement rose. By 1965, pressure to reduce the growth of public spending forced the government to take remedial measures. In particular, a vigorous programme of export promotion was instituted. In announcing this decision in the House of Commons on 25 January 1966, the Minister of Defence stated that 'we must . . . take what practical measures we can to ensure that this country does not fail to secure its rightful share of this valuable commercial market'.

There is also a conflict between industrial requirements and restrictive principles. The effectiveness of restrictive policies tends, therefore, to be related to the strength of the industrial pressure, and to the degree of control exercised by governments over the defence industry. For example, Switzerland exports a very large share of total military output and, for this reason, the restrictive Swiss policy has been rather ineffective in practice. Swiss arms have been supplied to a number of conflict areas, including the Middle East and South Africa, after the imposition of embargoes. Between 1964 and 1968, the Swiss firm Oerlikon-Buehrle illegally exported large amounts of weapons to countries under Swiss embargo.

Sweden is the only country with a very advanced defence industry which has an effective restrictive policy. The main reason for this is that the pressures to export, at any rate in the aircraft industry, are lessened by a careful planning of procurement which reduces the creation of surplus capacity. There is a steady and continual replacement of aircraft over time. In addition, there is only one aircraft company which needs to be kept occupied. This has enabled Sweden to reduce the number of aircraft types in the inventory and, by relying on multi-role combat aircraft, the benefits of long production runs can be reaped without exports. Thus Sweden possesses three basic combat types, compared with eight for Britain and ten for France, although all three countries possess roughly the same number of aircraft. Nevertheless, in certain sectors of the defence industry, there is a growing pressure to loosen the restriction on exports and there have been suggestions that Sweden should develop close military collaboration with European neutrals in order to minimize this problem.

Military collaboration is one way in which the Federal Republic of Germany, Japan, Canada and Italy resolve the conflict between industry and restraint. The bulk of their arms exports go to Western allies, and, for the Federal Republic of Germany and Japan, exports of arms to countries outside NATO are of marginal significance. Canada and Italy do not apply restrictions to exports of items of equipment which make an important contribution to their industries, for example, Canadian transports and Italian trainers and helicopters. Another factor limiting industrial pressures in the Federal Republic of Germany and Japan is the fact that their defence industries are relatively small and are highly integrated into civilian firms, so that there is less dependence on government orders and exports and greater dependence on related civilian production. Yet, as their defence industries grow, there are indications that the industrial establishments are exerting pressure for a more liberal export policy.

THE RECIPIENTS OF ARMS

Since 1950 nearly 30 per cent of major weapon supplies have gone to the Middle East, another 30 per cent to the Far East including Viet-Nam, and a further 15 per cent to the Indian sub-continent. In other words, three quarters of all major weapon supplies have gone to the Middle East and Asia. Moreover, major weapon supplies to these areas have shown enormous increases: in the Middle East the yearly rate of increase since 1950 has averaged 13·5 per cent and on two occasions, in 1955 and 1956, and in 1967, imports doubled.

In Viet-Nam major weapon imports between 1968 and 1972 were twenty-six times higher than they were in the second half of the 1950s – the region became an important recipient only in 1954. In the rest of the Far East, major weapon imports have declined somewhat since the peak year of 1958, when the United States supplied large quantities of major weapons, particularly a great number of Sabre fighters to Taiwan, South Korea, the Philippines and Thailand, the 'forward defence areas' in the Far East. (The countries designated by the US as 'forward defence areas' are those bordering on the USSR and China, including South Korea, Laos, Taiwan, the Philippines, Thailand, South Viet-Nam, Greece, Turkey, Iran and Pakistan.)

In two other forward defence areas, Greece and Turkey, there has been a similar decline. The major weapons supplied to these two countries were 40 per cent lower in the second half of the sixties than in the second half of the fifties. But, with the lifting of the partial US embargo on Greece imposed in April 1967, arms supplies have again increased. For example, in 1969 arms imports almost doubled compared with 1968, and since then a high level has been maintained.

Major weapon supplies to South Asia also reached a peak in 1958. India was then receiving aircraft and frigates from Britain, partly in response to US supplies of fighters, bombers and destroyers to Pakistan – another forward defence area. Supplies to both countries rose again from 1966, and a new peak came in 1968.

Africa, as a whole, has accounted for only 8 per cent of total arms supplies, although this share has been increasing. There has been an arms race in North Africa between Morocco and Algeria, and in addition Libya has been making large purchases of arms. Major weapon supplies to South Africa have increased from $1 million in 1960 – the year when many Black African countries achieved independence and the year of the Sharpeville massacres – to $50 million ten years later. In fact, South Africa imported more major weapons in 1969–70 than the total to the rest of Sub-Saharan Africa, despite the UN Security Council resolution of 1963. The increase in arms supplies to the rest of Sub-Saharan Africa was mainly due to the establishment of independent armed forces for the first time.

The level of major arms supplies to Latin America was about twice as high in the years 1968–72 as in the years 1950–54. The trends in arms supplies were different in Central America and in South America. In South America, major weapon supplies reached a peak in 1960 and 1961, when several countries acquired expensive naval vessels, and they have begun to rise again from 1968 as these countries re-equip their air forces and navies. The all-time high was reached in 1972. In Central America, major arms supplies reached a peak in 1961–2, when there was a heavy arms build-up in Cuba, but then declined sharply until 1969, when they began a new rise.

Factors influencing demand

With the big exception of Latin America, most of the developing world was under colonial rule before and during the Second

World War, and the multiplication of nations as a result of independence led to the multiplication of military units under independent control. Moreover, the circumstances in which these states were created often encouraged the establishment or expansion of armed forces.

Some states were created artificially – that is, their borders were not necessarily determined by geographical, historical or ethnic considerations – so that both internal and external divisions were built into them. In addition, the decolonization process brought with it sharp changes in social structure which also caused internal instability. All of these factors led to the requirement for supplies of weapons and while for some countries the acquisition of arms was limited by the scarcity of resources, for others the competition between the two great powers to provide military aid greatly facilitated their acquisition of weapons.

The acquisition of arms can satisfy three sorts of requirements of the recipient country. First, there is the purely military requirement; arms are needed for those external and internal conflicts in which force might be used. Secondly, the acquisition of arms can serve to unite divided groups by affirming the national identity. Although national independence movements were often based on mass parties, these parties were united on little save the struggle for independence, so that after independence, when ethnic and class divisions began to appear, the mass base often began to be whittled away. In bidding to retain their support or to mobilize new support, the new leaders often renewed their appeal to nationalism, and, because armed forces represent one of the main attributes of independence, the acquisition of arms is one way of doing this. Related to this is the need for strong armed forces to provide a backing for foreign policy. Thirdly, internal divisions are often reflected in the role of the armed forces. Governments can gain the support of the armed forces by satisfying their demand for weapons.

There is an interaction between these three factors. Where there are armed conflicts, the demand for weapons has generally been greatest: thus, in 1972 the Middle East accounted for a quarter of the developing world's defence expenditure and almost one third of its major weapon imports. Yet, the existence of armed conflicts cannot be separated from the other two factors which influence the demand for weapons. Often, the appeal to nationalism is associated with an external conflict: for example, the conflict with Israel is one aspect of the commitment to Arab nationalism in the Middle East, and the conflict with the white dominant regimes in Africa is an integral part of the African concept of true independence.

At the same time, the extent to which arms are demanded to affirm the national identity depends on the role of the armed forces. In some countries the armed forces are the most important element of the new and growing middle class: they are an important modernizing (a term generally synonymous with 'westernizing') force in society and they possess a monopoly of educative and technical skills. This role is often associated with the concept of nationality, of building a self-sufficient society. In other countries, where for example armies were recruited by the colonialists from particular 'warrior tribes', the armed forces initially had a less prestigious role to play because they were often in conflict with the ruling tribes or were regarded as colonial offshoots. This generally changed after independence when officers were recruited from the middle class.

In a circular fashion, the possession of weapons can intensify the factors which brought about their acquisition. Thus arms may increase the risk of conflict, strengthen national unity and enhance the political position of the armed forces.

These three factors alone do not represent conditions sufficient for the acquisition of weapons: they are all present in varying degrees in the Middle East, South East Asia and Africa, but the differences in the pattern of arms buying between these regions might be ascribed to their financial resources and to the attitude of the supplying countries. The countries of the Middle East are either regarded as strategically important by the major powers or are rich in oil resources, or both, so that either they can afford to fulfil their requirements for weapons or the supplying countries are ready to meet their demands at very low cost. The Far East is also regarded as vitally important to the supplying countries, so the pattern of arms acquisition has been, very largely, imposed by the interest of the supplying countries in that region. In contrast, Sub-Saharan Africa, with the exception of South Africa, is neither of sufficient strategic importance to be able to acquire arms at low cost, nor rich enough to purchase large quantities of weapons. It is not unreasonable to suppose that some conflict situations in Africa, constrained by lack of financial or military resources, could have developed into wars had there been greater interest from the two great powers.

Trends in the flow of weapons tend to support the contention that the interest of the great powers is the most important single determinant. For example, a big rise in arms supplies occurred at the end of the fifties, although there was no great increase in the number of conflicts, and the several African nations which achieved independence in that period had relatively low arms imports. The rise occurred because the United States was sending large quantities of weapons to the forward defence areas, and because competition between the two great powers intensified as the Soviet Union entered the market.

Thus, five broad interrelated factors can be identified as determinants of the flow of weapons: the three requirement factors – conflicts, nationalism and the role of the armed forces – and the two resource factors – the size of foreign exchange earnings and the interests of the two great powers.

INTERACTION OF SUPPLY AND DEMAND

The interaction between the demand for and the supply of weapons has three fundamental aspects which will be considered in this last section. First, there is the role of the arms trade in the relationship between supplier and recipient. The possession of strong armed forces is usually considered an attribute of political independence. The importance of nationalism and political independence to certain groups has been stressed. Yet the acquisition of weapons from outside powers may bring about a state of dependence. Where the interests of the regime in the recipient country and the supplying country coincide, this may not matter, but where they do not, the independence of the recipient country and thus the interests of the regime may be threatened. Because there is a risk that the supplying country may for political reasons terminate a contract, discontinue the supply of spares or 'overcharge' for spares deliveries, the recipient regimes may be concerned to weaken their ties with the supplying countries.

For the supplying countries, and more particularly the two great powers, the contribution of the arms trade to reinforcing hegemony depends on the ability of the supplying countries to acquire a monopoly or near-monopoly position. Thus, if the weapons supplied are to be used in the interest of the supplying country, if the supply of weapons enables the supplying country to exact conditions from the recipient country, or if personal contacts made as a result of supplying weapons are to succeed in influencing the recipient military establishment, then the supplying country generally needs to be in a position in which the recipient country has limited possibilities for turning to other suppliers.

There are two main ways in which recipient countries can avoid dependence on a sole supplier: either by the establishment of domestic defence industries or by the diversification of sources of weapons supply. Several of the more advanced Third World countries, Argentina, Brazil, Israel and South Africa for example, have attempted to develop their own domestic defence production, mainly with the aim of increasing military self-sufficiency and reducing dependence on outside suppliers. Only Israel, and to a lesser extent South Africa, however, have achieved any important degree of independence. But, while it is true that the Israeli and South African defence industries have the capacity to produce a very wide range of weapons, it must be kept in mind that this is not the same thing as 'self-sufficiency' or independence from outside suppliers. Israel does not design or even produce the combat aircraft it needs but imports them from the USA, and although South Africa plans to produce combat aircraft it depends on French designs. Further, foreign assistance or cooperation have been of the utmost importance for the establishment of their defence industries, and yet these two countries are comparatively industrialized and normally not classed as developing. The licensed production of weapons is actually militarily the most significant part of all Third World defence industries, rather than the few projects involving indigenously designed weapons. Usually R & D resources are simply too small to allow widespread indigenous design. In addition to requiring considerable outside assistance in the form of advice and imported parts, the experience in less industrialized Third World countries would indicate that domestic defence production – whether licensed or indigenous design – is much more expensive than importing. For instance, in India, all of the aircraft produced under licence are more than 50 per cent more expensive than the cost of importing complete aircraft, at current exchange rates.

It may still be possible to claim that a certain degree of independence *vis-à-vis* the supplier is ensured once the licence for a weapon is acquired and the programme has reached a stage of indigenization when most of the components are being produced in the recipient country. But as this involves heavy economic investments during the take-off period, the method is hardly open to all small countries.

Diversification – the spreading of military dependence over a number of supplying countries – enhances the freedom of action of the recipient countries in a number of ways. First, the recipient country need not fear the actions of any one supplying country. Secondly, the competition between the supplying countries in itself increases the independence of the recipient nation. Competition has a dual effect: on the one hand it limits the ability of the supplying country to exert conditions in return for supplying weapons, because recipient countries can threaten to go elsewhere; on the other hand, the threat of going elsewhere limits the ability of the supplying country to withdraw the supply of weapons for fear of losing influence. Thirdly, diversification prevents the development of an army élite trained together in a foreign country, which might increase the risk of a military takeover.

One type of diversification is to avoid acquiring arms from one or other of the two great powers, and to spread arms purchases over a number of medium-sized supplying countries. But this is possible only where weapon requirements are limited. First of all, the number of potential suppliers is reduced where the types of weapons demanded are rather sophisticated: only the United States, the Soviet Union, Britain, France and Sweden are capable of supplying, for instance, advanced combat aircraft and missiles, and Sweden is generally ruled out because of its restrictive policy. And, although the Federal Republic of Germany produces tanks, it also has a restrictive policy. Furthermore, to meet heavy requirements for weapons a poor country may need favourable terms, that is, gifts or subsidized prices, and this further reduces the number of potential suppliers to the Soviet Union and the United States.

Thus, countries with large weapon requirements usually adopt a second form of diversification, exploiting the competition between the major powers. But this form of diversification is not confined to arms supplies; it concerns all sorts of transactions between supplying and recipient countries. Several countries therefore diversify in yet another way, through acquiring economic and military aid from different sources.

There are some situations in which the supplying country has a monopoly over arms supply, and where the possibilities of diversification are therefore involuntarily limited. One occurs where the recipient country is dependent on the supplying country over a wide variety of transactions, and another where the recipient country is involved in an armed conflict.

Clearly, it hardly makes sense to talk about military independence for countries such as South Korea and Taiwan, which actually depend entirely on the United States. In such situations, it is in the interest of the ruling group to remain dependent on the supplying country. In less extreme cases, such interests may change, but the supplying country can take various sanctions against a client which seeks other arms supplies, or it can support a powerful opposition group.

Involvement in armed conflicts limits the ability of recipient countries to diversify their sources for weapons for a variety of reasons. For example, it is often militarily impracticable to switch suppliers. Because it takes time, which may be scarce in a dangerous military situation, to adapt armed forces to new equipment, recipient countries become, so to speak, 'hooked' on a particular brand of equipment.

Wars

A second aspect of the interaction between supply and demand is the relationship between the supply of weapons and wars. Perhaps the most important question about arms supplies is what effect they have on the development of wars – on the likelihood of wars breaking out, on the course of wars and on their general severity. This includes not only the general effect of arms races on wars – which is the same whether weapons are produced domestically or purchased abroad – but also the consequences of supplier entrammelment in conflicts, via the arms trade.

The connection between arms supplies and wars is one aspect of the old question of the consequences of armaments. In the inter-war period it was widely held that the build-up of armaments, in itself, was an important cause of war. And although since the Second World War armaments in general have been given less prominence, they are still usually included as one of the many factors which make outbreaks of war possible or, in some circumstances, likely.

Because of the complexity of international and internal developments, questions about the effect of armaments in conflict situations are difficult to answer. Those who argue for the importance of armaments as a factor in causing war usually do so along the lines that if a country has devoted a considerable quantity of resources to the military, and if those in power have devoted a good deal of time to military questions, then they will tend to consider military solutions to their disputes, looking for some return on their investment of resources and time. When a border conflict arises, for example, military measures are more likely to be one of the possible courses of action.

Against this, it is often argued that, in a situation of armed conflict, a 'balance' of arms supplies to both sides in the conflict will have a deterrent effect and help to restrain the outbreak of war. However, there is little meaning in the 'balance' of arms in a war fought between an industrial and a developing country. If such a war is fought with sophisticated weapons, the developing country is unlikely to achieve a victory. In a guerilla war, very great imbalance in arms supplies can exist and neither side may achieve a decisive victory. Thus it is useful to make the following distinction between levels of modern warfare, before trying to state the significance of arms supplies for the outcome of conflicts in more general terms. Broadly, there are two levels of warfare relevant to Third World conflicts – industrialized warfare and guerilla warfare.

Industrialized warfare involves the concept of a conventional war fought with sophisticated arms, such as supersonic combat aircraft, missiles and tanks, and including the operation of a variety of electronic equipment. The outcome of this kind of warfare depends very much on the availability of educated manpower and the infrastructure needed to operate and plan the employment of these weapons. There are several examples of countries at relatively low levels of industrialization which have been placed at a military disadvantage either through the possession of sophisticated weapons, as with Pakistan and Somalia, or through the participation in an industrialized war against an opponent with greater industrial and technical resources, as with Egypt.

The second type of warfare is guerilla warfare. This is the sort of war which is fought by, for instance, the liberation movements in South East Asia and Africa. Weapons more sophisticated than rifles and machine-guns are unlikely to be required; indeed, heavier arms may be a disadvantage, since they are more difficult to move and camouflage.

Of course, there is a wide range of intermediate levels of warfare between these two extremes. The above distinction, however, leads to the conclusion that it is more pertinent to consider the implications of a 'balance' of arms supplies in a conflict between more or less symmetrical parties, that is to say, parties at a similar stage of industrialization with similar manpower resources. Even in this situation, a 'balance' cannot easily be judged by the number of weapons available to each side. In peacetime, what matters is the subjective assessment of the balance – whether it is thought to be such that an attempted military solution will fail, or whether it is believed that the risk of failure is sufficiently small to be taken. A perceived 'balance' of arms supplies may restrain the outbreak of war. But such 'balances' are not very stable, and an influx of arms to one side in the conflict may alter the 'balance' and lead to war. In wartime, there is a less subjective test of 'balance' – the prolongation of war. An imbalance in arms supplies to two parties with similar technical resources could lead to the speedy conclusion of a war, while a correction of imbalances could prolong it, as illustrated in the Nigerian civil war. The relative strength of the Federal forces in August 1968 was such that a negotiated settlement, favourable to the Federation, seemed near. But the sudden influx of arms to Biafra, indirectly from France, was followed by renewed fighting. Large quantities of weapons were provided by the UK and the USSR before the Nigerian Federal forces achieved a decisive victory.

To sum up, it can be argued that it is mainly in a conflict between two parties with similar industrial resources that changes in the level of arms supplies will have a significant impact on the outbreak, length and outcome of wars. In a war between an industrial country and a developing country, the situation is very different. Where both sides plan for an industrialized war, the outcome is likely to favour the industrial country. Where guerilla warfare is undertaken, the outcome of wars is unlikely to be determined by the weaponry possessed by both sides. This does not mean that the weapons have no significance for the conflict. The amount of destruction caused by wars will depend on the quantity of weapons, and also on their sophistication. Generally speaking, the more sophisticated a weapon, the more lethal power it will embody.

Another important facet of arms supplies is the way in which they draw supplying countries into the conflict. The supply of weapons to countries in conflict can be seen as an indirect use of force; by providing weapons to a particular recipient in conflict, the supplying country implicitly lends support to that recipient. When that support becomes explicit, it may have enormous implications for the course of the conflict. Other things being equal, it is in the situation of armed conflict that the supplier–recipient relationship becomes closest. The recipient depends on the supplier to meet its military requirements. Yet, because of the risks of the situation, the supplier cannot always exploit this position. The indirect presence of a supplying country can alter the issues involved in the dispute, and wars may be exacerbated or restrained depending on its interests. The nature of these effects depends largely on the role of competing supplying countries: whether they are arming opposing sides to a conflict, whether they are arming the same side, or whether one supplying country provides arms to both sides.

When competing supplying countries support opposing sides in a conflict and the local conflict is subsumed into their own conflict, the conflict is said to become polarized. In other words, a local conflict is distorted into a conflict between the supplying countries themselves, and, more often than not, the interests of the local opponents become secondary to those of their respective supporters.

The spread of polarization has been a characteristic feature in large parts of the world since the Second World War, for example in Korea, Indo-China and the Middle East. There are several important implications of polarization. The transformation of a local conflict into cold-war issues implies that a solution will have to be sought within the international context, and that, because more parties are involved, the conflict may be more difficult to solve. Also, a 'solution' that merely satisfies the outside powers may be no solution at all, as evidenced by the Geneva conferences on Indo-China in 1954 and on Laos in 1962. Furthermore, polarization alters the nature of the supplying country's military commitment. The delicate distinction between military assistance and direct military intervention cannot always be maintained.

Economic development

The final aspect of the interaction between supply and demand is the relationship between the arms trade and internal social conflicts and its effects on economic development. The acquisition of arms uses scarce resources which might be better employed in developing an industrial base and in producing food and other material necessities, although whether a reduction in arms procurement is associated with an increased effort is another matter.

Each year, increasing quantities of resources in developing countries are devoted to the procurement of major weapons from abroad. The gross national products of all developing countries have grown at an average rate of 5 per cent a year since 1950, while their military expenditures have grown at a yearly rate of 7 per cent and their major weapon imports at a rate of 8 per cent.

The total average yearly expenditure on major weapon imports to developing countries over the past five years has been around $1·7 billion. This represents approximately 3 per cent of their total imports. In certain regions, the share is higher – expenditure on major weapon imports represents 8 per cent of total imports to the Middle East and 5 per cent of total imports to South Asia. Total imports of military equipment are about twice the size of major weapon imports, and thus represent around 6 per cent of the total imports of developing countries. But although these figures provide some indication of the size of the resources devoted to the trade in arms, they do not represent the foreign-exchange cost to developing countries, since more than half the trade in weapons is financed by supplying countries.

The trade in weapons also absorbs other kinds of resources. In particular, the infrastructure and skilled manpower required to maintain a major weapon in operational condition is quite considerable. To repair and maintain a tank in an advanced country, 400 man-hours are required per year. For a destroyer, 45,000 man-hours are required. For each aircraft, four men are required full time for operational maintenance and six men for overhaul. These figures do not include the costs and the skilled manpower requirement for establishing repair shops, nor do they include the various support services necessary for an effective field organization. So it is in the use of skilled manpower as well as in the absorption of foreign exchange that imports of major weapons bear heavily on the economies of poor countries.

It is argued that the importing of these weapons provides training which would not otherwise be given, and which is of considerable potential use in civil life. This is part of the general argument about the role of the military in Third World countries, but how far it is in fact true depends on what alternative provision of training there might be if arms supplies were lower, and on the extent to which the skills learned in operating and maintaining weapons can be transformed easily to the civil sector. Obviously mechanics trained to service army trucks can easily transfer to civilian vehicles, but the skills learned in the maintenance and servicing of aircraft – in a country where there are hardly any civil aircraft – are probably much less easily transferred.

Equally, it is sometimes argued that the acquisition of military weapons leads to the construction of roads, airfields or other items of 'infrastructure' which might not otherwise be provided. But the resources which are used to provide them for military use could just as well be employed to provide them for civil use, and, in any case, military roads and airfields are frequently in areas – border areas for example – where the potential civil use is minimal.

However, it is not very helpful to treat the problem of transferring resources from military to civil uses as a purely mechanical one. Most governments have some leeway in reducing expenditure on weapons and increasing expenditure on development; but it is generally not realistic to envisage large transfers of resources without other political and economic changes. Arms-procurement policy cannot be treated in isolation.

For example, in a number of countries in the Middle East and South Asia, heavy arms procurement has accompanied modernization and economic reforms because nationalist groups have been in favour of both. But elsewhere the link may be between heavy arms purchases and a general reactionary posture, as weapons are procured to bolster a feudal regime.

So in some cases a reduction in arms supplies could conceivably be followed by the overthrow of a modernizing government, while in others one could well envisage a disaffected military group overthrowing a relatively reactionary regime. So what would happen in any particular country as a consequence of a large change in arms-supply policy would depend on the way in which this change was associated with other policy changes or changes in regime.

Part Two

The Suppliers of Arms to the Third World

2 The United States

The United States is the largest supplier of military equipment in the world, accounting for nearly half the world's total trade in weapons. Since 1950, well over one third of all the major weapons acquired by Third World countries has come directly from the United States. The policy which governs this supply of weapons is an integra part of the general external policy arising from the dominant position of the United States in world affairs. The export of weapons represents one of the transactions, together with economic assistance, direct military intervention or heavy industrial investment, through which this dominant position is maintained.

Benefits to the defence industry from arms exporting play an insignificant part in this policy: less than 5 per cent of the total US defence production is exported and more than half of these exports go to the industrial countries of Europe and the Far East. Moreover, until 1962, nearly all US weapons supplied to Third World countries were provided free of charge. After 1962 there was an increased emphasis on the sale of weapons, but the policy governing these sales was not significantly different from that governing the gift of weapons, and of the one third of US arms exports to Third World countries which were sold rather than given away, half were provided on favourable credit terms, financed by the US government.

The US Administration is not a unified decision-making body. Military assistance appears under a number of different guises and programmes, each programme creating its own bureaucratic machinery with special interests in perpetuating itself. At the same time, there are other departments and outside pressure groups with competing programmes and interests. Thus any decision is likely to represent a compromise between the different arms of government and different sections of vocal opinion. This compromise may have little to do with the explicit objectives of policy.

Such conflicts are very often reflected in Congressional debates. From its inception, the military-assistance programme has been subjected to close Congressional scrutiny; Congressional attitudes have been reflected not only in the content of some of the military-assistance legislation but also in the strategic arguments used to justify the policy governing the supply of arms. The proliferation of military-aid programmes – there are no less than eight programmes under which military assistance is provided – can be attributed to the need to evade Congressional criticism.

MAIN TRENDS

The United States emerged from the Second World War as the richest and militarily the strongest country in the world, with the main challenge to its leadership in international affairs coming from the Soviet Union. Military-assistance programmes thus formed part of a policy dominated by the competition between these two powers.

In the early post-war period there was considerable debate within the United States about its future international role. Criticism of the Administration's actions came both from those groups who favoured a return to the isolationist stance of the pre-war period and from liberals who feared an international position based on the use of force. The Administration stood firm in its intention to 'contain communism' in the West. Military assistance was provided to Greece, Turkey and Iran. In Greece, military aid was designed to prevent the victory of an internal revolution which, in the US view, would add to the strength of the socialist camp. And in Turkey and Iran, the United States was concerned to limit the external extension of Soviet influence.

In the Far East the United States provided military assistance to South Korea, China and the Philippines. But there was a certain ambivalence in its attitude to the Chinese revolution and in its support for the South Korean regime. Towards China, opinion was divided: some believed that the situation was similar to that in Greece and that military aid should be provided accordingly; others were unhappy with the Nationalist regime and supported the communist movement, 'mistaking it', according to a report called *American Foreign Assistance*, published by the Brookings Institution in 1953, 'for a predominantly agrarian reform movement representative of the aspirations of the "common man"'. Towards South Korea there was fear lest the regime might be tempted to embark on unilateral adventures, and the Administration, accordingly, took the precaution to arm the South Korean army with light weapons only, and made it clear that it was not committed to defend the regime. This ambivalence was finally removed in 1950. The Treaty of Friendship between China and the Soviet Union signed in February 1950 confirmed the US opposition to revolution, while the outbreak of the Korean War in June 1950 focused attention on external threats.

In the early fifties, US military aid was concentrated on building up a Western collective security system. In 1955, SEATO and the Baghdad Pact, later to become CENTO, were formed, thus completing a chain of military alliances bordering the Soviet Union and China. The same year, Egypt signed an arms agreement with Czechoslovakia indicating, for the first time, the willingness of socialist countries to supply arms to non-socialist countries. The deal with Czechoslovakia marked the end of the Western monopoly over arms supplies and the end of any possibility of using the offer of military aid to persuade countries to join a Western military alliance.

From 1955, there were two distinct stands in the US policy towards Third World countries. The policy towards those bordering on the Soviet Union and China, known as the 'forward defence areas', was a continuation of the earlier policy and represented one part of the overall US military strategy. These countries have received approximately three quarters of all US major weapon exports to Third World countries since 1950. The policy towards the remaining Third World countries, known in the USA as the 'free-world orientation areas', which excludes

Table 4 USA: major weapon exports to Third World countries, by region

	Far East excl. South Viet-Nam	South Viet-Nam	Indian Sub-continent	Middle East
1950	21	–	1	3
1951	82	–	–	2
1952	37	–	–	2
1953	30	–	9	10
1954	107	4	30	16
1955	134	3	27	15
1956	127	4	16	43
1957	116	–	16	42
1958	165	1	47	50
1959	151	2	12	27
1960	251	12	13	27
1961	72	77	25	2
1962	87	84	58	5
1963	85	59	58	62
1964	125	19	42	12
1965	99	37	–	172
1966	130	35	3	43
1967	77	54	3	46
1968	40	64	*	188
1969	160	124	*	234
1970	115	181	1	312
1971	149	124	1	361
1972	30	418	*	164
Total[a]	2,389	1,302	365	1,838
Per cent of total	28·0	15·3	4·3	21·6

[a] Figures may not add up to totals owing to rounding.
* = less than 1

US$ mn, at constant (1968) *prices*

North Africa	Sub-Saharan Africa	South Africa	Latin America	Greece and Turkey	Total[a]
–	–	2	15	9	51
–	–	*	23	23	130
–	–	–	29	66	133
–	4	–	18	143	214
–	4	–	48	89	300
–	*	3	48	25	256
–	–	2	33	52	277
–	1	–	57	9	243
–	1	*	43	326	633
1	2	–	25	87	305
*	5	–	73	103	484
5	4	–	98	20	303
1	3	1	32	13	284
1	9	24	34	5	335
1	13	–	16	37	264
*	1	*	30	116	455
15	21	2	33	59	340
16	7	20	45	51	319
6	1	–	28	61	388
8	–	–	40	125	692
27	4	–	41	13	694
–	11	–	55	33	733
–	5	–	29	43	689
81	95	54	891	1,506	8,522
1·0	*1·1*	*0·6*	*10·5*	*17·7*	*100·0*

Source: SIPRI worksheets.

Latin America and countries in which the USA has military bases, was dominated by the competition with the Soviet Union and, later, China.

US major weapons exports to the forward defence areas reached a peak towards the end of the fifties, when the United States was consolidating SEATO and the Baghdad Pact. Sophisticated weapons were supplied not only to demonstrate the US commitment to defend these countries, but also to improve their ability to withstand external attack without US intervention. During the sixties, supplies of major weapons to the forward defence areas fell. The doctrine of flexible response propounded by the Kennedy Administration implied a willingness to commit US troops to fight limited wars. There was also an increased emphasis on the internal 'threat' to developing countries. Military assistance was increasingly designed to train local forces to combat guerilla activities. While total supplies of major weapons fell, supplies of inexpensive COIN equipment, such as helicopters, patrol boats and trainers, rose. Moreover, the share of those countries where the internal 'threat' was most prevalent – Thailand, Laos and South Viet-Nam – rose from 6 per cent of the total for the forward defence areas during the fifties to 37 per cent during 1960–72. Recently, major weapons supplies to forward defence areas have risen again. In part, this reflects payment by the USA to those countries participating in the Viet-Nam War. In part, it reflects the Nixon Doctrine, under which US troops will be withdrawn from the Far East and self-reliance among US allies is once again to be encouraged.

From the early sixties US exports of major weapons to the free-world orientation areas rose. With the entry of the Soviet Union into the market, the conditions under which governments were eligible for US aid had to be relaxed. Increasingly, military exports were designed to pre-empt exports by the Soviet Union. In addition, various legislation introduced in the early sixties enabled the Administration to sell arms on extremely favourable credit terms. The sales programme was able to by-pass Congressional scrutiny, which was important, as Congress was thought to be unwilling to authorize grants of military equipment for countries where the strategic significance of such equipment was small. An increasing share of exports to the free-world orientation areas was sold rather than given away.

The emphasis on free-world orientation areas was also associated with an increasing emphasis on the more indirect influence which could be exerted through the provision of military aid. The social and political role played by military forces in developing countries became a popular doctrine; the advantages of training 'tomorrow's political leaders', of establishing informal contacts between US military personnel and military personnel in developing countries, and of helping military forces to perform tasks which would contribute to economic and social developments were all given prominence.

THE FORWARD DEFENCE AREAS

The report of the President's Committee to study the Military Assistance Program (the *Draper Report*), published in 1959, concluded that 'the military assistance program has provided the mortar giving cohesion, strength and credibility to our collective security arrangements. It is the foundation on which our forward strategy is built.' By this time, the United States was committed to defend all the forward defence areas, through either bilateral or multilateral treaties.

The size and content of military assistance to the forward defence areas has depended on the US perception of the threat to these countries and the means available to the USA for countering such threats. These means were four-fold: the USA could rely on the threat of massive retaliation to deter a possible aggressor; it could undertake to defend the area with conventional troops and weapons; it could provide equipment and training to local forces to defend the area; and it could provide economic aid, both to support local forces and to prevent internal discontent, which might be exploited by communism.

The experience of the Korean War left the United States unwilling to become involved in another land war in Asia. It was

Table 5 US military assistance to Third World countries,[a] by region

	Far East[c]	Indian Sub-continent	Middle East	Greece and Turkey
1949–52	160·7	–	16·6	559·4
1953–7	2,403·7	160·4	163·6	1,350·2
1958	627·8	92·9	151·4	392·8
1959	606·7	102·7	113·5	290·8
1960	501·6	79·1	95·2	217·2
1961	495·4	56·7	60·6	128·7
1962	523·3	29·7	44·1	191·3
1963	651·8	108·4	91·3	258·0
1964	563·7	64·2	44·8	184·8
1965	648·9	64·0	77·9	222·4
1966	535·6	7·6	108·3	179·2
1967	673·0	6·0	164·9	162·5
1968	1,026·9	5·6	116·9	175·9
1969[b]	1,064·2	1·6	83·4	165·0
1949–69	10,483·3	778·9	1,332·5	4,478·2

[a] Includes Military Assistance Program, Greek-Turkish Aid, China Naval Aid, PL-454 Philippines aid, Vessel Loans, aid to Viet-Nam, 1967–69, and Thailand and Laos, 1968–69, in Department of Defense Budget. Excludes deliveries of excess stocks.

[b] Excludes credit assistance.

[c] Excludes undistributed assistance to Indo-China.

believed that the threat of massive retaliation would prevent another situation being created in which it might be necessary to deploy conventional US troops, a belief which depended on the notion that the 'communist threat' was an external threat and that all internal threats were externally directed by socialist countries and could therefore be prevented by deterring these countries. The effectiveness of nuclear deterrence depended on the credibility of the US commitment to defend countries

US $ mn; US fiscal years

North Africa	Sub-Saharan Africa	Latin America	**Third World Total**
–	–	0·2	**736·9**
–	4·6	151·8	**4,244·3**
1·1	8·8	47·9	**1,322·7**
1·6	5·3	54·0	**1,174·6**
2·7	7·3	53·7	**956·8**
5·1	6·4	111·4	**864·3**
5·0	18·6	132·8	**944·8**
12·2	14·0	82·3	**1,218·0**
11·6	16·7	75·7	**961·5**
5·8	11·8	67·3	**1,098·1**
5·1	16·8	82·0	**934·6**
13·8	18·0	76·5	**1,114·7**
10·8	22·7	99·2	**1,458·0**
6·9	14·4	37·9	**1,373·4**
81·7	175·4	1,072·7	**18,402·7**

Source: US Overseas Loans and Grants, 1945–66, and 1945–68, Agency for International Development, Washington, 1967 and 1969.

Military Assistance and Foreign Military Sales Facts, May 1967 and March 1970.

Military Assistance Facts, March 1968 and May 1969.

threatened by communism. So the early fifties were primarily devoted to pact-making.

As became evident in the Middle East, military assistance was provided, in part, to persuade countries to join the Western collective security arrangements. Although Greece and Turkey joined NATO in 1952, attempts to form an Allied Middle East Command were frustrated. In 1955, Iran, Iraq, Pakistan and Turkey formed a military alliance, the Baghdad Pact. But the membership of Iran, Iraq and Pakistan in the Baghdad Pact does not seem to have resulted from any awareness of a 'communist menace'; they joined in order to acquire weapons from the United States. At that time, Iran was concerned with keeping down rebellious groups and later with its interests in the Persian Gulf, and Pakistan was preoccupied with the conflict with India. Iraq's first commitment was to the Arab cause, and weapons were needed to cope with various internal problems, as well as certain border disputes. Iraq withdrew from the Pact after 1959 and it was renamed the Central Treaty Organization (CENTO). Although both Pakistan and Iran granted base rights to the United States and remained members of CENTO, their continued allegiance depended on the continued provision of military assistance.

SEATO, the South-East Asia Collective Defence Treaty Organization, was formed to meet the combined power of the Soviet Union and China in the East, just as NATO had been formed to meet the combined power of the Soviet Union and Eastern Europe in the West. The Baghdad Pact provided the link between these two treaty organizations. But the United States did not adhere to the Baghdad Pact for fear of jeopardizing relations with other Arab countries, so that Turkey achieved a privileged position as the lynch pin of the whole system, unable to honour its Baghdad Pact obligations without involving NATO.

Once these arrangements had been formalized, the United States could either provide the minimum amount of equipment necessary to demonstrate its continuing commitment, local forces being designed mainly to cope with internal security, or provide sufficient equipment and training to enable local forces to provide effective defence against undeterred aggression. The second role was the one adopted. During the late fifties, all the members of SEATO and CENTO received large quantities of sophisticated equipment. There may have been other reasons for the emphasis on external defence. The US had little experience of guerilla warfare. In addition there was a considerable pressure at the time to get rid of excess stocks.

When the Kennedy Administration came to power in 1960, the

doctrine of flexible response – that the response should be appropriate to the threat, for example that a conventional threat could be met by a conventional response – was adopted. This change in the nature of US military commitment was partly the result of the changed situation in Asia. It was clear that the threat of massive retaliation was failing to deter the increased guerilla activities in Viet-Nam, Laos and Thailand, and the Sino-Soviet split, although it did not come out into the open until 1962, meant that the appropriate strategy for Europe was not necessarily the appropriate strategy for Asia. It was believed that China would not risk external attack without Soviet backing, and would prefer to rely on 'infiltrating local revolutions', a view supported by the statements of Chinese leaders calling for wars of national liberation.

But there were also other reasons. Already by the late fifties there was growing concern about the risks involved in a strategy which relied on the threat of massive retaliation. The possibility that deterrence might fail and that local forces might be unable to defend themselves against undeterred aggression posed a serious dilemma for the United States. This possibility was enhanced by the internal and military weaknesses of many SEATO and CENTO countries. At the same time, many of these countries, especially the CENTO members Iran and Pakistan, were preoccupied with their non-socialist neighbours and not with the 'threat of communism'. Furthermore, it was believed by some circles in the West that nuclear deterrence might actually encourage internal revolutions as being the only form of communist attack able to avoid massive retaliation.

Given the readiness to commit conventional troops for combat, it was possible and desirable to concentrate more heavily on the internal 'threat'. One advantage was that it was no longer necessary to distinguish between genuine internal revolution and externally directed revolution: both could be dealt with in the same way. Major weapon supplies to the forward defence areas as a whole fell by about a third in the early sixties, but in four countries – Thailand, Laos, Viet-Nam and Iran – they rose. In Laos and Viet-Nam, major weapon supplies were almost entirely devoted to counter-insurgency. Both received substantial quantities of helicopters, trucks and COIN trainers and bombers. Similar types of equipment were also supplied to Thailand and the Philippines. The increase in arms supplies to Iran was due to quite other considerations, which are more relevant to the discussion of free-world orientation areas.

The supply of conventional sophisticated weapons continued, although on a much more limited scale than previously. There were increased naval build-ups in the late fifties and early sixties in Taiwan, the Philippines and South Korea, corresponding with a general US anti-submarine programme in Military Assistance Program countries. At the same time, the commitment to help certain countries defend themselves against external attack was not abandoned. There were increasing incidents in the demilitarized zone separating North and South Korea, the dispute between China and Taiwan was continuing, and Turkey and Greece still had a role to play in NATO.

In the late sixties, major weapon supplies were also limited by the embargoes on Pakistan and Greece. Pakistan had exhibited increasing friendliness towards socialist countries ever since the Sino-Indian conflict of 1962. On the outbreak of the Indo-Pakistan War in 1965, the United States imposed an embargo on both countries. And although the embargo was successively lightened in response to Pakistani procurement from China, France and the Soviet Union, it was not until October 1970 that the State Department announced that the United States would resume supplies of aircraft and armoured vehicles as a 'one-time exception'. A new ban was imposed in March 1971 after the outbreak of civil war in Pakistan. (This ban was lifted in the spring of 1973.) A partial embargo was imposed on Greece after the military coup of April 1967, but this embargo was very partial indeed and during 1968 and 1969 considerable numbers of aircraft, missiles and naval vessels were delivered. Official decisions to resume shipments of major items to Greece were taken temporarily after the entry of Warsaw Pact forces into Czechoslovakia in August 1968, and again in September 1970. In January 1973, the Greek government decided to renounce further US military assistance grants, a decision which followed severe Congressional criticism of the fact that Greece had not yet returned to constitutional government, and Congressional reluctance to authorize more military-aid funds for Greece.

From 1969 there has been an increase in major weapon supplies to most forward defence areas. Increased military assistance has been provided to Thailand, the Philippines and South Korea to persuade them to participate in the Viet-Nam War. The Philippines agreed to provide an engineer task force, which has cost the United States $35 million to maintain. Thai forces first arrived in Viet-Nam in 1966, and by 1969 there were 11,000 Thai troops there. The cost to the USA of supporting these troops was $200 million between 1966 and 1969. In an agreement of 9 November 1967 concerning the dispatch of additional Thai troops to Viet-Nam, the USA agreed to increase military assistance by $30 million in 1968 and 1969, and to provide and train Thai technicians in the operation of a Hawk anti-aircraft missile battery. The total cost of supporting 50,000 Korean troops in Viet-Nam in 1965–9 and of modernizing Korean forces in return for this participation was $927·5 million. Also, military assistance has increased in connection with the Nixon Doctrine, under which allied nations are supposed to provide the manpower needed, while the USA provides the weapons. Increased funds have been requested for Thailand, Laos and Viet-Nam under the defence budget. In addition $28 million has been provided to Northrop to develop an improved version of the F-5 Freedom Fighter F-5-21, especially to meet the needs of South East Asian forces. A former Secretary of Defense, Clark Clifford, told the Senate Armed Services Committee in April 1969: 'clearly the overriding goal of our collective defense efforts in Asia must be to assist our allies in building a capability to defend themselves. Besides costing substantially less (an Asian soldier costs about 1/15 as much as his American counterpart) there are compelling political and psychological advantages on both sides of the Pacific for such a policy.'

Military aid and economic aid

From an early stage, it was recognized that economic aid could play an important role, as both a substitute for and a complement to military aid, in 'containing communism'. Assistance designed to increase economic development has been partly conceived as an alternative method of dealing with material problems, by reducing internal discontent which might be exploited by communism. And assistance known as supporting assistance has been generally designed to support the build-up of local military forces and thus help to overcome a 'communist threat'.

Before 1952, supporting assistance was provided only to Europe, Indo-China and the forward defence areas, and was confined to the provision of non-military commodities for military use. The Korean experience gave a greater impetus to supporting assistance, primarily because it focused attention on the external threat. In the Mutual Security Act of 1953, Congress attempted to clarify the distinction between countries receiving only economic assistance and those receiving military assistance as well. The distinction between economic aid and supporting aid was seen in terms of the type of objective involved rather than in terms of the content of aid programmes.

The Mutual Security Act of 1957 redefined supporting assistance as 'economic and budgetary assistance designed to enable the country to maintain a desired level of forces', while economic aid was defined as aid 'to help the development of the country economically'. From 1958 to 1961 supporting assistance reached its highest level, averaging $1 billion a year. In fact, it covered programmes which had little to do with the level of military forces, such as programmes for malaria or population control, presumably because of the greater willingness of Congress to authorize defence-related assistance.

The mood of Congress was, however, changing. Many of the liberal Democrats who had previously supported the Eisenhower Administration became disillusioned with the military content of the aid programmes. The Mutual Security Act of 1959 expressly stated that increased emphasis should be placed on economic aid to developing countries, a change in attitude adopted by the Kennedy Administration, which changed the name of the Mutual Security Act to the Foreign Assistance Act. The new Secretary of Defense, Robert S. McNamara, propounded the doctrine that revolutions arise from poverty. From 1961, economic aid as a whole began to increase and the share of supporting assistance declined. Moreover, supporting assistance was given a wider definition; in addition to supporting the 'common defence', it is now said to be provided to maintain economic stability, as an alternative to excessive dependence on Soviet aid, and to ensure access to US bases.

In content, supporting assistance is extremely varied. It can be used to finance strategic imports, as in Korea; it can be used to build up infrastructure, such as roads and airfields, as in Afghanistan; or it can be used to provide budgetary assistance, as in Jordan. The summary presentation of the *Proposed Mutual Defense and Development Programs* for the financial year 1964 described the combined use of military and supporting assistance in South Viet-Nam: 'South Viet-Nam today is a vivid illustration of the several programs under strategic assistance in action. US helicopters fly US trained and equipped Vietnamese soldiers into jungle combat with the communist forces of the Viet Cong; American dollars finance the import of raw material and machinery into South Viet-Nam to keep the economy functioning; and American technicians and advisers and US economic aid are helping to create a police force, establish strategic hamlets for the protection of the civilian population and carry forward other counter-insurgency prospects.'

THE FREE-WORLD ORIENTATION AREAS

In the early fifties, military assistance was provided largely in order to bring recipient countries within the US sphere of influence. Because the Western powers had a monopoly in arms supplies, the USA was able to exact conditions for the receipt of military assistance.

With the entry of the Soviet Union into the market, two other functions of US military assistance became important. First, it was provided as part of the competition with the Soviet Union – to pre-empt and offset the supply of arms by the Soviet Union. Secondly, it was provided to influence individuals in the military establishment, which in many countries represented a powerful political force.

The conditions

There were two sorts of conditions which the United States required in the early fifties before providing military assistance – those conditions required by law, the eligibility requirements, and, for some countries, membership in military alliances.

The eligibility requirements were contained in the Mutual Security Act of 1951 and the Mutual Defense Assistance Control Act of 1951, the latter being better known as the Battle Act. Under the former, countries were required to sign a military assistance agreement, which, essentially, implied a commitment to the US camp. Among other things, they were required to make the full contribution permitted by their manpower, resources, facilities and general economic condition to the development and maintenance of their own defensive strength and the defensive strength of the free world.

In several countries, there were difficulties in acquiring compliance with the 1951 Act. Military assistance to both Iran and Burma was halted because the conditions were not met. In Indonesia an agreement led to a Cabinet crisis and there were also difficulties with Brazil and Mexico.

Under the Battle Act, the United States placed an embargo on the export of strategic material to 'any nation or combination of nations threatening the security of the United States, including the Union of Soviet Socialist Republics and all countries under its domination', and declared that no military, economic or financial assistance should be supplied to any country unless it imposed a similar embargo. Recipient countries were further expected to control other exports to 'communist-dominated'

countries. These requirements were, however, somewhat miti-
gated by the condition that the President, under unusual circumstances and having carefully considered the situation, could direct
continuance of aid to countries which export items, other than
arms, ammunition, implements of war and atomic energy materials, to the socialist camp.

The *Draper Report* recommended that the section of the Mutual
Security Act referring to the bilateral agreements should be
repealed and substituted by an authorization for the President to
decide what undertakings are deemed necessary. It also recommended that training assistance should not require the same
conditions as grant aid, and that the restrictions contained in the
Battle Act should be liberalized. By this time, the President was
allowed to waive Battle Act restrictions for assistance not
exceeding $30 million.

Not all the recommendations of the *Draper Report* were acted
upon. Bilateral agreements are not now required for grant aid
defence services, including training, or for the purchase of
defence articles and/or services through the Foreign Military
Sales Program. For grant aid defence material less than $3
million, bilateral agreements concern only the use, transfer and
security of equipment delivered. For grant aid above $3 million,
bilateral agreements are essentially the same as they were in 1951:
the President can waive these agreements if he determines that
such assistance is essential to the United States. The Battle Act
has been substantially revised since 1951, in the light of the
interests of Western countries in increasing commercial relations
with socialist countries, so that today only total embargoes on
North Viet-Nam and Cuba are necessary before a country may
receive assistance.

Membership in military alliances

In the Middle East, the temptation offered by the Western powers
to persuade countries to join a military alliance was arms. On 25
May 1950, Britain, France and the United States, in the Tripartite
Declaration Regarding Security in the Near East, declared their

opposition to the development of an arms race between the Arab states and Israel, announced that they would take action against violation of frontiers, and required assurances from arms-purchasing countries that they would not undertake aggression against any other state. Effectively this meant that only countries willing to join a Western-dominated alliance would be able to acquire heavy armaments.

The Soviet entry into the Middle East arms market in 1955 destroyed the Western monopoly which had been the basis for this policy.

Competition with the Soviet Union

Once the Western monopoly over arms supplies had been broken, the Western powers could no longer exact conditions in return for weapons. Instead, one of the main considerations became to ensure that a potential recipient did not acquire weapons from a socialist country. The supply of weapons thus became pre-emptive.

The first evidence of this new approach was the Eisenhower Doctrine. After the 1955 Czechoslovak arms deal and the 1956 Suez crisis, the United States was concerned to regain its position in the Middle East. Despite US condemnation of British and French actions, the USA was inevitably associated with its allies. Besides, the USA had played a leading role in the Aswan Dam negotiations and, after the nationalization of the Suez Canal, froze all Egyptian dollar assets. In a speech to Congress on 5 January 1957, President Eisenhower proposed an increase in economic and military assistance and authorization to use US troops 'to secure and protect the territorial integrity and political independence of such nations, requesting such aid, against overt armed aggression from any nation controlled by international communism'. In the understatement of the year he added: 'This program will not solve all the problems of the Middle East.'

After his tour in March, James P. Richards, the President's special ambassador to the Middle East, reported that the Eisenhower Doctrine, 'this new departure, this entirely American line of action, evoked a heart-warming trust from the nations of the area'. In fact, outside the Baghdad Pact, Lebanon was the only Arab nation to endorse the doctrine.

The Eisenhower Doctrine was welcomed by King Hussein of Jordan, in opposition to his government, which had terminated the Anglo-Jordanian treaty and the British financial subsidy. In April 1957, an internal crisis brought about the dismissal of the government. The King appealed to the USA, which stationed the Sixth Fleet in the Mediterranean and promised economic and military aid. In 1958, a civil war broke out in Lebanon mainly as a result of the Muslim opposition to the pro-US policy. Two days after the Iraqi monarchy was overthrown in June 1958, the United States landed marines in Lebanon. By the time the US troops had been withdrawn, the neutral Commander-in-Chief of the Lebanese army had been elected President, and the leader of the insurgents appointed Prime Minister.

Perhaps the Eisenhower Doctrine had been too explicit. It was only a 'new departure' in the sense that, unlike previous offers of military assistance, it did not require membership in a military alliance. But to the countries of the Middle East it seemed apparent that the United States was prepared to pay with cash and with arms for abandonment of a neutral position. It ended two years after its inception with the loss of Iraq and Lebanon, and the burdensome gain of Jordan.

In the years that followed, the United States moved still further away from the attempts to exact hard conditions for military aid. Limited amounts of supporting assistance were provided to the UAR, Syria, the Yemen, Iraq and Afghanistan, which by this time were receiving large quantities of Soviet arms. In 1962, a military-aid programme was started in the Yemen. The policy of wooing the more intransigent Arab states was associated with restraint on arms supplies to their rivals, the traditional US clients – Jordan, Saudi Arabia, Iran and Israel.

This policy was expanded to cover the newly independent nations of Africa. Apart from assistance to Ethiopia and some small-scale programmes to the French ex-community countries, military assistance to Africa was largely concentrated on those countries where the possibility of Soviet influence was greatest.

Military aid was extended to Tunisia, after President Bourguiba hinted at the possibilities of a Soviet arms deal. Similarly, weapons or supporting assistance were provided to Morocco, Ghana, Guinea, Mali and the Sudan after these countries had signed arms deals with the Soviet Union. In the Congo (Kinshasa), military aid served directly to limit the influence of internal socialist elements.

Already by 1965, the United States was finding it necessary to modify this policy of restraint to traditional clients. It had not increased the friendliness of such leaders as Nasser and Nkrumah, and, at the same time, the traditional clients in the Middle East were becoming restive. The Jordanian government was under pressure both at home and from other Arab nations to acquire weapons from the Soviet Union in 1966. After the June War of 1967 and the French embargo on Israel, it was no longer possible to withstand domestic pressures for increased arms supplies to Israel. According to Townsend Hoopes, Deputy Assistant Secretary for International Security Affairs, this, in turn, made it necessary to increase supplies to 'moderate' Arab states, not only 'to weaken the radical Arab potential' but also 'to avoid a situation in which the United States would have no friends in the Middle East, except Israel, while the Soviet Union would gain uncontested influence in the vast and populous Arab world'. Finally, various events in the Persian Gulf area, such as the Yemeni civil war, the impending British withdrawal, Soviet supplies to the Yemen and Southern Yemen, and Arab claims to Iranian oil installations, gave impetus to arms supplies to the traditional US recipients in the region – Saudi Arabia and Iran – so as to ensure the protection of US interests there.

This pattern of supplying arms to the rivals of Soviet recipients is not confined to the Middle East, where arms supplies to Israel and the monarchies have increased rapidly. From the early sixties, the increase in military assistance to Ethiopia was at least partly a response to the Soviet arms supplies to Somalia. After the 1963 border war between Algeria and Morocco, increased arms supplies to Morocco and also Tunisia were justified on the grounds of offsetting aid to Algeria.

Influencing the military establishment

Until 1959 the notion of using military assistance to influence military personnel in recipient countries was largely confined to Latin America. The doctrine that the important social and political role of the armed forces in developing countries should be encouraged by training and civil action first appeared in the *Draper Report*, which concluded that because of the concentration of managerial and executive skills in the armed forces, and because of their responsibility for internal security and the direct defence of borders, the role of the armed forces in developing countries was different from that in the United States. They were more closely related to domestic affairs on all levels. By means of increased emphasis on training for leadership and development, rather than specific weapons and technical training, American values would be more widespread and appreciated. The *Draper Report* also recommended increased emphasis on civic action, that is, the use of military forces for activities which contribute to economic development, such as building roads and bridges. It recalled the role of US army engineers in developing the West – a recollection which has been made many times since.

The adoption of many of the recommendations of the *Draper Report* was concomitant with the increased emphasis on counter-insurgency, not only in South East Asia, but in Latin America and Africa as well. The Joint Chiefs of Staff define counter-insurgency as 'those military, para-military, political, economic, psychological, and civic actions taken by a government to defeat the subversive insurgency'. This gave a wide scope to the uses of military forces and their type of training.

In pursuing a policy aimed at influencing and to some extent strengthening military establishments, the United States was not necessarily concerned to encourage military coups. Indeed, one of the objectives of training programmes for Latin America is said to give the Latin American soldier a 'professional' notion of his role, an objective which would appear to be defeated in the efforts to inculcate an understanding of the role of the armed forces in defeating communism.

Under President Kennedy, the Administration expressed its disapproval of military coups in Latin America and temporarily cut off aid in a few cases. But this policy was reversed by the Johnson Administration, which intervened to support the military government in the Dominican Republic in 1965, and welcomed the overthrow of Goulart in Brazil in 1964, of Nkrumah in Ghana in 1966 and of Sukarno in Indonesia in 1966. The United States halted delivery of major items to the military government in Greece, but as a European country Greece can perhaps be put in a different category. In Africa, there have been coups in eight of the seventeen countries to which the United States gives aid, and attempted coups in at least two others. General Paul Adams, responsible for military aid to Africa, in his testimony before the House Foreign Affairs Committee in financial year 1964, stated as the first objective of military aid to Africa: 'to foster an anti-communist, free-world-oriented military community'. The point seems to be that since these military establishments are bound to intervene in politics, it is worth ensuring that they are on the 'right' side.

During the whole period, training programmes have amounted to approximately 7 per cent of the total US military-assistance programme. There is a special emphasis on training in Latin America and Africa, where the proportion of military assistance devoted to training has been 10 per cent and 12 per cent respectively. In terms of numbers, Latin America and the Far East have accounted for more than 50 per cent of the training programme.

The training programme showed a rapid increase in Latin America and Africa after 1959. Between 1956 and 1958, an average of nearly 40 African soldiers per year were trained in the United States, while in 1967, 824 were being trained – 617 in the United States. In Latin America, nearly 2,000 were trained per year between 1957 and 1958: by 1967 the number had risen to 5,000.

Apart from courses at civilian colleges and universities, the courses which place most emphasis on non-military subjects are the counter-insurgency courses, for which participants come mainly from Latin America and South East Asia, and leadership programmes, which are designed for Africans. In the eight-week counter-insurgency course held at the counter-insurgency school of Fort Bragg in 1963, five of the seven subjects dealt with non-military aspects.

The notion of using the armed forces for non-military projects was not a new one. The first large-scale programme of this kind was the 'Armed Forces Assistance to Korea' programme immediately after the Korean War. Its function was seen primarily in terms of the image it would present of the United States to the local people. By the end of the fifties, civic-action programmes were being undertaken by most of the major recipients of military aid. Nevertheless, at that time there were still qualifications concerning these programmes, mainly a fear that they might provide a justification for maintaining large military forces, or might detract from the ability to carry out purely military missions.

Civic-action programmes were given a boost in the early sixties by the Kennedy Administration. The use of civic action in counter-guerilla operations in South East Asia, and particularly in Viet-Nam, the Philippines and Thailand, convinced military officers of their utility; in addition, funds for civic action could come from the economic assistance appropriations, which were less liable to be cut than those of military assistance. Also, and perhaps more important, the US image of the armed forces in developing countries had changed: civic action was seen as a method of changing the image of the armed forces in the eyes of the local population.

Congressional criticism

A striking feature of the increase in arms deliveries to free-world orientation areas after 1965 was the increase in credit sales, as opposed to grant aid, and it has been suggested that economic interests – the need to reduce the US balance-of-payment deficit – was the main explanation for this. But another and more important explanation can be found in the need to evade increasingly critical Congressional scrutiny. When the extent of the credit sales was made public, Congress imposed various restrictions on the sales programmes, restrictions that reflected increasing concern with the US overseas role and which also led to restrictions on the foreign-assistance programme as a whole. By 1969, a new method of overcoming limited appropriation for military assistance had evolved – the transfer of weapons, surplus to the requirements of the US armed forces, mainly in Viet-Nam, to foreign countries at no cost to the Military Assistance Program.

In 1961, the US Department of Defense set up the International Logistics Negotiations (ILN) office to organize and promote military sales. In the first few years of the programme, it was rather successful. Sales rose from $1·5 billion in financial year 1962 to $2 billion in financial year 1966. Thereafter they fell, but they fell because of a 50 per cent fall in sales to industrial countries. Sales to Third World countries actually rose, and by 1969 amounted to approximately half the total sales, or $800 million. By financial year 1971, total sales amounted to approximately $2·5 billion, of which about two thirds went to the Third World.

It was stressed that the objectives of the sales programme and objectives of the grant aid programme were essentially the same. The only difference was that sales were cheaper. They were considered to be an effective and relatively inexpensive implement of United States national security policy. In his message to Congress in January 1967, McNamara stated the principal goals of the foreign military sales programme as being:

1.   To further the practice of co-operative logistics and standardization with our allies by integrating our supply systems to the maximum extent feasible and by helping to limit proliferation of different types of equipment.
2.   To reduce the costs to both our allies and ourselves of equipping our collective forces, by avoiding unnecessary and costly duplicative development programs, and by realizing the economies possible for larger production runs.
3.   To offset, at least partially, the unfavourable payments impact of our deployment abroad in the interest of collective defense.

The third goal, the balance-of-payments motive, was the only reason for selling weapons rather than giving them away. Great emphasis was placed on the benefits to the balance of payments on defence account, that is to say, the need to offset the cost of US troops deployed abroad. It was also stressed that the programme was aimed at developed countries able to share in the 'common defense burden'. Included in the Pentagon's definition of 'developed' countries are the oil-rich countries of the Middle East.

But the evidence suggests that there was another very important motive for increasing sales, as opposed to grants, to Third World countries. The big increase in sales to Third World countries occurred after 1964: they rose from $84·6 million in financial year 1964 to $444·5 million in financial year 1966, and this increase coincided with various legislation which enabled the Department of Defense to extend large amounts of very liberal credit without Congressional scrutiny.

The 1964 Foreign Assistance Act provided that the Department of Defense could guarantee the financing of military export sales undertaken 'by any individual corporation, partnership, or association doing business with the United States', while demanding only 25 per cent of the loan as a reserve to back up the 100 per cent guarantee. This reserve came from the Military Assistance Credit Fund, set up in 1957 and known as the revolving fund because repayment of loans went back into it. In order to guarantee such loans, the Department of Defense was required to charge a fee for this service. However, in 1965 the fee was no longer deemed necessary for 'any agency of the United States'. This marked the beginning of the country X account. The Department of Defense and the Export-Import Bank worked out an agreement whereby the Bank lent to the Defense Department, under Defense Department guarantee. As Harold F. Lindes, President of the Export-Import Bank, explained during hearings before the Senate Banking and Currency Committee in July 1967, the Defense Department then used the loan to finance arms sales to countries to which 'the Bank was otherwise not prepared to extend credit for military goods. Under this arrangement, the Export-Import Bank provides financing, but does not deal with the buyer and is not informed of the buyer's identity.' The country X loans, which were not publicized, enabled the Department of Defense to finance arms sales up to four times the size of the revolving fund, without Congressional authorization.

While it is clear that there were important political reasons for increasing the export of arms and that sales, especially the country X loans, represented an ingenious method of avoiding the awkward and tedious necessity of asking Congress to appropriate increased funds, economic motives cannot have been entirely insignificant. It is probable that, although top officials regarded the political factors as of paramount importance, middle-level officials, who were involved with the arms sales programme, placed more emphasis on the economic benefits.

The Sales Office must inevitably have gained a momentum of its own. Meeting sales targets became ends in themselves. Deals with Iran and Saudi Arabia increased the prestige of the office. It seems likely that the programme got out of hand. Although it was stressed by officials that each deal underwent extensive review, the machinery of review was never adequately explained.

The revelations concerning the size of the sales programme, the country X loans, and the machinery of review led to vociferous public criticism both in Congress and in the press. The debate in Congress centred around two issues. First of all, Congress had not been informed of the country X loans. Secondly, it was felt that the Administration was trying to convert the Export-Import Bank from a peaceful institution for promoting trade into a 'prime source of credit for the arms race'. Senators were 'frankly shocked' when it was revealed to the House Banking and Currency Committee that a quarter of the Bank's business was devoted to financing arms sales – 70 per cent of this was direct loans to developed countries.

Behind this controversy lay a whole range of criticism of arms sales to developing countries, mainly voiced by the more liberal Congressmen. The tone was set by the Senate Foreign Relations Committee staff study, which argued that high-pressure salesmanship in Europe forced the Europeans to compete in the developing markets and try to sell surplus US equipment, that arms sales to developing countries caused arms races and thus conflicts and diverted desperately needed resources from development, and that there was inadequate government machinery to deal with these sales. While the Banking and Currency Committees concentrated on the role of the Export-Import Bank, the Senate Foreign Relations Committee, in 1967, argued the need for tighter control over specific sales. They expressed abhorrence at the notion that the USA had become the largest supplier of weapons in the world – 'a profiteer in blood money'. It was argued that the USA should not be carried away by the argument 'if we don't sell them, the Russians will' and that, as 'the most powerful nation on earth', it was up to the United States to put a stop to these arms races.

In 1969, the Administration introduced a military sales bill which involved many restrictions, including abolishing the revolving fund, thus requiring new obligational authority from Congress for credit sales each year, limiting the ability of the Department of Defense to guarantee loans for private banks, and abolishing Export-Import Bank loans to developing countries. It also suspended all military credit sales to countries 'which buy from foreign countries an amount of military hardware which we regard as excessive'.

In its final form, the Act imposed credit ceilings on foreign military sales of $300 million for financial years 1970 and 1971, and called for efforts to negotiate an arms limitation in the Middle East, for a review of the US military assistance and sales programmes and for multilateral discussions on the control of worldwide trade in armaments. In March 1969, the ILN office was abolished.

Surplus weapons

Various measures have been taken to overcome these restrictions. Because of the deadlock over the Military Sales Act, authorization for sales to Israel was transferred to the Military Procurement Authorization Act. The transfer of funds for Viet-Nam, Thailand and Laos, as well as for South Korean and Philippine forces in Viet-Nam, to the Defense Budget is also partly explained in terms of the limited appropriations for foreign assistance. For financial year 1971, $2·2 billion was authorized for these forces.

Another method of increasing exports without requiring increased appropriations is the supply of surplus weapons. These can include both equipment which is obsolete for US forces and has been replaced by new equipment, and new equipment which exceeds the forces' requirements. Only the cost of refurbishing and shipping is charged to the Military Assistance Program. The Defense Department is merely required to report such transactions annually to Congress, when it appears before Congress for military assistance appropriations.

The surplus stocks programme has been given a boost by the increased availability of such weapons, owing to the war in Viet-Nam. The Department of Defense estimated in 1970 that $27 billion in excess defence articles, valued at original acquisition cost, was available for distribution. In particular, a programme has been established in the Far East, known as the Military Assistance Pacific Excess (MAPEX), under which excess stocks available in Viet-Nam are supplied to third countries.

Action by Congress on this programme has already been taken. An amendment to the Military Sales Act, passed on 12 January 1971, subtracts grants of excess stocks, measured at utility value, from MAP funds and places a ceiling on such grants of $100 million.

3 The Soviet Union

While Western countries generally release official information about their arms supplies to developing countries or publicly discuss the principles guiding their supply policies – for instance, in parliamentary debates or Senate hearings – in the Soviet Union these matters are given no official publicity. With the exception of a few general statements made by Soviet leaders, it is virtually impossible to find any official document explaining either the principles of Soviet arms supply policy or the internal machinery responsible for its execution.

However, despite the lack of official information, there is a considerable quantity of published material on Soviet arms supplies. Apart from information from Western sources gained in part by their intelligence activities, a number of recipient countries officially disclose their arms deals with the Soviet Union either in statements to the press or in government debates. In addition, knowledge of the use of Soviet weapons in certain conflicts indicates that agreements must have been made to supply arms, even when neither side has issued a public confirmation. When information from sources of this kind is combined with general knowledge of Soviet internal structure and development, and of Soviet foreign policy, it is possible to build up a reasonably accurate picture of the flow of major Soviet weapons, of the main characteristics and basic principles of Soviet arms supply in general, and of the circumstances under which specific arms-supply agreements were concluded.

The internal decision-making process of the Soviet Union differs in one important respect from that of other suppliers: it is highly centralized. Decision-making at the highest level is carried out by top Soviet state and party leaders. Top military officials also play an important role in this process, particularly when requests are made for very sophisticated weapons or when arms deals involve surplus stocks. The preparatory work, negotiations and execution of agreements are carried out by various ministries, such as the Ministries for Foreign Affairs, Defence and Trade, but these ministries only execute directives issued from above. Consequently, when an arms deal between the Soviet Union and a developing country is carried out, there is no doubt that it represents the policy of the party and government.

Certain general points should be stressed before a detailed examination of Soviet arms supply policy is made. First, the arms supply policy of the Soviet Union, like that of other countries, must be seen as one part or factor of a general Soviet policy towards developing countries, and must be viewed within the broader framework of Soviet foreign policy as a whole. Secondly, in pursuing its arms supply policy, the Soviet Union has frequently relied on member countries of the Warsaw Pact. But because the armaments industries of most of these countries cannot produce either the type or quantity of weapons which the developing countries need, their role, particularly in the case of Poland, has been to provide training and technical assistance. Czechoslovakia is an exception: it had been a major arms manufacturer in the inter-war period and, very often acting on behalf of the Soviet Union, continued to export significant quantities of arms after the Second World War, especially in the mid-1950s, when the Soviet Union first entered the arms market.

Thirdly, Soviet arms-supply policy has primarily served political interests, and economic interests have been secondary. There are several examples of payment in kind for Soviet arms, for instance in rubber, copper, tin and so on. Also, the Soviet Union has made large economic investments in some countries, notably India and Egypt. However, this is not always the case with all the countries who receive Soviet arms. Further, the actual earnings from arms supplies have not been high. The main Soviet recipients either received arms as military assistance or have not yet been able to pay for them. For instance, North Viet-Nam received all arms supplies free of charge, Egypt has, after the June 1967 War, been allowed indefinite postponement of payment and Indonesia has never been able to pay its huge arms debt at all. Soviet prices are probably not economical; in most cases they have been much lower than they should have been if calculated on a profit basis. Actually, on a number of occasions, price was a determining factor in motivating purchasers to buy from the Soviet Union rather than from the West.

In addition, just as in the USA, the Soviet defence industry does not depend on arms exports outside the Warsaw Pact, hence there is no real economic pressure to export. The number of weapons supplied to developing countries, in relation to the number produced for the Soviet Union and the Warsaw Pact, has not been high enough to have a significant effect on production costs. The production of MiG planes provides an example. In the past twenty years the Soviet Union has supplied various developing countries, both socialist and non-aligned, with about 450 MiG-15s, nearly 700 MiG-17s, over 200 MiG-19s and nearly 1,300 MiG-21s, while the Soviet Union itself at present operates about 8,000 MiG aircraft. So total production over the past twenty years for domestic and Warsaw Pact use must have been many times this figure. In addition, a significant proportion of the MiG planes delivered to developing countries were types which, at the time, were being replaced in the Soviet forces by a more recent model.

BACKGROUND

Up to 1955 the Soviet Union supplied arms only to the European socialist countries, China, North Korea and North Viet-Nam. There are several reasons why the Soviet Union did not emerge as a large-scale supplier much earlier. In the immediate post-war period the Soviet Union had two objectives: to rebuild its economy as fast as possible and, in particular, to strengthen its security. The strengthening of security was aimed at improving the protection of the Soviet Union's long and vulnerable borders: the acquisition of control over the countries situated along these borders was the best way of achieving this. However, the US and its allies in Western Europe had no sympathy with the Soviet

Union's security requirements, which they saw rather as the beginning of the 'spread of communism', and consequently made strenuous efforts to 'contain the further spread of Soviet power'. This represented the beginning of the 'cold war' era. In the following years the Soviet Union pursued a policy of isolationism. It was preoccupied with economic recovery, the consolidation of the socialist countries and, above all, with catching up militarily with the West, that is, breaking up the US nuclear monopoly. The theoretical foundation of Soviet foreign policy during this period was expressed in the so-called 'two-camp theory', launched in September 1947, according to which the world was divided into an imperialist camp on the one hand and a socialist camp led by the Soviet Union on the other.

In accordance with the two-camp theory, the Soviet Union expressed complete distrust of non-communist governments in the developing countries. One particular aspect of the foreign policy of the developing countries met with Soviet disapproval. At the time, a number of developing countries, particularly Asian nations, were launching the so-called policy of neutrality, or of a 'third force', which advocated strict neutrality in the struggle between the two sides, and welcomed the establishment of friendly relations with countries in both camps. This met with Soviet disapproval because the two-camp theory did not leave any room for such a 'third force'; it considered all those who did not join the camp led by the Soviet Union to be opposed to it.

The changes in Soviet military capability in the mid-fifties, accompanied by the economic and political stabilization of the country, inevitably affected the political thinking of the Soviet leadership and brought about substantial revisions in Soviet foreign policy. The Soviet Union became more willing to take an active part in the life of the international community and, in particular, to contribute to the solution of pressing international problems. On many issues the Soviet Union took a far less rigid stand than earlier and expressed willingness to make substantial compromises with the West. This development was, *inter alia*, a clear indication that the Soviet Union was changing its policy of isolationism, and as a result was able to abandon the extreme form of the two-camp theory. It was developed into the theory of peaceful coexistence and a policy of active engagement in world affairs.

As part of this general change in foreign policy, the Soviet approach towards the developing countries underwent thorough revision. The change was particularly noticeable in regard to the Soviet attitude to developing countries' foreign policies, notably to their policy of neutrality, which at that time was gradually being transformed into a policy of non-alignment. The Soviet Union not only recognized this policy but acted to support it. Soon large-scale diplomatic and cultural co-operation was established. It also extended political support in international affairs, offered economic aid and proved willing to expand trade relations. And for the first time the Soviet Union was ready to meet their demands for arms. This policy grew from Soviet efforts to increase its influence and prestige, and to challenge the Western hegemony in the developing regions.

MAIN TRENDS IN ARMS SUPPLIES

The pattern of Soviet arms supplies to Third World countries clearly reflects the change in policy after the mid-1950s. The first non-socialist recipients of Soviet arms were some of the Middle East countries. By 1972 the number of recipients had increased by over twenty. In 1971–2 the Soviet Union surpassed the United States in supplies of major weapons.

Supplies to socialist countries fell away substantially after the Korean armistice, and began to rise again only in the sixties. There were a number of factors behind this recovery. With the revolution in Cuba, the Soviet Union's position as the major power in the socialist world meant that Cuba naturally turned to it for weapons. And the Viet-Nam War also left the Soviet Union with little option but to increase supplies. Finally, in the sixties, there was the factor of competition with China. On a number of occasions when the Soviet Union temporarily reduced supplies to one of the socialist countries, that country began to obtain

Table 6 USSR: major weapon exports, by region

	Far East, incl. Viet-Nam	Indian Sub-continent	Middle East
1950	16·9	–	–
1951	30·0	–	–
1952	18·9	–	–
1953	121·3	–	–
1954	0·8	–	–
1955	30·6	2·0	15·8
1956	11·1	2·5	67·1
1957	4·6	9·5	146·8
1958	15·3	6·3	96·6
1959	7·4	6·8	63·1
1960	20·6	30·9	44·5
1961	51·5	36·4	111·6
1962	132·0	39·1	182·4
1963	61·1	40·6	84·1
1964	71·0	5·6	95·6
1965	52·3	46·8	52·7
1966	214·2	168·3	84·0
1967	251·5	110·4	522·7
1968	218·2	245·6	260·6
1969	38·7	108·8	176·3
1970	63·2	76·2	299·6
1971	148·7	194·7	368·4
1972	280·6	37·8	236·4
Total[a]	**1,860·6**	**1,168·4**	**2,908·3**
Per cent of total	*28·5*	*17·9*	*44·5*

[a] Figures may not add up to totals owing to rounding.
Source: SIPRI worksheets.

US $ mn, at constant (1968) *prices*

North Africa	Sub-Saharan Africa	Latin America	Total
–	–	–	**16·9**
–	–	–	**30·0**
–	–	–	**19·0**
–	–	–	**121·3**
–	–	–	**0·8**
–	–	–	**48·4**
–	–	–	**80·8**
–	–	–	**161·0**
–	–	–	**118·2**
–	–	3·8	**81·0**
–	4·4	17·5	**118·0**
4·4	13·0	79·6	**296·5**
16·2	0·2	148·8	**518·8**
10·7	2·9	12·8	**212·1**
5·4	2·0	11·6	**191·2**
41·5	19·5	5·3	**218·1**
37·9	5·7	3·9	**514·0**
37·3	5·9	2·2	**930·1**
3·1	2·4	–	**729·9**
3·0	7·8	–	**334·6**
9·3	29·6	1·2	**479·1**
11·5	11·5	7·0	**741·8**
–	0·2	18·7	**573·7**
180·3	**105·1**	**312·4**	**6,535·2**
2·8	*1·6*	*4·8*	*100·0*

supplies from China; later Soviet supplies were again increased. Despite the increase, socialist countries, which until 1955 had been virtually the sole Third World recipients of Soviet weapons, received only 32 per cent of Soviet supplies to the Third World in the period 1955–72.

The pattern of supplies to non-aligned countries also illustrates the way in which Soviet arms-trade policy developed. In the Middle East the Soviet Union's initial objective appears to have been to render ineffectual the Western attempt to construct an anti-Soviet military alliance there. However, long after this had been achieved, the Soviet Union continued to supply increasing quantities of arms, having become identified with the Arab side in the conflict with Israel. In total, the Middle East has received considerably more weapons than any other area.

In the late 1950s and early 1960s, the Soviet Union began to supply weapons to both Indonesia and India – after the Middle East, the next most important recipients among the non-aligned countries. Here, too, the Soviet Union's objective was to support the non-aligned policies of Indonesia and India and thereby strengthen the opposition to SEATO and CENTO. But there were other important considerations as well, in particular rivalry with China. Supplies to India could have helped to maintain that country as a countervailing military force to China in Asia, and supplies to Indonesia could have prevented its possible alignment with China at the time when the Indonesian Communist Party, the strongest political force in the country, was siding with China in the Sino-Soviet ideological conflict.

After 1960, the number of countries to which the Soviet Union supplied arms increased. Whenever a country turned away from Western arms supplies and approached the Soviet Union, the Soviet Union generally appeared willing to sell arms, for this served to reduce the Western monopoly and expand Soviet influence. A growing number of countries recognized the Soviet Union as a possible alternative source of supplies, and acted accordingly. These competitive arms supplies were particularly important in African countries.

SOCIALIST DEVELOPING COUNTRIES

Several factors have influenced Soviet arms-supply policy towards socialist developing countries. First there was Soviet interest in strengthening their position militarily, both against possible internal opposition and against external threats, and in defending the interests of the socialist camp in general. This factor still plays the most important role in Soviet arms supplies to these countries. The second important factor has been the state of Sino-Soviet relations; once the ideological conflict between China and the Soviet Union had come into the open, the competition between them often forced the Soviet Union's hand in the matter of arms supplies. Thirdly, there has been the state of relations between the Soviet Union and the socialist developing countries themselves. From time to time all of them have attempted more independent policies, or have accused the Soviet Union of sacrificing their interests in the cause of détente with the West; and from time to time the Soviet Union has reduced, or indeed cut off, arms supplies as a sign of its displeasure. The fourth factor has been the state of Soviet relations with Western countries, particularly the United States. The Soviet Union has in general avoided situations in which its arms supplies might provoke a direct confrontation with the United States (the installation of missiles in Cuba is, of course, the major exception), and this has been an important constraint on Soviet supplies.

During the most intense period of the cold war, 1947–55, North Korea was the only developing country to receive arms supplies from the Soviet Union. These supplies started immediately after the withdrawal of Soviet forces from Korea in January 1949, and continued at a high level during the Korean War, which broke out in June 1950. The peak year was 1953, with the delivery of some $20 million worth of major weapons. At first the Soviet Union was reluctant to support the North Korean attempt to reunify the country by the use of force, as the Soviet leaders were still occupied with the problem of internal consolidation of the socialist camp and catching up with the West militarily. However, when the advance of the North Korean troops was halted and indeed reversed, Soviet reluctance diminished and it provided North Korea with substantial military aid, indicating the Soviet Union's readiness to prevent the total defeat of the socialist regime. North Korea was an entirely Soviet-sponsored state and its defeat would have been a serious setback for Soviet interests in the region.

The same reasoning guided Soviet policy towards North Viet-Nam. The Soviet Union took an active part in the 1954 Geneva Conference and fully supported the agreements reached between the parties concerned. Following the Korean armistice and the Geneva Conference, the Soviet Union continued to support both countries but showed restraint in regard to further military aid. Arms supplies fell sharply from some $190 million in 1950–54 to only $60 million in the next five years. The basis of this policy was to avoid military confrontation between the two great powers, in line with the principles of peaceful coexistence launched by the Soviet Union in February 1956. Consequently, military aid to North Viet-Nam was primarily designed to strengthen the internal position of the Vietminh government, and arms supplies to North Korea were designed to do no more than keep the balance between the two parts of the country.

However, Soviet policy was on occasion regarded with some suspicion by the two recipients, although they complied with Soviet requests; they considered that the Soviet Union had held them back when victory was possible, and that consequently their tremendous losses had been in vain. This view was strongly held in North Viet-Nam, where it was generally believed that the Vietminh could easily have succeeded in reunifying the two parts of the country. The bilateral relations of both countries with the Soviet Union became strained from 1957 to 1958, and particularly from 1960 onwards, when the Sino-Soviet dispute began to intensify and the two powers began to compete for the allegiance of developing countries. Unlike the Soviet Union, China supported the North Viet-Namese government when it decided to back the National Front for the Liberation of South Viet-Nam (NLF), established in December 1960, while, at the same time,

Soviet military and economic aid to North Korea was being replaced by Chinese aid. From 1958 onwards Chinese arms supplies also included major weapons, mostly aircraft. Indeed from 1962 to 1965 all Soviet aid to North Korea was completely halted. During this period North Viet-Nam was closest to the Chinese in the Sino-Soviet dispute: the North Viet-Namese government joined China in condemning the Soviet leadership for 'revisionism'.

This situation changed only in the mid-sixties, after Khrushchev's fall from power. The new Soviet leaders seemed determined to regain Soviet influence in these two countries and to strengthen their position in their own country by successes in their foreign policy, while at the same time challenging the spread of Chinese influence. Their success was the consequence of factors largely beyond their control: increased US involvement in the Viet-Nam War posed an acute threat to North Viet-Namese security, and the inception of China's cultural revolution led China to reduce its relations with the outside world, including both North Korea and North Viet-Nam.

The North Viet-Namese government was first to accept the realities of the changed situation. Under the circumstances the Soviet Union was the only country which could fill its requirements. Beginning in 1965, and particularly in 1966–7, Soviet major weapons supplies to North Viet-Nam rose rapidly and for the first time included such highly sophisticated defensive weapons as surface-to-air missiles. The value of Soviet major weapon supplies in the three-year period 1966–8 is estimated at about $580 million. This massive Soviet military aid was one of the main reasons for North Viet-Nam's decision to incline once again towards the Soviet view in the Sino-Soviet conflict. Soviet arms supplies to North Viet-Nam, particularly surface-to-air missiles, were reduced only after the US bomb halt in late 1968, and for a few years North Viet-Nam received a relatively small amount of arms, which suggests, again, that the Soviet Union was still concerned not to provoke a serious confrontation with the United States and that its aid was closely tailored to the military requirements of North Viet-Nam.

During 1971 Soviet supplies to North Viet-Nam appear to have increased again, and the five-day US bombing campaign in December 1971 was followed by renewed promises of military aid. Despite heavy US bombing of North Viet-Nam's supply lines and the mining of its coastal waters, major arms supplies, mainly surface-to-air missiles, surpassed the 1967 peak in 1972.

Soviet military supplies to North Korea were resumed in 1965, coinciding with the deterioration of North Korean–Chinese relations. However, unlike North Viet-Nam, North Korea refrained from taking sides in the Sino-Soviet dispute and continued to pursue a fairly independent policy.

Soviet arms-supply policy towards Cuba to some extent met the same problem as its policy towards North Viet-Nam and North Korea. Arms supplies to Cuba began in 1960 after the revolution, and rose sharply until 1963. At first the supplies were designed to support a country which had been ostracized by the United States and which later became a member of the socialist camp. The Soviet Union posed a more serious direct challenge to the United States by attempting to site missiles on Cuban territory in 1962 and the account of the US response is a familiar story. Soviet arms supplies to Cuba dropped sharply after 1963, and Soviet–Cuban relations deteriorated considerably. The Soviet Union displayed a lack of enthusiasm for Cuba's desire to help establish revolutionary movements in Latin America. In recent years, however, relations have improved and Soviet arms supplies have increased.

NON-ALIGNED DEVELOPING COUNTRIES

Once the decision had been taken around 1955 to reorient the general direction of Soviet policy towards developing countries, there was a gradual evolution of arms-trade policy towards them. During an initial phase the Soviet Union's dominant concern was to weaken the military alliances which the West was forming round its borders. Secondly, Soviet arms supplies were provided to other countries where the Soviet Union considered it had some strategic interest. Finally in recent years the Soviet Union has negotiated arms agreements more generally, as part of its apparent readiness to compete for influence on a worldwide basis. Although these three phases constitute a convenient way to describe the evolution of the Soviet policy, it should be understood that, in reality, the changes were not clear-cut, but were part of a process of gradual development.

Weakening the Western military alliances

The policy of breaking through the Western military encirclement, as seen by the Soviet Union, was the basic objective of Soviet foreign policy in the second half of the 1950s: it was directed first at weakening the strategic advantage of the West, and secondly at establishing the Soviet Union as a recognized great power in the world strategic context. By 1955 the belt of military alliances along the southern borders of the Soviet Union and China had been nearly completed, and only one big gap remained – the Middle East. The Western powers, particularly the United States, had been making strenuous efforts to fill this gap since the early fifties, but to prevent this the Soviet Union was ready to associate itself with any country in the region which could help in its efforts.

The emergence of the new political and social forces in the Arab world in the early fifties created the necessary basis for close co-operation between the Arab countries and the Soviet Union. Some of the new regimes were more nationalistic and more hostile to the vestiges of Western colonialism than the old ruling classes, and were as determined to eliminate the dominant position of the West as was the Soviet Union. Thus the Soviet objectives in the Middle East – to get the West out of the region and to prevent the establishment of a pro-Western military alliance – coincided with the national policies of a number of the Arab countries, particularly those of the new regimes in Syria and Egypt. When the Western countries intensified their pressure upon those Arab countries unwilling to join any military alliance in the Middle East by displaying reluctance to supply weapons on terms acceptable to them, these Arab countries turned to the

Soviet Union, which had no hesitation in declaring its willingness to extend political support and supply them with the weapons they requested.

The first arms deal between a socialist and a Third World country was concluded early in 1955 between Czechoslovakia and Egypt, the former acting on behalf of the Soviet Union. The deal caused great anxiety in the West, since it challenged the traditional Western monopoly of arms supplies and was thus a clear indication of the decline in the political influence of the West over the countries in this region. On the other hand, the Soviet arms supplies considerably increased the prestige of the Soviet Union amongst the new Arab leadership, so much so that the Soviet Union was considered the saviour of the Arab world.

Soviet readiness to meet Arab demands for weapons contributed to the rapid consolidation of anti-Western nations, for example, the emerging Egypt–Syria–Yemen group which counterbalanced the Baghdad Pact coalition. From a strategic point of view the refusal of the Arab countries, with the exception of Iraq, to join the Baghdad Pact considerably weakened the Pact's military advantages for the West, while the Soviet Union, by supplying the Arab countries with weapons, became actively involved in Middle East affairs, and was thus in a position to establish itself as a power in the region. In 1956 Soviet leaders made attempts to obtain official recognition of this status from the West, as well as to dismantle the Western alliance structure, by inviting the Western powers to undertake a joint action for enforcing a general embargo on arms shipments to the Middle East. And although the Soviet offer was rejected by the West because the halt of arms shipments to Iran and Iraq would have meant the disintegration of the Baghdad Pact, it became obvious that no solution to the problems in the Middle East was possible without Soviet consent. The Suez crisis of October 1956 only further strengthened the Soviet position. By meeting the heavy replacement requirements of the Arab countries and by supplying them with considerable quantities of new weapons, the Soviet Union became an inevitable participant in any decisions about the future political solution in the Middle East.

The Iraqi revolution in 1958 was a final blow to efforts by the West to maintain its Middle East defence system. The key country in the Baghdad Pact, Iraq, became a recipient of Soviet arms in November 1958, only four months after the monarchy was overthrown. Thus, within a few years after the first deal with Egypt, all the major Arab countries had enlisted themselves as recipients of Soviet weapons. In the second half of the fifties, Soviet major weapons supplies to the Middle East reached a value of $390 million, or some 40 per cent of all arms supplies to the region.

The Middle East was not the only strategically important area where the Soviet Union made efforts to break through the Western encirclement. Beginning in the mid-fifties, Soviet relations with Afghanistan, India and Burma improved considerably. Between 1955 and 1959, India alone received over $500 million in economic aid from the Soviet Union, and substantial credits, amounting to $120 million, were also extended to Afghanistan. The purpose of heavy Soviet economic commitments to these countries was clearly to strengthen their independence, which, it was feared in the Soviet Union, might have been put in jeopardy by exclusive reliance on the West both for military and economic aid.

Soviet efforts also proved successful in the Far East. From 1956 close relations were established with Indonesia, whose denunciation of military pacts in general and refusal to join SEATO in particular coincided with Soviet policies. The first arms deal between the two countries was concluded in 1958. Previously Indonesia had relied exclusively on arms supplies from Western countries, particularly the United States.

Thus the general world situation at the end of the 1950s was an encouraging one for the Soviet Union. By means of generous arms supplies it had succeeded in establishing close relations with a number of non-aligned countries which played important roles in international affairs, and thus had strengthened its image as a promoter of the interests of the non-aligned countries. Politically it was a setback for the West. The military alliances along the southern Soviet borders, originally envisaged as a cohesive belt, now showed important loopholes. In the Middle East they were Egypt, Syria and Iraq: in South Asia, Afghanistan, India and Burma, though India and Burma were not recipients of Soviet weapons at that time: and in the Far East, Indonesia – one of the largest countries in the region.

Strategically important regions

Having accomplished its initial objective of breaking the Western military encirclement, the prevailing concern of the Soviet Union in the sixties appeared to be to strengthen its position further in strategically important regions around its borders, and then more generally to play the role of a world power in more distant regions as well.

In pursuing the first objective, the Soviet Union continued to concentrate on the Middle East, whose share in the total quantity of major weapons supplied by the Soviet Union grew rapidly from about \$390 million in the second half of the fifties to some \$520 in the first half of the sixties. In the next five years, from 1965 to 1969, the value of arms supplies to the Middle East doubled, representing 40 per cent of all Soviet arms supplies to developing countries (including Viet-Nam) during that period. Between 1970 and 1972 the share of the Middle East had increased even further, representing 50 per cent of total supplies. Egypt continued to be the main recipient, but arms supplies to Iraq and Syria also rose.

The arms which the Soviet Union supplied to the Arab countries in the fifties were primarily intended to strengthen the Arab position against the West and to weaken the Baghdad Pact. However, by the early sixties the Baghdad Pact was no longer a decisive issue. Furthermore, Arab relations with the West were no longer so strained as before, and the West finally accepted their non-alignment. Iraq entered into an arms deal with the UK in 1960, Syria received some weapons from France during the same year, and Western economic aid to the UAR and Syria was also resumed. Thus the Arab countries remained primarily concerned with Israel, rather than with the West, and their arms purchases were designed to maintain or strengthen their military potential in regard to Israel. Later, when Arab relations with the West deteriorated again, it was because of the support which the Western powers were extending to Israel. Consequently, if the Soviet Union hoped to maintain its position in the region and to advance it further, it had to extend its support to the Arab cause.

In the aftermath of the June 1967 War, the Arab reliance on the Soviet Union moved into a decisive phase. The Soviet Union not only replaced Arab losses but also supplied a very sophisticated air-defence system, with large numbers of Soviet troops closely concerned with its operation. In return for military and political support, the Soviet Union obtained naval landing and refuelling rights in Syria and the UAR, facilitating the maintenance of the Soviet fleet in the Mediterranean and enabling the Soviet Union, for the first time, to challenge the NATO nations' supremacy in the region.

However, the unwillingness of the Soviet Union to supply greater quantities of arms, in particular offensive weapons, and thus to risk a confrontation with NATO, brought about a severe strain in Soviet–Egyptian relations. In July 1972, President Anwar Sadat terminated the mission of the Soviet military advisers serving in Egypt. After the withdrawal of the 15–20,000 experts, Soviet arms supplies were limited to spare parts and replacement items. One consignment of surface-to-air missiles also arrived in Egypt. Instead, relations developed with Syria and Iraq, followed by increasing quantities of arms to these countries.

The Soviet Union has also negotiated arms-supply agreements with other countries not directly involved in the Arab–Israeli conflict – for example Algeria and Southern Yemen. All had some strategic importance for the Soviet Union. Algeria first received Soviet arms during the national liberation struggle against France in the 1950s, but large-scale supplies started only after Algeria had obtained independence in 1962. Soviet supplies to Algeria were particularly high between 1965 and 1967, and, in addition, the Algerian army has largely been trained by the Soviet Union. Algeria had also provided the Soviet Union with naval landing and refuelling facilities. But relations between the two countries were somewhat strained after the June 1967 War because of Algeria's open criticism of Soviet reluctance to replace the Arab losses in offensive weapons, and Algeria has taken steps to obtain some French weapons as well.

Very close relations were established with Southern Yemen after its independence in 1967, and the first Soviet arms shipments were delivered in 1968. Soviet relations with this country are part of its overall strategy towards the entire region of the Gulf of Aden. Three key countries – Southern Yemen, the Yemen and Somalia – have received Soviet weapons. Arms supplies to the Yemen, which first received Soviet weapons in 1956, were renewed after the Egyptian withdrawal from the country following the 1967 UAR–Saudi Arabia agreement. Somalia applied for Soviet weapons in 1963 because it was dissatisfied with arms supplies from the West. Since then the Soviet Union has been Somalia's main arms supplier, while a number of Somali cadets have attended military academies in the Soviet Union. There were no doubt strategic reasons for the Soviet Union's interest in these three countries at the junction connecting the Red Sea and the Indian Ocean.

There were also strategic and political considerations in the Soviet Union's arms supplies to a number of Asian countries, especially India. The first arms-supply agreement with India was concluded in 1960, but it was only after the Sino-Indian armed conflict in October 1962 that Soviet military aid became significant. This conflict placed the Soviet leaders in the unique position of having to decide which side to support – a socialist country, China, or a non-aligned country, India. By confirming its readiness to supply previously promised arms, after an initial hesitation the Soviet Union sided with India. Two basic reasons seem to have prompted the Soviet Union to take this stand: the worsening of the Sino-Soviet party relations and India's strategic and political importance within the overall context of Soviet strategy.

In the following years, Soviet influence in the region increased, particularly after the 1965 Indo-Pakistani War. When the conflict broke out the Soviet Union acted cautiously: it took a neutral position and supported the efforts of the UN Secretary-General to arrange a ceasefire. When this was achieved, the Soviet Union unilaterally continued its efforts to bring the two sides together. The Tashkent declaration of January 1966, in which Prime Minister Shastri and President Kahn announced their resolve, *inter alia*, to restore peaceful as well as diplomatic relations between their countries, was a major political victory for the Soviet Union. It convinced India of continued Soviet support and later opened the door for improved Soviet–Pakistani relations. However, during the 1971 crisis, caused by the civil war in Pakistan which subsequently grew into the war between India and Pakistan, the Soviet Union extended full material and political support to India. This relationship was formalized in a treaty of friendship and co-operation concluded in August 1971. Chinese support for Pakistan in the conflict with India again placed the Soviet Union and Chinese on opposing sides in a conflict, thus continuing earlier developments.

Iran was the first member of a Western-sponsored military alliance to receive Soviet weapons. The deliveries were concentrated in two years, 1968 and 1969. Economic co-operation between the two countries continued, with Soviet investment in various Iranian companies amounting to about $250 million during 1966–9. Although Iran continued to rely on the West for arms supplies, it pursued a much more independent policy than before; and its military commitments to CENTO weakened.

In the Far East, Soviet efforts have on the whole been less successful, owing to internal political changes in two important recipient countries, Indonesia and Cambodia. In the first half of the sixties Soviet arms supplies to Indonesia far exceeded those to both North Korea and North Viet-Nam, and the Soviet Union had a very influential position in the country. However, towards the mid-sixties the Soviet Union became rather reluctant to continue its heavy arms shipments and appeared anxious to improve its relations with the West: Indonesian regional policy could have been an obstacle to achieving this aim. But from about 1960 Sino-Indonesian relations, which for a long time had been rather strained, improved considerably and China became a champion of Indonesia's 'crush Malaysia' policy. The Indonesian Communist Party (PKI), which was very influential in the country and one of the largest non-ruling communist parties in the world, supported China in the Sino-Soviet dispute. There was at the time a widespread belief that the PKI might take power in Indonesia. Under these circumstances the Soviet Union in 1964 reluctantly consented to conclude a new agreement with Indonesia and to accelerate the deliveries of weapons which had been previously promised, apparently to neutralize Chinese influence and also to move the PKI towards a neutral stand. However, the 1965 coup completely changed the situation. With the ousting of Sukarno, Indonesia turned to the West for both military and economic aid. The Indonesia–US rapprochement reached its culmination during President Nixon's visit to Indonesia in July 1969, and at the same time relations with the Soviet Union became cool.

Soviet–Cambodian relations developed in a similar way. Cambodia first received Soviet arms in September 1963. At that time, relations with the United States had been deteriorating for some time and Prince Sihanouk broke off relations completely in December 1963. Soviet commitments to Cambodia are difficult to judge; it is, however, clear that the Soviet Union wanted to preserve Cambodia's independence and neutrality. Chinese influence in the area might also have played a role. The overthrow of Prince Sihanouk's government in March 1970 and the subsequent US invasion of Cambodia have significantly altered the strategic environment in Indo-China.

In the long term, the organization and alignment of a future post-war Indo-China is, of course, of great importance. The Soviet Union has already taken several initiatives for the creation of a collective security zone.

General competition for influence

In the early part of the period the Soviet Union, as a general rule, entered into arms deals only with countries which were not on good terms with the West: the Soviet Union was their only choice as an alternative supplier if they did not want to give in to Western pressures. Later, particularly in the late 1960s, the Soviet Union proved willing to supply weapons also to countries which maintained good relations with Western countries and which continued to receive both economic and military assistance from them. Arms supplies to such countries might well have increased Soviet influence and prestige and possibly reduced the influence of other suppliers. Little strategic gains, if any, were sought, which distinguishes this group of arms recipients from, say, India, Iran or Pakistan. At first the Soviet Union was competing for influence with the West; when the Sino-Soviet ideological conflict came into the open, the USSR began to compete with China as well.

The effects of this policy can best be observed in Africa, which, although neglected to a certain extent throughout the fifties, aroused considerable Soviet interest in the beginning of the sixties. The Soviet Union proved ready to supply arms to a large number of emerging African states, so that between 1959 and 1970 agreements were concluded with the Sudan, Guinea, Morocco, Ghana, Mali, Congo (Kinshasa), Tanzania, Kenya, Uganda, Nigeria and Mauritania. All these countries had been recipients of Western military aid and continued to receive aid after they had concluded arms-supply agreements with the Soviet Union. These arrangements were often just single deals: Soviet arms supplies continued regularly in only a few cases, and even then they usually did not entirely displace supplies from other sources. Soviet expectations were apparently not very high: the least it could do was to break the Western monopoly of arms supplies, while at most it might establish a position of significant influence in the country concerned and give support to those forces oriented towards the Soviet Union. But in most cases the Soviet Union did not in fact achieve any major change in the foreign-policy orientation of the recipient countries.

The demand for weapons: Soviet response

The Soviet Union's success in establishing itself as a major arms supplier to non-aligned countries is to be explained as much by the policies of these countries as by its own. If it had not been for the interest shown by the recipients, Soviet efforts would have been much less successful.

The most typical and frequently occurring situation was that in which Western countries displayed reluctance to supply arms, refused to supply the kinds of weapons demanded or were willing to supply arms only on terms unacceptable to the recipients. This has been the situation with Egypt, Syria, Afghanistan, Iraq, Indonesia, Guinea, Nigeria and Iran. All these countries considered that they had a pressing need for weapons – a need which was quite independent of any Soviet willingness to supply. In most cases, they were actively involved in disputes or armed conflict. The Soviet Union simply took advantage of the situation to meet their needs and at the same time to promote its own interests.

Another group of countries received Soviet weapons simply because they preferred to. The West would probably have continued to supply arms had they been asked, but the Soviet Union was preferred. The most typical examples are Algeria and Southern Yemen: both countries started receiving regular Soviet arms supplies as soon as their struggles for national liberation were complete. Close relations with the Soviet Union, including arms supplies, were also an expression of their determination to build their societies along socialist lines.

The third situation in which recipient countries resorted to the Soviet Union for arms supplies occurred when their otherwise cordial relations with the West for various reasons became strained, or when the recipients wanted to pursue a more radical or independent policy in general. This was the case with Morocco, Tanzania, Uganda, Mali, Ghana, Iran, Pakistan and to a certain extent also with India and the Sudan. All these countries have regularly received Western arms supplies and only at certain stages preferred to obtain them from the Soviet Union. With a few exceptions these were isolated deals rather than arrangements for continued supplies.

AID TO LIBERATION MOVEMENTS

The Soviet support of liberation movements also reflects the changes in Soviet foreign policy, as well as the competition with China. Up to the mid-1950s only communist-led liberation movements were officially recognized. After the 20th Party Congress in 1956 the Soviet Union expressed unreserved support for all anti-colonial movements, although for several reasons aid to these movements did not markedly increase. First, the process of decolonization was largely complete in Asia, except for Indo-China, and nearing completion in North Africa. In the rest of Africa, the anti-colonial struggle began later. The Soviet Union was at this time improving its relations with the West, so that military aid to liberation movements would have been counterproductive. Secondly, in Asia, Africa and Latin America, the risk of conflict with Western powers was too great. Only the Pathet Lao in Laos received weapons for a short period in 1960–61. The FLN in Africa received only small quantities of Soviet arms before the independence of Algeria in 1962, owing to Soviet relations with France.

From the mid-1960s the Soviet attitude changed. In Africa, those anti-colonial movements still existing were directed against Portugal and the white regimes in Rhodesia and South Africa, and Soviet military aid to them did not entail any risk of serious confrontation with Britain or France. By supporting these struggles, the Soviet Union often improved relations with Black African nations. Another consideration was the competition with Chinese influence in the Third World. Today the Soviet Union is the main arms supplier of most of the African liberation movements.

In other areas, there is little evidence of direct Soviet aid. The NLF and Pathet Lao in Indo-China do receive Soviet weapons via North Viet-Nam, but the Cambodian liberation movement apparently gets no aid, being based in Peking. The Ceylonese government received Soviet arms when the guevarist guerilla uprising occurred in 1971. The PLO in Palestine has acquired some Soviet arms, but not the ELF in Eritrea.

4 The United Kingdom

Changes in British policy towards military exports reflect changes in Britain's international role. In the first post-war decade, Britain was the second largest exporter of weapons in the world, and British defence industry was the only one in Europe, apart from Sweden's, to have continued uninterrupted throughout the war. Because of its far-flung military commitments, many countries were dependent on Britain for military equipment, and, in turn, weapons exports served to secure and maintain Britain's overseas interests. In 1955, the government White Paper on the export of surplus material stated that: 'The general policy of HM government on the sale of arms is primarily governed by political and strategic considerations: only when these have been satisfied are economic considerations – i.e., the contribution of arms sales to export earnings – taken into account.'

As Britain withdrew from its overseas territories, military exports began to fall, partly because traditional recipients of British equipment turned to other sources, and partly because Britain failed to produce the types of equipment, particularly aircraft, most suitable for export. At the same time it was becoming increasingly expensive for Britain to maintain a defence industry on the scale that was considered commensurate with its international position. In order to reduce or stabilize the rising costs of domestic military procurement, it became more important to export.

This function of exports was officially recognized in the mid-sixties. In order to improve British organization for selling defence equipment abroad a Head of Defence Sales with a small sales organization was appointed in 1966. His duties were to promote exports and to see that foreign requirements were taken into account when drawing up specifications for new weapons. Since then, official statements have stressed the economic importance of exports.

THE FLOW OF WEAPONS

British exports of major weapons to developing countries reached a peak in 1958 of $250 million. And although they began to rise rapidly again from 1965, in 1972 they still amounted to only $180 million. The fall in the demand for British major weapons was at least partly the result of a decline in worldwide demand for such weapons from developing countries. But while total exports of major weapons to developing countries fell by only approximately one third between 1958 and 1959 and 1963 and 1964, British major weapon exports fell by two thirds over the same period. During the fifties, Britain was responsible for 21 per cent of total major weapon exports to developing countries. Between 1960 and 1972, this share had fallen to 12 per cent.

An important part of the story of British military exports is the way in which traditional recipients turned to other sources. To some extent, the decline in the demand for British weapons lagged behind the decline in Britain's world role. British withdrawals were often accompanied by aid agreements which provided for the supply of arms, because many countries whose armed forces had been trained by the British and had experience of British weapon systems preferred to continue with British equipment. Nevertheless, by the end of the 1950s the change in the pattern of British supplies had already begun. Traditional recipients were already acquiring arms from other sources, both because they could acquire more favourable terms elsewhere and because they wished to avoid association with British 'imperialism'. Thus, in the early fifties, British weapon exports were concentrated on former dependencies which Britain regarded as strategically important – Egypt, Iraq, Jordan, India, Pakistan and South Africa. Today, while India still accounts for a large share, British major weapons exports are concentrated on the oil-rich countries of the Middle East.

India is the biggest purchaser of British weapons in the Third World. During the fifties, India and Pakistan together accounted for 49 per cent of British exports of major weapons. During the

Table 7 UK: major weapon exports to Third World countries, by region

	Far East	Indian Sub-continent	Middle East	North Africa
1950	*	31	25	–
1951	*	16	6	–
1952	*	15	5	–
1953	*	30	30	–
1954	3	18	37	–
1955	9	49	26	–
1956	3	68	21	–
1957	6	123	9	1
1958	6	186	14	–
1959	1	85	6	*
1960	3	106	9	1
1961	8	107	7	1
1962	7	15	13	–
1963	23	3	23	*
1964	27	*	20	*
1965	4	14	10	–
1966	21	24	40	7
1967	11	25	17	6
1968	12	36	91	7
1969	3	23	135	16
1970	11	13	60	4
1971	28	25	108	–
1972	8	28	98	13
Total *a*	**195**	**1,040**	**807**	**55**
Per cent of total	*6·6*	*34·9*	*27·1*	*1·8*

a Figures may not add up to totals owing to rounding.
* = less than 1.

US $ mn, at constant (1968) *prices*

Sub-Saharan Africa	South Africa	Latin America	Greece and Turkey	Total[a]
–	2	16	*	73
4	–	6	–	31
3	13	*	–	36
8	11	41	–	121
9	13	42	–	121
8	9	30	–	131
*	13	21	9	136
*	13	7	35	193
1	9	39	–	256
31	9	10	–	141
4	1	42	1	166
3	–	51	–	177
13	5	2	–	55
6	14	11	–	80
10	16	4	1	78
10	83	21	–	142
8	1	12	1	116
3	–	–	–	62
4	–	31	–	181
2	1	16	–	196
1	3	10	*	102
14	10	20	–	206
10	–	25	–	182
152	**225**	**457**	**47**	**2,979**
5·1	*7·5*	*15·3*	*1·6*	***100·0***

Source: SIPRI worksheets.

sixties and up to 1972, this share had fallen to 23 per cent, since both countries found that they could obtain more favourable terms from the two great powers.

In the early 1950s Britain was supplying arms to a number of countries in the Middle East – Egypt, Jordan, Iraq, Syria and Israel – but after 1956 supplies fell. The reasons for this fall are rather different from those applicable to the Indian sub-continent. In 1955 Egypt signed an arms deal with Czechoslovakia, and Syria followed suit the following year. Both countries could obtain weapons from the West only under conditions which would mean a firm commitment to the Western camp, but by obtaining weapons from Czechoslovakia they could remain non-aligned. Furthermore, there was anti-British feeling in Egypt about that time, enhanced by the Suez crisis of 1956. And in 1958 a radical army group overthrew the pro-West monarchy in Iraq, after which they also purchased arms from socialist countries.

The situation in Jordan was rather more complex. Growing anti-British feeling in 1956 culminated in an election immediately following the Suez crisis in which an anti-West government came to power. As a result, British troops were withdrawn and Egypt, Syria and Saud i Arabia agreed to provide financial support to substitute for British aid. By the time relations with the West were restored in 1957, the United States had taken over Britain's role in providing aid, and although Britain continued to supply weapons, mainly aircraft, Jordan began to receive an increasingly large proportion of weapons from the USA. Another factor in the preference for US weapons was that, while Jordan paid for all the British weapons, those from the USA, with the exception of F-104 Starfighters delivered in 1969–70, were nearly all supplied on a grant basis.

Since 1965 the primary demand for British weapons has come from Iran and the oil-rich countries of the Arabian peninsula, a situation associated with the British withdrawal from the area. Iran has ordered 700–800 of the sophisticated Chieftain tanks and has also bought missiles and advanced fighters. The biggest deal for Lightning fighters and Provost trainers was negotiated with Saudi Arabia at a time when Britain was considering withdrawal from Aden. In 1966, a deal for Lightnings was also signed with Kuwait. The treaty with Kuwait, under which Britain undertook military protection of the country, expired in 1968, and this is one reason why Kuwait was building up its military forces; in 1968, a deal with Kuwait for the purchase of Vickers tanks was also signed. Britain's announcement of its withdrawal from east of the Suez in July 1967 led to a rising demand for equipment from the small Persian Gulf States, many of which were establishing armed forces for the first time.

The demand for weapons from the countries of Sub-Saharan Africa became significant only after 1958, when most of the ex-British colonies became independent, and weapons were provided as part of aid agreements accompanying independence. Before that date, Britain was supplying arms to the Central African Federation, the Sudan and Ethiopia.

Nevertheless, the size of British major weapon exports to Sub-Saharan Africa has remained small, averaging only $7 million a year during 1960–72. The demand for weapons is not, in any case, large, and although Britain still remains the second largest supplier to Sub-Saharan Africa (after the Soviet Union), all the larger ex-British colonies with the exception of Kenya have attempted to diversify their weapon sources. Generally, they have also bought weapons from European and from Commonwealth countries. South Africa received most of its weapons from Britain until 1966, when the British embargo of 1964 came into force.

In North Africa, the main demand for British weapons has come from Libya. Until 1970, British troops were stationed in Libya under a defence agreement signed in 1951, and since 1957 Britain has proffered $3·7 million in military aid. In 1968 and 1969, Libya, with the aid of its new huge oil revenues, ordered large quantities of weapons from Britain, including Chieftain tanks and anti-aircraft missiles. But in September 1969 a radical army coup overthrew the Libyan monarchy, the withdrawal of British troops was negotiated and the missile deal was reconsidered. The British firm BAC finally cancelled the deal when instalments were not forthcoming. Libya then decided to purchase Mirage planes from France. The Chieftain tanks have not yet been delivered and late in 1972 it was reported that Libya had instead ordered the A M X-30 from France.

British major weapon exports to the Far East have gone primarily to Indonesia, Burma and Malaysia. Substantial military aid has been provided to Malaysia and Singapore, and the demand for weapons has increased in connection with the British withdrawal from the area in 1971.

The considerations which govern the demand for British weapons in Latin America have been somewhat different from those governing the demand in other areas. Britain is the second largest supplier of weapons to Latin America, and supplies have consisted mainly of ships and combat aircraft. Often sales agreements have occurred when the United States has been unwilling or unable to supply equipment: for instance, Britain supplied Meteor fighters to Brazil in 1953, at a time when the United States was having difficulty in persuading Brazil to comply with the eligibility requirements necessary for the provision of military aid.

The demand for major weapons from Latin American countries fell after 1960. During 1967–72, it increased again as Latin American armed forces embarked on a period of re-equipment. Because of US attempts to limit the supply of sophisticated weapons to Latin American countries, many countries have adopted a deliberate policy of purchasing weapons from Europe, and both Britain and France have benefited from this.

THE INSTITUTIONAL STRUCTURE

During 1967–9, Ministry of Defence, that is, government, sales averaged $130 million a year out of total arms exports of approximately $400 million a year. The sales fall into four main categories. Sales of equipment from the Royal Ordnance Factories, together with sales of surplus military equipment from government stocks, form the bulk of exports. Sales from the Royal Dockyards are a third source, but do not amount to very much. Finally, there are sales by the government of sophisticated equipment produced by private firms. Some foreign governments prefer to deal with the government rather than with private firms, and, in this situation, the government merely buys from the firm and resells to the foreign government.

Export prices are nearly always higher than the procurement price paid by the government. In addition to the basic cost of production, there are certain extra costs involved in exporting: the cost of alteration to suit the customer's requirements, warranty, after-sales services, the costs of export promotion, credit charges and so on. Normally the government also charges a Research and Development levy on each weapon exported to recover its own contribution to R & D. According to government officials, the price is normally determined by what the customer is prepared to pay over and above the costs of producing and exporting the weapons.

In addition to direct government-to-government sales, the government plays an important role in sales from private firms; for example its procurement policy determines the export price, the Export Credit Guarantee Department determines the terms of payment and the government sales organization promotes exports.

Weapons are automatically sold on credit unless the customer prefers to pay cash, which is rare. Credit terms vary according to the nature of the goods rather than according to the country concerned, the exception being for 'off-cover' countries, that is countries which are not considered credit-worthy at all. Brazil was 'off-cover' during the fifties, Ghana was 'off-cover' at the end of the Nkrumah period and Indonesia was 'off-cover' during the sixties.

Until 1966 the task of promoting exports rested with the sales organizations of the Royal Ordnance Factories, the Ministry of Aviation and the Admiralty, and the defence attachés in foreign countries. The sales organizations were very small and it is unlikely that they were able to do much more than handle requests for exports. Concern with the inadequacy of the government's role in export promotion was expressed in the report of the Committee of Inquiry into the Aircraft Industry (Plowden

Report) of 1965, which recommended the establishment of a government sales organization. A Head of Defence Sales was appointed in 1966 with a sales organization, which co-ordinated and centralized the previous organizations. In addition to promotion, the defence sales organization has been directed to ensure that foreign requirements are taken into account when drawing up weapon specifications.

Control over exports

All private exports of weapons require a government licence. The Board of Trade, now the Department of Trade and Industry, is required to issue licences for all military equipment except warships, which are dealt with by the Ministry of Technology. The procedures for vetting government sales are the same as those for private sales. Theoretically, four ministries are consulted before a licence is issued: the Board of Trade, the Ministry of Technology, the Ministry of Defence and the Foreign Office, but in practice the relevant ministries are consulted only where a proposed sale does not fall clearly within a defined policy. For politically sensitive deals, a high-level inter-ministerial committee, known as the Strategic Exports Ministerial Committee, meets to discuss the issue.

The licensing procedures in Britain are generally simpler than those operating in other countries. There is no legal provision for end-use. If desired, the government can negotiate a separate agreement forbidding resale, but it is not automatically included as it is, for instance, in the United States. Nor are there any legal sanctions to ensure final destination, as there are in France and the Federal Republic of Germany, where deposits are demanded as a guarantee against resale. Further, there are no agreements concerning the use to which weapons will be put, as is the case again with US exports. Nevertheless, the suitability of a weapon for a particular use is taken into account when granting licences, so that, for example, Britain does not sell to Portugal weapons appropriate for counter-insurgency which might be used in the

Portuguese colonies, although it continues to supply weapons to support Portugal's role in NATO.

There are no fixed criteria for determining whether an export licence should be granted. The British government prides itself on its 'pragmatic' attitude, and it is usually stated that each case 'is decided on its merits', an expression that has been liberally applied to recent arms deals in the Middle East. Arms embargoes have been applied on South Africa after 1964, on India and Pakistan between September 1965 and March 1966 and on the Middle East for two days in June 1967. There have also been several published instances of individual licences being refused, for example the British refusal to supply Hunters to Cuba in 1959 and Chieftain tanks to Israel.

Export licences are not required for the sale of production licences abroad, as this is not considered practicable. Moreover, it is assumed that all production licences will in any case be subject to some form of government control, because the sale of licences will normally be accompanied by the sale of parts and associated equipment, and the government will have responsibility for determining whether know-how which has been built up with the use of government finance should be sold. While all this is true, the failure to insist on licences for the export of know-how can represent an important loophole where third-country sales are concerned. This is particularly relevant for the effectiveness of the arms embargo on South Africa, as several planes delivered from France and Italy have British-designed engines. In particular, the Macchi M.B. 326, which South Africa is building under licence from Italy, has a Rolls Royce–Bristol Viper engine originally licensed to Piaggio. The Transall transport aircraft sold by the French to South Africa also has a Rolls Royce engine.

THE DEFENCE INDUSTRY

When the Labour government came to power in 1964, concern was already being expressed about the state of the defence industry. As this concern intensified, steps were taken to remedy the situation, including the establishment of the defence sales organization and the cancellation of three major aircraft projects, including the TSR-2 bomber, in 1965.

One of the main reasons for this situation was the rising cost of government procurement, due in part to the increased sophistication of weapon systems, which were much more costly to produce and, at the same time, were produced in much smaller quantities. The fact that Britain neither needed nor could afford to buy weapons in larger quantities had serious consequences both for unit costs and for productivity in the industry. The rising cost of procurement was also due to the numerous cancellations in the aerospace industry, and the wide spread of projects. Out of seventy-three combat aircraft and military transport projects undertaken between 1945 and 1965, only twenty-five were produced in quantities greater than 100, only 5 in quantities greater than 500 and only 2 in quantities greater than 1,000. The total cost of cancelled programmes over the period 1952–62 has been estimated at $672 million.

The second major fact which gave cause for concern was the dramatic fall in exports, particularly of air-force equipment, which forms the greater share of British major weapon exports and which fell by half. As well as decisions on the part of traditional recipients to turn to other sources, the over-sophistication of British weapon systems, and, in particular, the absence of a competitive fighter aircraft during the sixties were additional factors. The only new combat aircraft produced between 1958 and 1965 were the Buccaneer naval bomber and the Lightning interceptor. The Lightning, chosen in preference to a supersonic variant of the Hunter, costs $2 million, compared with around $1·5 million for its French and US counterparts, the Mirage III and the F-104 Starfighter. The MiG-21 costs even less. Moreover, the Lightning has a pure interception role, whereas the Mirage and Starfighter are fighter bombers. Only Saudi Arabia and Kuwait have so far proved rich enough to buy the Lightning, and of the Third World countries which originally purchased the Hunter, Lebanon, Pakistan and Peru have replaced it with the Mirage, Jordan and Pakistan with the Starfighter, and India and Iraq with the MiG-21. All the European countries which previously used the Hunter have purchased their successors from other countries.

Two solutions were proposed to invigorate the ailing industry. The first was international collaboration in producing weapons, the argument being that this would spread the burden of costs and ensure a larger market. For convinced Europeans, there was also a political argument. But collaboration has tended to lead to an increase in costs through duplication, and the division of responsibilities is usually made on political rather than on economic grounds. Moreover, it is argued that, although the market is larger, the return to each country is only proportional to its contribution and, since total costs are larger, exports are still important.

The second solution was to make a positive effort to increase exports. While the importance of exports has always been recognized, their advantages had previously been seen in terms of political and strategic considerations and the contribution to export earnings, and it was taken for granted that British weapons would remain in demand because they always had been in the past. For the industry, the increased emphasis on exports provided, according to Sir George Edwards, Managing Director of BAC, a means to become 'less dependent on government work and thus on the whims of governments and their policies'. For the government, exports provided a means of slowing down the rising costs of procurement, which could be achieved by increasing the number of units of each type produced and by helping to maintain stability in the industry. Since 1965, both the industry and the government have demonstrated a great enthusiasm for exports, and aerospace exports are rising continuously. It is notable, however, that a large share of the rising exports (nearly half in 1972) is accounted for by sales of spares for past successful projects.

After aerospace equipment, the second most important component of British military exports is naval vessels, which, particularly to developing countries, represent a much larger

Chart 2. UK: aircraft sales

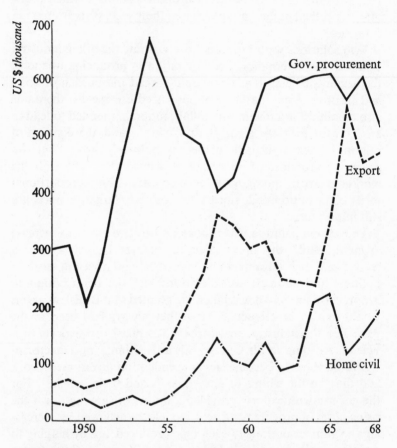

Note: 1949 exchange rates: \$4/£ up to mid-September and \$2·8/£ after mid-September. Average \$3·65/£ .

Sources: 1948–59, *Plowden Committee Report*, Appendix D, Table 1; 1960–68, *Elstob Committee Report*, Annex C.

share of total military exports for Britain than for other supplying countries. Moreover, in value terms (although not in terms of number), British exports of ships to Third World countries are higher than those from either the United States or the Soviet Union.

Total British exports of naval equipment fell after 1959. And unlike exports of air-force equipment, they have not recovered. Compared with other countries, the British shipbuilding industry has been geared towards naval work and also towards exports, and while there has been a relative rise in the world demand for simple ships, such as tankers, bulk carriers and dry cargo ships, this has not been the case for highly specialized naval vessels. British shipyards are designed to produce both types of ships, unlike those in other countries where naval and merchant ship-yards are separated, which has meant that merchant ships tend to be more expensive than those produced by Britain's growing competitors, particularly Japan. Throughout the post-war period, there has been a continuing and serious unemployment problem in the shipbuilding industry.

Thus the failure to keep up with world competition in merchant ships and the run-down of many European navies, particularly the British Royal Navy, has meant that the export of naval vessels to developing countries where there is a demand is an important way to keep shipyards occupied. Since 1964, exports of naval vessels to developing countries have risen, although they are still not as high as they were in the late fifties. But with the large orders from Latin American countries from 1969, they can be expected to rise further.

POLITICAL CONSIDERATIONS

The Labour government of 1964–70 made no secret of the fact that its main interest in exporting weapons was economic. Yet, although exports as a whole are defended on economic grounds, individual sensitive deals are defended in political terms. Thus, the recent deals with Jordan have been defended on the grounds that they prevent Jordan from turning to the Soviet Union for equipment. Similarly, the Conservative government's proposal in 1970 to renew the sales of weapons to South Africa has been largely described in terms of the strategic need to defend the Cape route.

While it is clear that the present role of exports in supporting the defence industry is of overriding importance, it must also be remembered that, having dismantled an empire in twenty years, there remain British political interests in the ex-colonies which have some bearing on the arms trade. This section considers three areas where political considerations have been of overriding importance to arms supplies.

Military aid

Between 1964 and 1968, British military aid reached its peak, averaging $67 million per year. It has tended to be concentrated on a few countries, the main recipients having been Jordan, Malaysia, India, Kenya and South Arabia, now Southern Yemen. The military aid to Kenya, India and South Arabia after 1963 accounts almost entirely for this peak.

British military aid falls roughly into four categories: training and technical assistance, loans for the purchase of British equipment, supporting assistance and gifts of military equipment. There are two functions of training and technical assistance. First, it is a way of maintaining ties with the ex-colonies. Secondly, it has an economic function in that it can promote the sales of British military equipment. The British are very conscious of the sales advantages to be gained from the fact that so many armed forces have had experience with British military equipment. Loans also have an economic function, of course, besides a political function in some cases, for instance to Turkey, which is both a NATO and a CENTO member. Supporting assistance has almost always had a strategic function. It has been provided to countries which have a defence agreement with Britain, providing for the presence of troops or other military facilities. British gifts of weapons have been rare, and associated with special political circumstances. Between 1958 and 1960 the Sudan received $1·5 million worth of arms, after having rejected a Czechoslovak military-aid offer and after having granted overflying and staging rights to the RAF. Other military-aid recipients have been Jordan, Iraq, Lebanon, Muscat and Oman, and India.

With the withdrawal of troops east of Suez, supporting assistance is likely to be confined to Malaysia and Oman. Gifts of weapons are likely to become increasingly rare. In the future, therefore, one can expect military aid to become even more confined to training and technical assistance, and possibly loans. Thus, the function of military aid in promoting military sales is likely to become the predominant one.

Nigeria

In answer to questions in Parliament, it was stated on several occasions that Britain was supplying, throughout the war, 15 per cent of all arms supplied from abroad to the Federal force. Figures calculated from Nigerian trade statistics show that the quantity of arms delivered by Britain under the category of 'Firearms of War and Ammunition thereof' amounted to $225,000 in 1966, $6·8 million in 1968 and $25 million in 1969. This covers most equipment delivered to ground troops. For 1967–8 the British estimate of 15 per cent is probably correct, but in 1969 this would imply that Nigeria's total arms imports amounted to as much as $164 million. So far as is known, Britain supplied no air-force equipment during the war and the only reported naval equipment delivered were six seaward defence boats in 1967. The refusal to grant a Nigerian request for fighter aircraft on the outbreak of war appears to have been a major factor in the introduction of Soviet weapons.

There was considerable controversy in Britain over the issue of arms supplies to Nigeria, both within Parliament and outside. Opposition ranged from those who believed that Britain should give outright support to Biafra, to those who believed that Britain should remain neutral and refuse to supply arms to either side, to those who believed that Britain should continue to give qualified support for the Federal forces but should press for a multilateral embargo under international supervision and should increase food supplies to Biafra. The last position was that held by the official opposition.

In view of the controversy aroused and the smallness of the commercial gain from selling arms to Nigeria it is clear that reasons for continuing to supply arms were not strictly commercial. The government's lines of defence were several. For example, it was stressed in the House of Commons that cutting off arms supplies was not a neutral policy: 'The traditional supply of arms to the Federal government could not have been stopped without our being far from neutral.' Also, the government emphasized its beliefs in federation, its fear that the secession of Biafra would be the first step in the 'balkanization' of Africa.

Thirdly, the government argued that British influence in bringing an end to hostilities would be greater if Britain continued to supply arms. Even if it imposed an embargo, it would not appear neutral because, as the creator of the idea of federation, it could not pretend to have abandoned the Federal cause. It would therefore be impossible for Britain to introduce an acceptable peace initiative. On the other hand, by continuing to supply arms, Britain could bring pressure to bear upon the Federal government.

A variant of this argument was that other countries, in particular the Soviet Union, would continue to supply arms and would gain the position of influence which should rightfully be British. There is no doubt that Britain did attempt to put pressure on the Federal government, but its effectiveness is not clear. Thus, for instance, in March 1969 Britain threatened to stop the supply of arms unless the Nigerian High Commissioner in London gave assurances that bombing of civilian targets in Biafra would be stopped. Bombing attacks on civilian targets were later stopped, but whether this was due to British pressure, the pressure of world opinion or simply their ineffectiveness is not known.

On the question of seeking a multilateral embargo, it was argued that such an embargo would be ineffective without the agreement of both sides because of the large preponderance of private dealers. But this argument was a weak one, as even the private dealers had to have the support of at least one government. Most of them operated from Portugal, and a multilateral agreement with the support of Portugal could virtually have ended the supply of outside weapons. This would not necessarily have ended the war – Nigeria has a small arms factory and Biafra was producing crude weapons itself – but it might at least have slowed the tempo.

It seems clear from their failure to make any efforts towards a multilateral arms embargo that the British interest was to bring about a Nigerian victory, presumably at the earliest possible date. Press reports suggest that the British government had expected a quick Federal victory at the beginning of the war, but when this failed to occur they remained committed to the Federal side. The reasons for this commitment are not hard to find. First, the British always believed, rightly in the event, in a Nigerian victory, and did not want to see an extension of Soviet influence there. British economic interests were at stake. Secondly, there was a genuine belief in the importance of federation, the need to build nations on the basis of different ethnic groups and the fear that secession might be infectious and create instability in Africa, again contrary to British interests. It has always been hoped that Nigeria would provide the model of decolonization and the test case of federation.

Perhaps the most interesting feature of the Nigerian issue is the way in which it illustrates a dilemma of arms control. To the British, cutting off supplies to Nigeria or a multinational arms embargo was not a means of ending the war but rather a means of prolonging it. A victory for the Nigerians was seen as the quickest way of ending the war. Until the French began to supply weapons to Biafra, the balance of arms was tipped strongly in favour of Nigeria, and the British government view was that supplies to Biafra from August 1968 prolonged the war by a year and a half. Similarly, a total arms embargo on both sides would have maintained the balance of arms and might also have prolonged the war.

The wider questions raised are these. If ending hostility is a priority, is it justifiable to do so by ensuring the victory of one side? If so, how is it to be decided who should win?

South Africa

The issue of arms sales to South Africa is one of the few issues which clearly divides the two major political parties. It has aroused intense feelings, on the one side from the defence industry and those companies responsible for over $2,400 million of British investment in South Africa and over $1,400 million of British exports, and, on the other side, from the various political and religious groups active in the movement against apartheid. Outside Britain, feelings have been equally intense. When the new Conservative government announced in 1970 its intention to resume arms sales to South Africa, at least three countries threatened to resign from the Commonwealth and several hinted that reprisals of various sorts might be taken.

Before 1964, Britain was the foremost supplier of arms to South Africa. South Africa, in turn, was one of Britain's largest customers for defence equipment, particularly naval equipment. In 1955, Britain concluded the so-called Simonstown Agreement with South Africa, under which Britain handed over the Simonstown naval base to South Africa, while maintaining base facilities which could be used even in a war in which South Africa remained neutral. The agreement also provided for joint operations to ensure 'the safety . . . of the sea route round Southern Africa' and for the supply of $50 million worth of naval vessels.

On 7 August 1963, the Security Council of the United Nations passed a resolution calling on all states 'to cease forthwith the sale and shipment of arms, ammunition of all types and military vehicles to South Africa'. Britain and France abstained. A further resolution, which was adopted unanimously on 4 December 1963, extended the arms ban to 'equipment and material needed for the manufacture and maintenance of arms and ammunition in South Africa'. While supporting these resolutions and a further resolution of June 1964, the British representative made it clear that Britain reserved the right to supply equipment for external defence. This distinction between weapons for external defence and for internal suppression had been made as early as 1955 when the Simonstown Agreement was signed.

On 17 November 1964, within days of coming to power, the Labour government announced a total embargo on arms to South Africa. The embargo, however, excluded 'firm contracts' which were still to be carried out. Thus, following the imposition of the embargo, Britain delivered to South Africa six refurbished Canberra B(1)58 bombers, four Wasp helicopters and sixteen Buccaneer naval bombers.

There were several important loopholes in the embargo. First, Britain has no power to prevent the delivery or sub-licensing of equipment built on British design. In particular, the Atlas Impala jet trainer and light-strike aircraft, built under licence from Italy, has a Rolls Royce–Bristol Viper engine. And Britain has continued to supply spare parts for British equipment already in South Africa, including spare parts for aircraft such as Canberra and Buccaneer bombers and Shackleton maritime reconnaissance aircraft, for naval equipment, and, reportedly, for Centurion tanks and Saracen armoured cars. Britain also continued to supply ammunition for naval equipment and, according to some reports, for Centurion tanks and 25-pounder guns. Thirdly, Britain released $70–80 million worth of radar equipment manufactured by the British electronics company Marconi, for an air-defence system. And a number of British firms opened new factories in South Africa, producing, among other things, electronic equipment and hovercraft. Hovercraft are considered useful COIN weapons.

The Labour government also continued to co-operate with South Africa on defence matters, stationing a naval officer with a small staff in Cape Town. Joint British–South African naval exercises continued to be performed.

In opposition, members of the Conservative party indicated their firm intention to reverse the embargo on regaining power, so that the Conservative victory of June 1970 was greeted with acclaim in South Africa. The South African Foreign Secretary

Muller was among the first to arrive in London for talks with the new government. The defence industry eagerly awaited a decision that might bring in orders for Nimrod maritime reconnaissance aircraft and Buccaneer naval bombers, for destroyers and frigates, and for Sea Dart missiles. Sir Alec Douglas Home, in his initial speeches as Foreign Secretary, gave priority to the defence of the Cape route.

But it seems that the extent of the opposition to resuming arms sales had been misjudged. Not only were there protests from the Labour and Liberal parties and from pressure groups within Britain, and not only do Foreign Office officials appear to have opposed a resumption, but the majority of the Commonwealth members criticized the proposed action in strong terms and several warned of the possible consequences. Tanzania and Zambia even threatened to leave the Commonwealth. In a letter from Canadian Prime Minister Trudeau, quoted in *The Times* of 27 July 1970, the government was urged to 'take full account of the likelihood that the provision of any military assistance to South Africa will be interpreted by many Commonwealth governments as an implicit gesture of acquiescence in the policy of the South African government towards the African population'.

The effect of these protests was to weaken the resolution of the government. In addition, the South African government appears to have had second thoughts. Much of the equipment, particularly naval vessels, which South Africa might purchase from Britain would take several years to deliver, and there was no guarantee that a future Labour government would fulfil contracts entered into during the Conservative period of office. On 10 July, South African Defence Minister Piet Botha made a speech in which he stated that the Simonstown Agreement would have to be revised before South Africa buys British weapons because, as it stands, 'it apparently can be interpreted by alternative British governments as it suits them'.

On 20 July, Sir Alec Douglas Home finally made a statement in the House of Commons on the government's position on arms trade to South Africa, announcing its intention to consider, within the context of the Simonstown Agreement, 'applications for the export to South Africa of certain limited categories of arms, so long as they are for maritime defence directly related to the security of the sea routes'. This was essentially a modification of the previous Conservative position, when arms were to be supplied for external defence and not only for maritime defence. Sir Alec also stated that no final decision would be taken before consultations with Commonwealth governments had been completed.

This statement was followed by strong reaction from all Commonwealth members except Australia, Malawi and Mauritius. Even Singapore and Malaysia opposed a resumption of arms supplies, although their protests were less severe because of their desire for a British presence east of Suez. In a note to Britain on 23 July, quoted in the *Financial Times*, 24 July 1970, Sierra Leone stated that the government 'would find it extremely difficult, if not impossible, to continue its membership of the Commonwealth if the supply of arms by the British government becomes effective'. And President Obote of Uganda, in a letter to the government, stated that Uganda would follow Tanzania's lead in leaving the Commonwealth if arms supplies to South Africa were resumed. However, at the Conference of Commonwealth Prime Ministers in January 1971, a crisis appears to have been averted: the countries most opposed to the resumption of arms sales did not leave the Commonwealth, and at the same time it appears that a face-saving formula was found for the government. The White Paper published in February 1971, on the 'Legal Obligations of Her Majesty's Government Arising out of the Simonstown Agreements', concluded that Britain's only obligation is to supply Wasp helicopters for use on the three anti-submarine frigates, supplied as part of the original agreement. In February 1971 it was announced that South Africa wanted to buy seven Wasps. Delivery of these was expected in 1973.

What was at issue? The main argument used by the Conservative Government has been the strategic one. It is an argument tempered by an imperial past and a global notion of defence. The Cape route, the only alternative to the Suez Canal, is vital for British trade, particularly oil supplies. And the Soviet fleet in the

Indian Ocean is increasing in strength. The argument was put in its proper context by Lord Chalfont in the House of Lords on 14 July 1970:

> Does anyone ... seriously believe there is any kind of situation in which these submarines [Soviet] would be able to interfere with our shipping in the South Atlantic except in circumstances of such a grave crisis, if not a war, that the whole of the Western Alliance would be involved? ... The only threat to our sea routes in the South Atlantic is the threat of war, and the next war is not going to be a war of naval engagements in the South Atlantic. The nuclear weapon has changed all that, and those who talk of 'showing the flag in the traditional way of a great naval Power' are ... indulging in the ... worst excesses of pre-nuclear fantasy.

It is clear that commercial stakes remain uppermost in the minds of many who support a resumption of British arms sales to South Africa. The argument of those who object is not so much that South Africa will obtain weapons which would not be obtained in any other way, nor is it that the particular weapons supplied can be used for internal suppression (though this may be true for some of them). It is rather that the provision of weapons enables the South African government to claim that, for all its protests about apartheid, the British government regards the South African government as a fully legitimate one and that the provision of weapons is a practical demonstration of this.

5 France

Arms exports have played a vital role in the expansion of the French defence industry in enabling France to maintain a self-sufficient armaments base, and in demonstrating this to the world. Because of this, French arms-trade policy has helped the country to establish an independent position in international affairs.

French actions can best be described as those of a country seeking the best available markets without strong political restraints. For example, when Britain imposed an embargo on South Africa in 1964, France became the principal supplier to that country. After the United States embargo on India and Pakistan in September 1965, France sold Mirages and sub-marines to Pakistan. And France received orders for major weapons from Greece when the USA imposed a selective embargo, and has supplied counter-insurgency weapons to Portugal for use in the African colonies when other countries have more closely adhered to the UN Security Council resolution of 1963 on this question.

Even the Middle East embargo can be interpreted in this light. The June War of 1967 provided the opportunity to exchange the Israeli market for the potentially more lucrative Arab market, and for commercial and other gains in an Arab world disenchanted with Britain and the United States and not entirely satisfied with the Soviet Union.

This course has not merely increased French arms exports, but has brought France commercial and political gains as well. Moving into Anglo-American markets increased the French sphere of influence and demonstrated French independence from other Western countries. This improved the French international position in general, but it did not always do so. For instance, French arms supplies to Portugal, Greece and South Africa met with the strong disapproval of Third World countries. In view of

Table 8 France: major weapon exports to Third World countries, by region

	Far East, incl. Viet-Nam	Indian Sub-continent	Middle East	North Africa
1950	–	–	1	–
1951	–	–	1	–
1952	–	–	1	–
1953	–	30	2	–
1954	3	30	14	–
1955	3	–	35	–
1956	3	–	88	19
1957	*	30	23	2
1958	1	79	18	2
1959	1	–	32	3
1960	1	–	8	1
1961	1	15	6	*
1962	6	–	49	1
1963	4	5	55	4
1964	4	–	63	5
1965	9	–	11	*
1966	2	5	2	–
1967	3	7	6	2
1968	*	59	58	*
1969	5	2	27	11
1970	*	17	17	23
1971	1	*	28	55
1972	2	12	7	93
Total [a]	**51**	**290**	**554**	**221**
Per cent of total	*3·1*	*17·6*	*33·5*	*13·4*

[a] Figures may not add up to totals owing to rounding.
* = less than 1.

US $ mn, at constant (1968) *prices*

Sub-Saharan Africa	South Africa	Latin America	Greece and Turkey	Total[a]
–	–	–	–	1
–	–	–	–	1
–	–	–	–	1
–	–	–	–	32
–	–	1	–	48
–	–	3	–	41
–	–	8	–	118
–	–	–	–	55
–	–	4	–	104
–	–	–	–	37
5	–	7	–	23
4	2	1	–	29
2	6	2	–	67
5	38	1	–	111
2	8	3	*	87
7	26	1	–	54
4	47	9	–	69
9	15	2	2	46
8	9	9	–	144
6	31	24	–	106
5	40	15	1	118
16	36	5	19	161
3	6	52	27	200
77	**264**	**148**	**48**	**1,653**
4·6	*16·0*	*8·9*	*2·9*	*100·0*

Source: SIPRI worksheets.

the overriding importance of exports for the defence industry, this criticism has not brought about substantial changes in French arms-supply policy.

French exports of major weapons have increased very rapidly – at a rate of 16 per cent per year since 1950, compared with 10 per cent for the world total. In 1971 and 1972, French supplies of major weapons to Third World countries amounted to a yearly average of $180 million, compared with less than $2 million in 1950.

Three countries, Israel, India and South Africa, have accounted for 56 per cent of all French major weapon exports. France also supplies weapons to all its ex-colonies in Africa, with the exception of Guinea, and has supplied weapons to Viet-Nam during the fifties and to Cambodia throughout the period. France has also periodically sold weapons to Latin American countries, especially towards the end of the sixties and even in the seventies, when a number of Latin American countries – Peru, Brazil, Argentina, Colombia and Venezuela – purchased Mirage fighters.

THE INSTITUTIONAL STRUCTURE

A large part of the French armaments industry is government-owned, the biggest exceptions being Dassault and Breguet, which merged in 1967. There is close co-operation between private and national firms and the sales of weapons are strictly supervised.

Attempts to regulate the trade in war material have been made since 1933. The present regulations are based on a law of 18 April 1939, which laid down the principle that war material and related items require export licences. A decree of 14 August 1939 established a list of equipment requiring such licences, and also provided for exemptions for certain types of equipment – civil aircraft, spare parts, temporary imports or *matériel* in transit. But these exemptions can be suspended for exports destined to certain countries, and in such cases, in addition to the export licence, a deposit is required to guarantee the final destination of the equipment and prevent its re-export to countries where such deliveries are prohibited.

Export licences are issued by the Ministry of Finance, after approval by the Minister of Foreign Affairs, the Minister of the Interior, the Minister of War, Navy or Air depending on the type of equipment, and the Minister of Defence. The Minister of Foreign Affairs can make his approval for an export licence conditional on proof that the government in the recipient country approves the delivery of equipment and will not re-export it. The burden of proof is placed on the exporter, and the final destination of the equipment is guaranteed by a deposit which is repaid only on the presentation of a certificate by the French consul, confirming that the equipment has arrived at its destination and has not been re-exported to a third country. This certificate can only be issued three months after the delivery of the equipment.

By a decree of 10 June 1949, an inter-ministerial commission was established. Its functions were, first, to consider requests for authorization to produce and export war material, and, secondly, to study the policy that should govern the production of war material for foreign countries and the methods of influencing the quantity and quality of the production and export of war material. Today, this commission, in which the most important role is played by the Ministry of Foreign Affairs, is directly responsible to the Prime Minister. The office most closely concerned with the sales of weapons is the Délégation Ministérielle pour l'Armament (DMA).

Following the smuggling of five gunboats by Israel out of Cherbourg on Christmas Day 1969, there has been a re-examination of the rules governing arms exports, and Debré, then Minister of Defence, announced his intention of making the procedures for the supervision of exports more rigorous. An improvement and acceleration of the procedures for examining exceptional cases is also envisaged.

Active government promotion has been instrumental in the increase in French weapons sales to developing countries. From 1967, exhibitions have been held at Satory to display French armaments to prospective buyers, with a special emphasis on arms for developing countries. In arms deals with Third World countries, the government usually provides the required training and technical support through the relevant branch of the armed services. As in Britain, the government has also placed emphasis on the design of military equipment to meet foreign requirements. For example, the Mirage 5 has been specially designed for the Third World market. Following a fall in exports in 1969, Debré instructed the French armed forces to take export potential into account when choosing military equipment.

The Direction des Affaires Internationales (DAI), under the Délégation Ministérielle pour l'Armament, is primarily responsible for the promotion of weapon exports on the government's behalf; in addition, there are special missions dealing with arms sales in the United States, the Federal Republic of Germany and Britain. There are also independent private selling agencies which undertake the promotion of weapon exports. The Société Française de Matériel d'Armament (SOFMA), the agency responsible for promoting the sale of tanks and infantry weapons, is owned jointly by the government (with a 35 per cent share) and a consortium of interested firms. The structure of the aviation agencies, Office Français d'Exportation de Matériel Aéronautique (OFEMA) and the Office Général de l'Air (OGA), is very similar.

In offering credit for arms purchases, a distinction is made between weapons and equipment goods. A gun or a missile is a weapon, but a weapon platform, such as a tank or an aeroplane, is an equipment good. For weapons, cash is generally demanded. For equipment goods, credit is extended up to eight years. In theory, the credit period is five years, but this can be extended by two or three years through initiating the credit period on delivery, and in fact this is normal practice for evading the agreements on credit arrangements concluded at Berne in 1934.

Interest rates vary. The normal rate is said to be about 7 per cent, but examples of other rates can be found. The French deal with Argentina for the sale of AMX-13 tanks was based on a five-year credit arrangement at 3 per cent interest, while credit arrangements with Israel were generally for five to seven years at 5 to 6 per cent interest.

France does not generally accept barter payments. A Brazilian request to buy helicopters with raw materials in 1964 was rejected. A report by the Brazilian Air Minister, however, concerning the possible purchase of Mirages in January 1968, indicated that the French had agreed to accept partial payment in coffee and raw materials over a period of ten years.

French arms exports have been closely associated with commercial gains in recipient countries, and often arms agreements are part of wider commercial agreements, as was the case, for instance, with the recent Mirage deals signed with Libya and Brazil. Around the same time as Argentina signed the AMX-13 deal with France, providing for the assembly in Argentina of thirty of these tanks, the government-owned Régie Nationale des Usines Renault acquired a controlling interest in the main vehicle-producing firm in Argentina, Industrias Kaiser Argentina.

An interesting feature of these commercial agreements has been the association with uranium. In South Africa, an agreement concerning uranium was signed in 1964 simultaneously with the signing of a general arms-trade agreement.

THE DEFENCE INDUSTRY

The growth of the French industry has been closely associated with the growth of its exports. The industry, not re-established in any important sense after its wartime interruption until the mid-fifties, had its most rapid expansion after 1960, particularly after 1962, and exports played a vital role in this expansion. Between 1960 and 1971, French arms exports rose at a rate of more than 20 per cent a year, and in 1970 they amounted to more than 20 per cent of total defence production. The importance of exports in the French aerospace industry is even more striking: total turnover has risen threefold since the 1960s and the share of exports in total aerospace industry production has risen from 25 per cent in 1960 to over 70 per cent in the record year, 1970.

The role played by exports in maintaining the French defence industry has been stressed on numerous occasions both in the press and in the National Assembly. It is pointed out that exports have brought with them the benefits of economies of scale, and it is also stressed that exports have protected the industry from fluctuations in government demand, thus helping to ensure a stable level of employment.

A major problem of the French defence industry is that of limited domestic resources, and international co-operation has been regarded as a possible solution to this. France is under-taking joint production projects with the Federal Republic of Germany and Britain, but despite the political advantages – their contribution to European policy and to breaking the domination exercised by the USA in the provision of essential *matériel* – both government and industry spokesmen, like their British counterparts, have found the results of such projects disappoint-ing commercially. In fact, in 1969, international production was cited as one of the main reasons for the fall in French exports, and it is generally considered that licensed production and exports are a more efficient form of international specializa-tion.

To meet these growing problems and to improve the possi-bilities for export, the French aerospace industry has been reorganized. As well as the 1967 merger between the private firms Dassault and Breguet, the three main nationalized com-panies – Sud Aviation, Nord Aviation and SEREB – have been merged to form one company, the Société Nationale Industrielle Aéronautique et Spatiale (SNIAS). This company is now called Aérospatiale. At the same time, it was recognized that the reorganization would, in itself, require a more determined effort in the export market. In June 1967, the Minister of Services told the Commission of National Defence of the Assembly that one result of the mergers would be a contraction in employment, so that an increase in foreign orders would be essential in guarantee-ing the level of employment. Similar reorganization is now taking place in other sectors of the French defence industry. In May 1970, the National Assembly approved the creation of a Société

Nationale, with a controlling government interest, which will have a monopoly over the production of explosives.

The attempt to increase foreign orders suffered as a consequence of the 1969 embargo on the Middle East. Since 1960, Israel has been the third largest customer of the French aerospace industry after the United States and the Federal Republic of Germany, accounting for 13 per cent of total orders, and it had been estimated that approximately $200 million would be lost by the industry following the embargo. In fact, in 1969, not only did the industry lose more than $350 million in orders, owing equally to co-production and the embargo, but the discontinuation of spare-part deliveries for the materials purchased by Israel reportedly made customers conscious of the risks inherent in the dependence of their policies on that of France. In October 1968, however, Jacques Hébert, special rapporteur on the defence budget for the Finance Commission, had argued in the National Assembly that 'the authorities and the industry have immediately reacted to the embargo through the search for new markets', and that the international circumstances 'mitigate the effect which the embargo might otherwise have had'. Among these, he cited the war in Viet-Nam, which has limited the export potential of the US industry, the British withdrawal east of Suez and the entry into the Kuwait, Saudi Arabian and Singapore markets, and the US and British embargo on South Africa 'which places us in a very privileged position in this market'. His predictions did not reach fruition until 1970. Orders for Mirages by Libya, Spain, Brazil and Argentina are worth more than the entire military orders during 1969, and arms exports in fact tripled between 1969 and 1970. Later, however, exports have fallen back, though they are still higher than the pre-1960 level.

One other benefit that exports bring to the defence industry should be mentioned – the contributions to Research and Development. South Africa and Israel have both financed major projects. The anti-aircraft missile Cactus-Crotale was developed by means of finance provided by the South African government. Israel financed Dassault's development of the MD-660 medium ballistic surface-to-surface missile. Israel has also made indirect contributions to the French defence industry by the modification and design improvements undertaken by Israeli engineers. In particular, the Mirage 5 is based on modifications requested by Israel to the Mirage III, such that certain electronic equipment was removed and replaced by an extra fuel tank, giving it greater range and less complexity.

POLITICAL CONSIDERATIONS

Increased arms exports and commercial activity have therefore been of overriding importance to the French defence industry and the economy in general. Thus, economic considerations were the determining factors influencing French supply policy. But this policy has also brought about benefits of a political nature: it has contributed to an increase in French political 'presence' in the world, and to the establishment of France as an international world force independent of the two major power camps. This is, however, a consequence of promoting the export of arms, additional to the economic consequences, rather than a motivation for initiating this policy. In only one case – French military aid to its ex-colonies – did political considerations obviously predominate. In others – French policy towards the Middle East and towards Biafra – it is not clear. In South Africa, political opposition to arms supplies has been ineffective in preventing the conclusion of lucrative transactions.

Military aid

France provides military assistance to members of the French community and to its ex-colonies in North Africa. But the extent of this aid is difficult to estimate, since it is included in the Co-operation Budget which also covers economic and technical assistance. French military assistance is primarily provided to the ex-French colonies in Sub-Saharan Africa, and is one of the many instruments with which France maintains its influence and interests in the region.

The bulk of French military assistance is devoted to training assistance. In 1970, there were 1,400 officers and non-commissioned officers (NCOs) acting as military advisers in the ex-French colonies in Sub-Saharan Africa, and approximately 400 French officers and NCOs in Morocco, Algeria, Tunisia, Cambodia and Laos. In addition, 800 Africans are trained in France each year, and in 1969 France agreed to establish a flying school at Bou Sfer in Algeria, intended also for personnel from Libya, Morocco and Tunisia.

French supplies of equipment, on the other hand, are limited. All the ex-community countries in Africa received, at independence, a package of equipment including one or two light liaison planes, one helicopter, some armoured vehicles and one or two patrol boats. The total supplies in the first two years after independence have been estimated at $80 million, and in the late sixties about $2 million per year. The North African and Asian ex-colonies have generally purchased French equipment, although the credits for 1969–70 included some provision for aircraft and armoured vehicles for Tunisia.

The armies of the ex-community countries are small, often representing little more than police forces. The provision of equipment, services and training permits close relations between the French military establishment and its local counterparts, thus maintaining French influence. On the one hand it is in the French interest that the armies should remain small, so that French support continues to be necessary and the likelihood of instability is reduced. On the other hand, close military co-operation paves the way for future arms purchases, as it has already done in North Africa, when these states reach a level of development compatible with large acquisitions of arms.

Biafra

In June 1968, France imposed an embargo on both parties to the Nigerian Civil War. The first reports that Biafra was receiving French technical assistance, military equipment and mercenary personnel came in August 1968.

Although Biafra did not receive any military equipment directly from France, French arms were, according to Stanley Diamond, writing in *New York Review of Books* in February 1970, purchased either on the black market (presumably with the knowledge of the French government) or indirectly through the government of Gabon with francs from the Ivory Coast. It seems clear that the motives for supplying arms to Biafra were not strictly economic, as the quantities supplied were not sufficient to make a significant contribution to the French defence industry. Biafra's oil sources may have been an important consideration. But perhaps the most convincing interpretation of France's limited support for Biafra is the political, or perhaps long-term, economic explanation – the size and wealth of Nigeria could represent a counterbalance to French influence in West Africa. Already Nigeria is developing closer co-operation with its francophobe neighbours, and in aiding Biafra France might have been able to reduce the possible influence that could be exerted by a strong Nigeria. Furthermore, French support for a successful Biafra might have achieved far more for French interests in the region than French support for a successful Nigeria, given the support Nigeria was already receiving from Britain and the Soviet Union.

However, support for Biafra was very tentative. France not only never supplied arms directly to Biafra, maintaining the fiction of an embargo on both sides, but also never recognized Biafra and never restricted commercial dealings with Nigeria. In November 1969, President Pompidou ordered a cooling of dealings with Biafra, and restrictions were imposed on private and unofficial arms supplies. Whether this represented a reversal of Gaullist policy – Debré, the Gaullist Defence Minister, was reportedly opposed to this decision – or whether it was merely a recognition that the gamble would not pay off is a matter for speculation.

The Middle East

France was a party to the Tripartite Declaration of 1950, restricting arms supplies to the Middle East. In 1953 and 1954 France, like Britain, supplied limited amounts of matching equipment to Egypt and Israel. British Mosquitoes sold to France for scrap were also supplied to Israel in 1953, but it is not clear whether the French government was involved in this transaction.

The first French aircraft deal with Israel in 1954 was opposed by both the Defence Ministry, who felt that French forces should receive priority, and the Foreign Ministry, who feared to irritate the Arab countries. Opposition was muted, however, when the Algerian War broke out at the end of 1954, and deliveries of Ouragan fighters began in 1955. As the Algerian War intensified, support for Israel as a second front against the Arabs increased. After the Egyptian arms deal with Czechoslovakia in 1955, Israel ordered Mystères from France. Nationalization of the Suez Canal acted as a catalyst in French–Israeli relations. In July 1956, an agreement was signed in which France engaged to supply Israel with all the arms necessary for its defence. Large quantities of arms were supplied in 1956 as part of their joint preparation for the Suez–Sinai campaign. On the eve of the war Israel received Sherman tanks and thirty-six Mystères. By this time it was clear that the arming of Israel was part of a French troop disposition stretching from Cairo to Morocco.

Between 1956 and 1967, Israel continued to receive most of its equipment from France, but it was clear that the relationship would not survive the conclusion of the Algerian War. Already in the mid-sixties, France began to offer arms to Jordan, Lebanon and even Egypt. Only Lebanon took up the offer, ordering Mirage fighters, although a Jordanian attempt to purchase the Mirage was foiled by the United States.

The turning point came with the June War of 1967. On 3 June, President de Gaulle announced that France would impose an embargo on the aggressor in the Middle East, and on the outbreak of hostilities on 5 June France imposed a total embargo on the region. However, on 20 October 1967, the embargo was lifted for countries which had not been direct participants in the war, such as Lebanon, Iraq and Saudi Arabia, and at the same time the embargo became 'selective': essentially this meant that France continued to supply all equipment to Israel except the Mirage, because this was 'the symbol of the offensive and its role was very important in the development of the conflict'. During this period there were essentially two French policies towards Israel – the official policy and the policy of the industry. While the official policy condemned Israeli actions, the industry continued to supply arms, accept new orders and cement the already close ties between France and Israel in the military domain. This situation lasted until the Israeli attack on Beirut on 28 December 1968, in which Israel used Super Frelon helicopters delivered after the imposition of the embargo. This was interpreted as open defiance of the official French policy, and the limitations of the 'selective' embargo were apparent to all observers.

On 3 January 1969, the total embargo was reimposed; it was imposed, without a deliberation of the Council, by a directive addressed direct to the customs by the administration. There was considerable opposition to the embargo in military industrial circles, as well as in the French press, as, quite apart from the political considerations – the popular support for Israel – it was felt that this precipitate action might endanger the confidence of prospective arms clients. The embargo also, of course, represented a serious loss to the defence industry.

During the presidential campaign of the spring of 1969, all the candidates made it clear that the embargo needed to be reconsidered. On 10 July 1969, soon after becoming President, Pompidou held a press conference at which he said that France desires only that 'all powers cease to furnish arms to countries in the Middle East which would be without doubt a factor in favour of peace'. He stated that there might be a return to the 'selective' embargo if the situation should warrant it. In his announcement of the Libyan deal on 21 January 1970, Defence Minister Debré said that France had continued to supply spare Mirage parts to Israel during 1969. In addition, the establishment of a Turbo-meca factory in Israel to build aircraft engines went ahead. Spare parts and, reportedly, other 'non-offensive' *matériel* were apparently stopped after the smuggling of the five gunboats out of France by Israeli sailors on Christmas Day 1969.

The gunboat affair represented a defiance of French official policy similar to the raid on Beirut. It seems clear that, so long as Israel played along with the official policy, it could benefit from the policy of the industry. When Israel defied the official policy, the policy of the industry was clamped down upon.

The embargo was imposed in an effort to improve relations with Arab states. France's traditional ties with the Arab countries were temporarily interrupted by the supply of weapons to Israel and by the Algerian War. In the long term, France stands to gain more both commercially, in terms of oil and arms markets, for instance, and politically in the wider Arab arena. In addition, the influence of the other Western powers in Arab countries is being eroded, a process which was speeded up by their support for Israel during the June War of 1967. Psychologically, the June War provided the ideal opportunity for France to disclaim identification with Israel in the Middle East conflict.

The deal for 110 Mirages signed with Libya in January 1970 is the most spectacular of French gains, made after the embargo on Israel. All the necessary conditions for a French success were present. After the overthrow of the Libyan monarchy in September 1969, which represented a victory for radical Arab nationalist forces, the first target of the new Libyan government was Anglo-American influence. The withdrawal of British and US troops was negotiated, and, as we have seen, an order for British anti-aircraft missiles was cancelled by BAC after Libya failed to pay its dues. At the same time, the Soviet alternative was not necessarily the most attractive. Libya, rich in oil revenues, could afford to pay for the French option.

The gains were obvious: Libya stands at the crossroads of North Africa, the Middle East and the French ex-community, so that the deal was heralded as part of a new French policy to expand French presence in the Mediterranean. Moreover, the Libyan oil-rich market is a lucrative one – not only for arms, but also for other commercial transactions. Such a deal would not have proved possible had France continued as the principal supplier to Israel.

South Africa

France began to deliver major weapons to South Africa in 1961. In August 1963, when the UN Security Council resolution called for an arms embargo on South Africa, Britain and France abstained. In 1964, the new British Labour government decided to join the embargo, leaving the field clear for France to become the main supplier of arms to South Africa. Today, South Africa is France's fourth largest aerospace customer. Between 1961 and 1969, France supplied almost 55 per cent of South Africa's total major weapon imports.

The first intimation of arms transactions with South Africa came with the visit of Major-General Viljoen, Chief of Staff of the South African Air Force, to France in 1957. Four years later, the South African press reported an imminent order for Mirages. The South African Minister of Defence announced on 27 August 1961 that South Africa would build under licence the Panhard armoured car and heavy machine-guns, and in April 1962 the first orders for Mirages were announced. Since then France has supplied considerable numbers of Mirages, helicopters, transports, air-to-air missiles and three submarines, has provided help in building the factory to produce the Italian Macchi trainers, and has developed the anti-aircraft missile system, Crotale – or Cactus, as it is called in South Africa – especially for South Africa. The most recent agreement, concluded in June 1971, covers the production under licence in South Africa of the Mirage III and the more advanced F-1 Super Mirage.

The commercial benefits of these transactions are clear – South Africa is a lucrative arms market, with few competitors – but politically France has been under attack both at home and abroad. Numerous questions have been asked in the National Assembly, critical articles have been published in the French press, and both Britain and the United States have attempted to prevent deliveries of certain equipment. The United States vetoed the supply of the Breguet Atlantic 1150 in 1965 and three Mystère 20s in 1966, and when South Africa expressed interest in Jaguar, the joint Franco-British fighter project, the British government announced on

30 May 1969 that it was under embargo and opposed such a sale.

The defence of the French position has been on the following lines: when the Security Council resolution was debated in 1963, the French representative, Seydoux, declared: 'I have specified that the French authorities would take all the measures they consider necessary to prevent the sale to the South African government of arms which could be used for repression.' Such a distinction between arms for national defence and arms for internal use has been used in arguments on this subject both by the Italians and the former British Conservative government. But it is difficult to see how France can ensure that armoured cars, machine-guns, helicopters, transports and even fighter bombers will be used only for external defence.

The other argument used by France in support of its position is that arms embargoes are ineffective. On his visit to Johannesburg in April 1965, M. Schmittlein, Vice-President of the National Assembly and President of the France-Afrique parliamentary group, after reassuring South Africa that France would continue to supply arms and maintain its cultural and commercial ties with South Africa, declared that: 'France cannot agree with all aspects of South Africa's policy but she cannot concede to other countries the right to take punitive measures to force South Africa to change its policy. General de Gaulle has emphasized during his recent talks with the British Prime Minister the fact that each country has the right to have the government it chooses.'

After severe criticism from the OAU and a number of African states, it was announced in October 1970 that France would impose certain restrictions on the sale of arms to South Africa. No new contracts would be signed for the delivery of weapons that could be used for internal suppression – for example, helicopters and armoured cars. But nothing has been said about the supply of spare parts, current contracts are not affected, and France will probably fulfil the agreement to supply between fifty and one hundred helicopters. In some Black African countries, doubts were expressed whether the embargo would be effective .

Compared with the US and Soviet arms supplies, Chinese exports of major weapons to Third World countries have been very small, amounting to 2·1 per cent of the total. These supplies are concentrated on a very small number of recipient governments – North Korea and North Viet-Nam have accounted for more than 90 per cent of Chinese major weapons exports – and have often been short in duration. However, Chinese military aid, in the form of the provision of small arms, training assistance and infrastructure building, has been extended to a much larger number of revolutionary movements in Asia, the Middle East and Africa.

As for the United States and the Soviet Union, Chinese arms supplies must be regarded as an integral part of China's overall foreign policy, and in particular there are two aspects of this policy which have influenced Chinese strategy and choice of allies. The first element represents a more traditional factor: the need, conditioned by its pre-1949 weakness, for China to regain its status as a first-ranking power with an independent say in world affairs. This includes the need to reduce US influence, especially in Asia, as well as Soviet influence, in particular since 1960 when the split between the two governments over economic, military and ideological matters became apparent. In general this policy coincided with Chinese official ideology.

Related to this, a common factor in Chinese foreign-policy decisions up to 1971 remained the need to break the isolation imposed on China by events beyond its control. For example, China needed neutral border states for reasons of security as well as for commercial and other relations.

The second element in Chinese foreign policy, of relevance to its arms-supply policy, is the ideological component – the desire to support revolutionary movements and to see an extension of socialism. However, China's support, for security reasons, of the non-aligned nations in Asia and Africa, and the need to avoid direct confrontation with the US, have often conflicted with its willingness and ability to support revolutionary movements. For instance, China has supported Pakistan since 1965 – both countries have been in dispute with India – and remained firmly committed to the military regime in Pakistan during the 1971 war with the Bengali liberation movement, the Mukhti Bahini. From China's point of view it was not desirable to see a pro-Indian government in power in East Pakistan, now the state of Bangla Desh. The situation would perhaps have been different if the radical anti-Indian faction of the Mukhti Bahini had not been ousted by Mujibur Rahman's followers. The case of Ceylon in 1971 was very similar. Ceylon's non-aligned government received Chinese, as well as Soviet, arms to suppress the 'guevarist' guerillas on the island.

In pursuing this foreign policy, China's arms supplies have had the following functions, in addition to a purely military one: they have provided the means of developing closer relations with recipient governments, of preventing or competing with Soviet and Western influence, and of achieving support for China's admission to the United Nations and its policy against Taiwan. Chinese arms supplies have not had any economic function, although they may have led to economic benefits. Nearly all Chinese weapons supplies are gifts. In the case of sales, as for Pakistan, long-term credits at low interest rates are granted. Some transactions may also have been made on a barter basis. Further, like the USA's, but unlike the Soviet Union's, a large part of Chinese military aid has consisted of training assistance and the building of infrastructure projects, such as harbours, roads and railways.

The provision of Chinese arms has often had political consequences, particularly outside Asia, which are disproportionate to the quantities of at least major weapons supplied. The appearance of Chinese arms in a new area tends to focus attention on the conflict and is often taken as an indication of a radical shift in the orientation of the recipient. This was the case for instance when

Table 9 Chinese aid to revolutionary movements

Country	Recipient movement	Weapons[a]	Training[a]	Financial aid[a]	Verbal support[b]
Asia					
Burma	Burmese Communist Party (BCP)		[1951–5] 1970	[1958–69]	1965–9
Cambodia	National United Front of Cambodia	1970–72			1972
India	Mizo and Naga tribes		[1967–70]		1965–8
	Naxalites				1967–9
Laos	Pathet Lao	[1969–72]	early 1950s; early 1960s; 1967–70		1960–72
Malaysia	National Liberation Army				1967–70
Philippines	Huks		1943–50	1943–50	1965–70
Thailand	Thai Patriotic Front	[1969–72]	[1960s]		1965–72
South Viet-Nam	National Liberation Front	1962–72			1960–72
Middle East					
	Palestine Liberation Organization (PLO)	1965–72	1965–72		1964–72
	PFLOAG (Dhofar) guerilla	1968–70	1968–70		1968–70
North Africa					
Algeria	National Liberation Front	1959–62	1959–62		1958–62
Africa					
Angola	MPLA				1961–72
Cameroun	Union des Populations du Cameroun (UPC)		1961–4		1961–4
Chad	Union National Tschadienne (UNT)				1964

Table 9 – contd

Country	Recipient movement	Weapons[a]	Training[a]	Financial aid[a]	Verbal support[b]
Africa – contd					
Congo (K)	Lumumba government			1960	1958–61
	Mulele uprising (in Kwilu province)	1964		1964	1964
	Patriotic Armed Forces of Congo (K) (in Kwilu province)				1965–70
Ethiopia	Eritrean Liberation Front				1965–70
Guinea-Bissau	PAIGC		1960–72		1960–72
Mozambique	FRELIMO	[1969]			1963–72
	COREMO				1967–70
Niger	guerilla				
Nigeria	Biafra		[1961–3]		1968–9
Rhodesia	ZAPU			1964	
	ZANU				1967–72
Rwanda/Burundi	Watusi tribe	[1963]	1963–5	1963	
South Africa	ANC				before 1959
	PAC				1959–72
South West Africa	SWANU				1967–72

[a] Includes only those cases with substantial reports on a flow of weapons or training assistance, the latter either in China or from Chinese instructors in local training camps.

[b] Chinese sources.

[ ] = date estimated

Pakistan received Chinese weapons in 1965–6, and also when Syria received a limited amount of Chinese small arms in 1969.

ASIA

During the 1950s, China developed close relations with India and encouraged the formation of a non-aligned group of nations. During this time, only North Korea and North Viet-Nam received major Chinese weapons. The Indo-Chinese resistance movements were closely related after 1951, and it is known that members of the Pathet Lao received some training in Chinese guerilla camps at the same time as members of the Viet-Minh. Supplies of small arms from China were channelled via North Viet-Nam.

No liberation movements in non-aligned states received any Chinese weapons at this time. On the contrary, at the 1955 Bandung conference Chou En-lai made it clear to Cambodia, Burma and Pakistan that China had no intention of supporting forces opposed to the governments within those countries. The Huk movement in the Philippines, however, may have received Chinese aid up to 1951. China attempted to establish good relations with all governments opposed to Western influence and willing to recognize China instead of Taiwan, and this remained a consistent policy until 1971.

The break in Sino-Indian relations, evident from 1956, meant that China had to find new allies. Further, the public escalation of the Sino-Soviet dispute from 1960 brought a new aspect into Chinese arms-supply policy: socialist recipients had to be at least neutral in the Sino-Soviet conflict, and arms supplies to the non-aligned states in Africa and Asia and to the liberation movements became related to the competition with the Soviet Union. Sukarno's Indonesia was initially adopted to succeed India as China's partner in Asia. The two governments shared the objectives of eliminating Western influence in the area, of organizing a radical alternative to the United Nations, and of emphasizing the

Third World as a force separate from East–West power camps. But there is no evidence of Chinese arms supplies to Indonesia between 1960 and 1965, except for a limited amount of small arms to the air force. In 1965 an agreement was signed for the supply of Chinese small arms to equip a People's Militia but the agreement never materialized. And the army coup of October 1965 that ousted Sukarno from power brought an end to relations with China.

During this period the two socialist governments in Asia – those in North Korea and North Viet-Nam – remained largely neutral in the Sino-Soviet conflict, except for the years 1962–5, which was the most pronounced anti-Soviet period. China was actually the sole supplier of arms to Korea during this time. Although, in the case of Viet-Nam, Chinese arms supplies were very low and did not approach the scale of the Soviet military aid programme, China was first to recognize the NLF in South Viet-Nam and to supply small arms from 1963.

AFRICA AND THE MIDDLE EAST

The early sixties also marked the beginning of an increase in Chinese activity in Africa. In fact, from 1959 the FLN of Algeria had been recognized and had received some small arms, largely as a result of contacts made at Bandung. The competition with the Soviet Union was evident in the support of African liberation movements. China often came out in support of those small movements which opposed those supported by the OAU and received Soviet aid, for instance the UNITA in Angola, COREMO in Mozambique, ZAPU in Rhodesia, the UNT in Chad and SWANU in Namibia. A vivid illustration of this competition was the withdrawal of China's aid to the ANC in South Africa owing to the impact of the Sino-Soviet conflict, and probably on the initiative of the ANC itself. Instead China directed its aid to a group that left the ANC in 1959, the Pan Africanist Congress (PAC). In Rhodesia Chinese aid to ZAPU was transferred to ZANU because of the former's good relations with the Soviet Union. Chinese support is often determined by the liberation groups themselves: the PAIGC in Guinea-Bissau, for example, sent a group of trainees to China in 1960, and FRELIMO in Mozambique receives Chinese aid in addition to Soviet aid as a result of a meeting in Peking in 1963.

Related to this is the Chinese assistance in guerilla training and in setting up bases for this purpose in African host countries; this was the case in Zambia, Tanzania, Guinea, Ghana, Uganda and Congo (Brazzaville). Between 1960 and 1965 China also supported the UPC guerilla movement in Cameroun, some members being trained in China. In 1964 there were reports in Niger about a group of Chinese-trained guerillas, based in Ghana. For this reason both Cameroun and Niger opposed China's admission to the UN. Some odd political moves were made by China in Africa before 1965: small arms seem to have been supplied to the opposition party led by Odinga in Kenya, and also to the Watusi tribe in the Rwanda–Burundi civil war.

The competition with the Soviet Union was also reflected by African governments that accepted military and economic aid from China. Chinese aid was at its height in 1964–5 during the preparations for a 'second Bandung' conference, on the Chinese initiative, when China aimed at excluding the Soviet Union. Mali, under President Keita, was one of the few African states that supported China, and received military training and military advisers up to 1968. But the 1968 coup resulted in a reduction of Chinese assistance in favour of aid from the Soviet Union. From 1964, the Lissouba government of Congo (Brazzaville) accepted large quantities of Chinese arms, as well as a number of military instructors. The cabinet reshuffle of 1968, however, brought the same change in relations as in Mali: China had to withdraw its huge military mission and embassy staff.

China also channelled arms to the Kwilu rebels in Congo (Zaire) in 1964, via Brazzaville, Uganda and Burundi, and subsequently to the Stanleyville regime, but it never recognized either the Tschombe or Mobutu governments in the Congo. China's relations with Uganda were related to the civil war in the Congo, and in 1965 Premier Obote revealed that he had received military aid from China. But eventually the Soviet Union was chosen to train Uganda's air force in 1968.

Tanzania remains the most important African recipient of Chinese military aid, a situation which dates from Chinese interests in Zanzibar before the creation of Tanzania in 1964. Zanzibar received military aid from the Soviet Union, China and the German Democratic Republic at the same time, but later the Tanzanian government continued to accept the aid agreed upon with China, while the other suppliers were phased out. China has acquired the task of training the air force, and will supply the first jet fighters to Tanzania. It has also undertaken important infrastructure work, for example the building of the Tanzania–Zambia railroad.

Another aspect of the competition with the Soviet Union is evident in the Middle East: while the Soviet Union has concentrated on aid to the nationalist Arab governments, China has concentrated on aid to the Palestinian guerillas (PLO). From 1965 a PLO mission was allowed to open a permanent office in Peking. Chinese support for the PFLOAG guerillas (the People's Front for the Liberation of the Occupied Arab Gulf) was initiated in 1968. China also supported the Eritrean Liberation Front in Ethiopia until 1971, when relations were established with the Ethiopian government.

THE CULTURAL REVOLUTION

During the period 1965–8, the height of the cultural revolution in China, there was a marked shift of emphasis in favour of liberation movements, while contacts with foreign governments almost came to a standstill. Verbal support for revolutionary movements covered for instance the Burmese communist party, the Mizo, Naga and Naxalite rebels in northern India, guerillas in Indonesia and Malaysia, the Thai Patriotic Front and so on, but there is no definite evidence of actual arms supplies. Arms continued to be channelled to the Pathet Lao and the NLF in South Viet-Nam, however. Pakistan was the sole new recipient of

Chinese arms during this period. It can be noted that up to 1965 Pakistan had not supported China's admission to the UN. After the end of the cultural revolution, Chinese contacts with governments were re-established, and arms supplies are on the increase, mainly because of the commitment to Pakistan. Also, the coup in Cambodia in 1970 brought about the establishment of Prince Sihanouk's exile government in Peking, and the organization of a resistance movement directly supplied with arms by China.

Part Three

The Recipients of Arms in the Third World

7 The Far East

In the Far East the supply of arms represents only a minor part of a great-power involvement. Whereas in the Middle East the hegemony of the great powers has largely been established through the supply of arms, in the Far East direct intervention – certainly on the part of the United States – has been much more important. In Thailand, Laos and South Viet-Nam, the weapons supplied to the governments of the countries have been, relatively, of minor importance: the resources which the United States has put into direct intervention have exceeded the resources devoted to arms supplies by a factor of some 50:1.

The pattern of arms transfers to Far Eastern countries has been dominated by the conflicts in the area. For instance, North and South Korea received nearly three quarters of the major arms imports to the Far East in 1950–53. Taiwan's share during and immediately after the 1958–9 crisis in the Taiwan Strait was about one third. Indonesia and Malaysia also received about a third of the area's arms supplies during their confrontation. And North and South Viet-Nam have accounted for some two thirds of the Far Eastern major arms imports since 1965.

The weapons acquired have been closely related to the military requirements of the parties. For example, North and South Korea received aircraft and tanks suitable for conventional land and air warfare, and Taiwan's arms procurement was devoted to the build-up of air and sea power. On the other hand, Laos, Thailand and Viet-Nam – the scene of predominantly guerilla-type warfare – have received mostly COIN equipment, such as trainers and helicopters. The peaks in North Viet-Namese arms imports in 1966–8 and 1971–2 are explained by the massive supply of surface-to-air missiles to counter US bombing attacks.

But the nature of the conflicts and the accompanying arms supplies cannot be divorced from the role of the suppliers. A

Table 10 Far East (including Viet-Nam): supplies of major weapons, by supplier
US $ mn, at constant (1968) *prices*

Supplier:	USA	UK	France	USSR	China	Other	Total[a]
1950–54							
$ mn annual							
average	56	1	1	38	16	10	**121**
per cent	46·3	0·5	0·5	31·0	13·1	8·5	**100·0**
1955–9							
$ mn annual							
average	141	5	2	14	42	31	**234**
per cent	60·1	2·1	0·7	5·9	17·9	13·3	**100·0**
1960–64							
$ mn annual							
average	174	14	3	67	8	12	**280**
per cent	62·3	4·9	1·2	24·0	3·0	4·6	**100·0**
1965–9							
$ mn annual							
average	164	10	4	155	6	11	**350**
per cent	46·8	3·0	1·1	44·2	1·7	3·3	**100·0**
1970–72							
$ mn annual							
average	339	16	1	164	12	14	**545**
per cent	62·1	2·9	0·2	30·1	2·1	2·5	**100·0**
1950–72							
$ mn total [a]	**3,690**	**195**	**51**	**1,861**	**396**	**369**	**6,652**
Per cent of							
total	*56·2*	*3·0*	*0·8*	*28·4*	*6·0*	*5·6*	*100·0*

[a] Figures may not add up to totals owing to rounding.
Source: SIPRI worksheets.

cold-war pattern has been established through the involvement
of the two great powers. This is reflected in the striking predomin-
ance of the great powers as suppliers; together the Soviet Union
and the United States are responsible for 85 per cent of total arms
supplies, compared with 67 per cent for the Third World as a
whole. Nearly all Chinese major arms have gone to Far Eastern
countries. Britain and France have a far smaller share than in the
Third World as a whole, accounting for only 4 per cent, and most

of their exports going to ex-colonies such as Burma and Malaysia, and former French Indo-China. Other medium and smaller suppliers have virtually no major arms trade with the Far East.

In the Far East, perhaps more than in any other area, the process by which local conflicts are transformed into confrontations between the two rival systems can be observed. This process of polarization occurred first in the division between North and South Korea and the subsequent conflict on the Korean peninsula. Then the conflict between Taiwan and China became internationally significant with the US commitment to support Chiang Kai-Shek. In the states which once formed French Indo-China, there is an intricate pattern of ethnic rivalries and inherited hostilities, further complicated by the fact that these states have never been able to complete the transition from colonialism to independence, since the colonial wars have so rapidly developed into part of the East–West conflict. With the arming of various groups by one side or the other, these local conflicts have become part of the cold war.

The process of polarization was described by Senator Symington in February 1970, during hearings before the Subcommittee on United States Security Agreements and Commitments Abroad of the Senate Foreign Relations Committee:

We have now gone to country splitting, you might say. First we split Germany. Then we split China. We stay with billions and billions of dollars and hundreds of thousands of people in the case of Germany [*sic*], China we stay with billions of dollars and thousands of people [*sic*]. Then we split Korea, and stay there . . . Then we split Viet-Nam . . . Now we split Laos, and go in there with hundreds of millions of dollars and lots of people. Do you know of any other country we plan to split pretty soon?

A month later, Prince Sihanouk of Cambodia was overthrown and, following the US and South Viet-Namese invasion of April 1970, that country was split too. Indeed, the only countries in the Far East which remain relatively untouched by the process of polarization are Burma, Malaysia and Indonesia.

US RECIPIENTS

Throughout the period, the regimes in Taiwan, South Korea, South Viet-Nam and Thailand have been dependent on the United States for support and, in particular, for military assistance. These countries, together with Laos, are the US 'forward defence areas' in the Far East. The story of their arms imports is largely the story of US strategy towards the conflicts in which they are involved. Fluctuations in the level of arms supplies have reflected the intensity of the conflicts and the form of US participation, whether it be the supply of soldiers or merely of arms. In the various wars that have taken place in the Far East over the past twenty years, the US has intervened directly, as in Viet-Nam and Korea, and/or indirectly, by equipping indigenous armed forces or by persuading other countries, such as the French in Indo-China, or Thailand, Korea and the Philippines in Viet-Nam, to intervene on its behalf, with the help of US funds and weapons.

The relationship between the United States and these regimes has largely resulted from their common interest in 'containing communism'. The US commitment to South Korea, Taiwan and South Viet-Nam was a direct result of their conflicts with communist forces. Military aid to the Chinese Nationalists began during the Chinese revolution. It was temporarily halted after the Nationalists escaped to Taiwan in late 1949 because, at that time, the US was avoiding 'a course which will lead to involvement in the civil conflict in China'. But it became important after the Treaty of Friendship between China and the Soviet Union, and the outbreak of the Korean War in 1950 convinced Americans of the need to prevent the spread of communism in the Far East. Military aid to South Korea was a consequence of the US occupation during the Second World War but, again, it did not become important until after the outbreak of the Korean War. Finally, aid to South Viet-Nam grew out of the support provided to the French during the Indo-China War; what was for France an attempt to retain its colonial empire became for the United States a battle against communism.

Thai interest in 'containing communism' must be viewed in its historical perspective. Viet-Nam has functioned through the centuries as an antipode to Thailand in the political dynamics of the area. Thailand is often said to fear a strong Viet-Nam, that is a united Viet-Nam, more than it fears China. Further, the historical Thai dominance over what are now Laos and Cambodia has led to active Thai participation in the internal affairs of Laos and to problematic relations with Cambodia. Thus, Thailand shares the US interest in preventing the reunification of Viet-Nam and in supporting right-wing regimes in Laos and Cambodia.

Unlike the support for other Asian clients, US support for the Philippines cannot be said to have arisen from any particular conflict. Rather, it stems from the former colonial relationship. In the post-war period, there existed a substantial insurgent group, the Huks, but today even US officials admit the smallness of the 'communist threat' to the Philippines. It is clear that the Philippine government largely regards military aid as a rental for US base facilities; it expects the United States not only to supply weapons but also to maintain them.

Despite the common interests between the United States and its clients, there is not always an identity of interests. Polarization has the effect of producing a state of mutual dependence between supplying and recipient countries, in which each partner can influence the other's policies. The fact that the supplier cannot withdraw its support without risking the defeat of its client gives the recipient a chip with which to bargain. Very often recipients may be bribed with arms and money to prevent extreme action, and this has been apparent in South Korea, Taiwan and Thailand.

Throughout the period, there has tended to be an inverse relationship between US military aid and the number of US troops deployed in the area. Until 1954, weapons supplies to indigenous armed forces were relatively low. Prior to 1950, limited amounts of military aid had been extended to the Chinese Nationalists, South Korea and the Philippines, but these countries were not considered part of the US 'defensive perimeter' until the outbreak of the Korean War. Arms supplies to indigenous armed forces remained low during the next few years mainly because US participation in the Korean War took the form of direct intervention, while in the Indo-China War it took the form of military aid to the French. The United States also began to supply arms to Thailand during this period, as a *quid pro quo* for Thai participation in the Korean War.

In 1954 and 1955, Mutual Defense Treaties were signed with all the Asian forward defence areas except Viet-Nam and Laos: the USA, in the protocol to the South East Asia Collective Defense Treaty, unilaterally committed itself to defend these latter two countries. From then until 1960, arms supplies rose substantially in line with the view, which became prevalent in the United States, that local forces should carry the burden of meeting united attacks. Indeed they were five times higher in the second half of the fifties than in the first half. Since it was widely believed that the 'communist threat' would take the form of external attack, these supplies were concentrated on Taiwan and South Korea. In particular, large amounts of sophisticated equipment, including 320 F-86F Sabres, armed with Sidewinder and Falcon air-to-air missiles, F-100 Super Sabres and F-100A fighter-bombers, were supplied to Taiwan after limited Chinese attacks in 1954–5 and the hostilities in the Taiwan Strait in 1958. Taiwan also received long-range surface-to-air missiles – two Hawk battalions and ten batteries of Nike Hercules – and a number of Honest John artillery rockets. It has been suggested that the massive military aid provided by the United States was also due to the pressure to get rid of surplus stocks, which were purchased from the US services at their replacement cost, and to inefficiency on the part of the recipients as well as the US military advisers. For example, until 1960 there was no effective inventory of supplies inherited from the Korean War, so that, since nobody knew what was in the stocks, shipments to South Korea were in excess of requirements.

From 1960, an increasing emphasis was placed on the need to combat internal revolutions. Military aid to South Viet-Nam began to rise substantially, and in 1961 and 1962 arms imports reached a peak which was only surpassed in 1969. Large amounts of COIN equipment were supplied, and the strike capability of the air force was virtually trebled by the delivery of T-28 trainers, A-1E/H Skyraiders, B-26 bombers, helicopters and transports. The number of US military advisers also increased, from 327 in 1957 to 23,300 in 1965.

Military aid to Thailand also increased during this period, from $22 million between 1957 and 1960 to $70 million in 1961–3. Thailand received, *inter alia*, large quantities of F-86 fighters, trainers, transport and liaison aircraft. Initially, these arms were supplied to strengthen Thai participation in the Laos war, in support of the rightist faction, but later they acquired another function – to appease Thai fears about US intentions in the area and to secure its loyalty. Thailand had expressed severe criticism of SEATO's passive stand on the Laotian crisis, especially when the USA opted for negotiations in the spring of 1961. And Thailand was also critical when US aid was extended to Cambodia.

At the same time, arms supplies to South Korea, Taiwan and the Philippines fell substantially: these countries faced no internal threat. Military aid was increasingly devoted to the replacement and maintenance of equipment. By 1965, ammunition, parts, food and training accounted for some 80 per cent of military assistance grants to Korea, while maintenance accounted for around two thirds of the military aid to Taiwan.

The arrival of regular US troops in Viet-Nam in 1965 brought a further change in US military-aid policy. On the one hand, direct US presence limited the necessity to arm local forces and this is reflected in the relatively low level of arms supplied to South Viet-Nam. On the other hand, military aid was increased in Thailand, South Korea and the Philippines in return for participation in the war. Thailand provided base facilities for US air attacks as well as troops. Because, as stated in 1969 in hearings before the Subcommittee on United States Security Agreements and Commitments Abroad of the Senate Committee on Foreign Relations, 'the Thais expressed concern that in sending their best troops out of the country they would be weakening their ability to deal with the insurgency at home', the US began to assist in accelerating the modernization of the Thai forces by adding $30 million to the military-assistance programmes in 1968 and 1969. Similarly, when 50,000 Korean troops were dispatched to Viet-Nam in 1965, the United States promised to equip fully three of the ten South Korean reserve divisions and to expedite the modernization of the Korean forces in firepower, communications and mobility. The Philippines have also received additional funding and arms supplies in return for the provision of an engineer task-force to Viet-Nam.

In addition to their participation in the Viet-Nam War, Thailand and South Korea faced new military contingencies at home. In Thailand, traditional ethnic and cultural conflicts have led to the growth of socialist guerilla movements in the southern and north-eastern parts of the country. In 1965, the Thai Patriotic Front was formed, and since then the guerillas have been receiving arms from China as well as North Viet-Nam. US equipment supplied to Thailand in the latter part of the sixties has, for the most part, consisted of COIN material, including F-5 fighters, a considerable supply of helicopters – HH-43, KH-4, UH-1, CH-34 and Boeing Vertol 107 – and a large number of infantry weapons, M-79 grenade launchers and M-16 rifles, vehicles and communications equipment. In 1966 and 1967, US-manned helicopters were leased to the Thai authorities for counter-insurgency operations, but these were withdrawn at the end of 1967 when the training programme for Thai helicopter pilots was sufficiently advanced.

Since 1968, there has also been a sharp increase in the number of incidents between North and South Korea, and after the Pueblo incident in January 1968 US arms supplies and military assistance were increased. In addition to the $170 million in regular military aid and $32 million for anti-infiltration equipment scheduled for 1968–9, a $100 million request was added at the last minute to the President's annual foreign aid message. It was to be spent on anti-aircraft equipment, patrol boats, ammunition and aircraft – the Phantoms which South Korea had been requesting for a year.

The Nixon Doctrine, introduced in 1969, led to further increases in military aid to the Asian forward defence areas. Troops were to be withdrawn from Viet-Nam, South Korea and Thailand, and to be replaced by US-equipped local forces. According to US Secretary of Defense Laird in October 1970: 'The US Military Assistance Program and the US Foreign Military Sales Program serve as key instruments in the implementation of the Nixon Doctrine.' So far, the effects of this policy have been most apparent in South Viet-Nam. To carry it out, large transfers of weapons, especially counter-insurgency equipment, such as Cessna A-37 ground attack planes, 300 helicopters and several hundred patrol boats, took place in 1969. In anticipation of the cease-fire agreement, which would ban the further introduction of arms to Viet-Nam, except as replacements, a huge airlift was carried out in October and November 1972. In less than a month, the 'Vietnamization' programme, scheduled for several years, had been completed, with the supply of 230 fighters, more than 50 transports, 270 helicopters and large amounts of army equipment.

SOCIALIST RECIPIENTS

As with the clients of the United States, the military requirements of the socialist states in the Far East stem from the conflicts in which they are involved. Arms supplies were at their highest during the Korean and Indo-China wars of the early fifties and during the Viet-Nam War since 1965. Unlike the US clients which they oppose, however, the socialist states have not depended on a single supplier and have acquired arms from both the Soviet Union and China. In practice, Soviet aid has been greater, but the availability of Chinese support has enabled these two countries to defy Soviet wishes when necessary to ensure their independent development. When the Soviet Union halted all forms of aid to North Korea in 1962, the official North Korean party paper *Nodong Shinmun* commented: 'certain persons propagandize as though a certain country's armed forces alone were safeguarding the entire socialist camp . . . no socialist country should try to rely solely on the military power of another country'.

By avoiding reliance on the Soviet Union and by exploiting the Sino-Soviet dispute, North Korea has managed to pursue an independent economic policy and North Viet-Nam was able to pursue an independent military strategy: in particular, North Viet-Nam was able to support the insurgency in the South at a time when both China and the Soviet Union were somewhat unwilling to take actions which might provoke an escalation of the US presence.

The two countries came into being in very different ways. North Korea was the creation of the Second World War. Soviet troops occupied the area from Japan's capitulation in 1945 until January 1949, and during this period a regime was established in which the key positions were awarded to Korean communists who had spent the war years in the Soviet Union. The Soviet Union was the sole supplier of arms and ammunition, as well as essential foodstuffs and other material, while China, at that time, had no resources with which to aid Korea either economically or militarily. The Soviet Union continued to supply substantial quantities of arms during the Korean War. It built up the air force, which had been established in 1948, and which, by the end of the war, comprised five air divisions, operating MiG-15, Yak-9P and La-9 fighters, Il-10 and Tu-2 bombers, plus a small number of Il-28 twin-jet bombers. China's aid commitments included the provision of air bases and the participation of 300,000 volunteer troops.

Unlike North Korea, the Democratic Republic of Viet-Nam had existed for many years – under a strong government headed by Ho Chi Minh – before either the Soviet Union or China had substantial influence in the country. The war against the French was conducted up to 1950 without aid from either the Soviet Union or China. In January 1950, Chinese People's Republic troops reached the Tonkin border, and on 18 January 1950 China became the first country to recognize North Viet-Nam, fifteen days before the Soviet Union. Military aid immediately began to flow across the border. Some 40,000 Viet-Minh troops were trained in China up to 1954 and China also provided a limited number of military personnel – in technical and advisory capacities – and supplied considerable quantities of arms, mostly of US origin but including Soviet trucks, Czech bazookas and rifles and Chinese-made light arms and ammunition.

The Korean armistice of 1953 and the Geneva Agreements of 1954 respectively led to some disillusionment in the two countries; it was widely held that victory had been denied them by collusion between the major powers. During the following years, they continued to receive military aid from both the USSR and China, but in practice their relationships with China were the more cordial. This was particularly evident in North Korea, where Kim Il Sung consciously attempted to undermine the Soviet and Soviet–Korean influence in the country; the presence of Chinese troops greatly facilitated Korean opposition to the Soviet system of control. In addition to building up an indigenous power-base, Kim Il Sung embarked on an independent economic policy which was clearly inspired by China. When the collectivization programme was completed in 1958, North Korea undertook the 'Flying Horse Campaign', much like China's 'Great Leap Forward', in order to expand production as rapidly as 'a horse that travels one thousand li per day'. China did not, however, begin to supply major weapons until 1957, when Korea received a number of patrol boats and some ex-Soviet An-2 transport planes. (North Viet-Nam also received patrol boats during this year.) From 1958, China began to supply large numbers of aircraft, particularly MiG-17s, to Korea.

The period 1961–4 was the most pronounced pro-Chinese period in the history of both North Viet-Nam and North Korea. In September 1960 the Third National Congress of the Viet-Nam Workers' Party took the decision to support the insurgency in the South with arms, and in December of that year the National Front for the Liberation of South Viet-Nam was officially created. This decision was taken independently of the Soviet Union and China, who were avoiding provocative actions towards the United States. Although the Soviet Union and China formally recognized the NLF, they did not immediately increase military aid. However, in September 1962, an NLF mission visited Peking for the first time, and by July 1963 Chinese semi-automatic weapons began to appear in the South. Liu Shao-Chi visited Hanoi in August 1963 and a joint communiqué was issued, attacking 'revisionism' and condemning 'bourgeois ideologists who try to kill the revolutionary spirit of Marxism-Leninism'. It is believed that this communiqué formalized a bargain made earlier: China was to receive Hanoi's support in the Sino-Soviet dispute in exchange for military support for the NLF.

North Korean differences with the Soviet Union largely stemmed from its independent economic policy. The Seven-Year Plan, introduced in 1961, once more defied Soviet efforts to organize co-operative planning in the socialist camp. In the same year, mutual-defence treaties were concluded between North Korea and both the Soviet Union and China, but Korean insistence on an independent policy soon brought reaction from the Soviet Union, which halted all forms of aid in 1962. In response, Chinese military aid increased substantially in the early 1960s; for example the Chinese air force shared its supplies of jet fuel and spares with the Koreans, and also supplied considerable numbers of aircraft. In fact, the Korean air force fighter regiments were re-organized along Chinese lines with five fighter regiments receiving new Shenyang MiG-17s produced in Manchuria. And by 1963, the Korean air force had received 380 Chinese-built MiG-15s and MiG-17s, additional Il-28 bombers, Chen Shenyang Yak-18 trainers and Fong Shou No 2 transports – a Chinese version of the Soviet An-2 aircraft. Estimates at the end of 1963 credited the Korean air force with 700 aircraft, of which 465 were combat planes.

From 1965, relations with the Soviet Union improved. The intensified US bombing of North Viet-Nam, the landing of US combat forces in South Viet-Nam and the constant Chinese criticism that Soviet support for wars of liberation was being sacrificed to détente with the United States were factors which contributed to the Soviet Union's more active intervention in both North Viet-Nam and North Korea. Further, the fall of Khrushchev enabled the Brezhnev–Kosygin government to disclaim identification with the policies of the past. In May 1965, North Korea signed an agreement for additional military aid from the

Soviet Union, a deal which probably included MiG-21s, since these were reported for the first time in 1965. The rapprochement did not, however, lead to a 'pro-Soviet' policy in general, and North Korean media continued to stress the necessity for North Korea to remain economically, culturally and even ideologically independent of the Soviet Union. The independent economic policy enabled North Korea to produce its own small arms, such as rifles, ammunition, machine-guns and mortars.

North Viet-Nam concluded a new military-aid agreement with the Soviet Union in February 1965. The Soviet Union did little to strengthen North Viet-Nam's offensive capabilities, but whether this was due to caution or to recognition that North Viet-Nam could not match the strength of the United States is not clear. However, it was very generous in supplying defensive weapons. Substantial numbers of radar-controlled anti-aircraft guns were supplied during 1965, and in mid-1966 North Viet-Nam's defence was supplemented for the first time by the highly sophisticated Soviet missiles, the SA-2, and with MiG-21s equipped with Atolls. At this time, the Soviet Union also promised to let Soviet volunteers go to Viet-Nam if the North Viet-Namese government requested such help. Soviet aid further increased in 1967; besides additional contingents of SA-2 missiles and MiG-21s, the Soviet Union supplied North Viet-Nam with Mi-6 heavy helicopters, An-24 transports and a small number of Il-28 medium bombers. According to Western estimates, Soviet economic assistance increased in value from $300 million in 1965 to $720 million in 1967, while Chinese economic assistance rose from $120 million 1965 to $250 million in 1967.

During this period, relations with China were strained. As far as Korea was concerned, this largely stemmed from the cultural revolution in which North Korea was accused of revisionism and Kim II Sung was personally attacked. A number of border incidents were also reported.

It also appears that China placed more importance on its dispute with the Soviet Union than on the war in Viet-Nam. The Chinese response to the escalation of the war was cautious and few public statements referred to aid. Military assistance extended by China to North Viet-Nam during 1966 comprised the provision of some 20,000 army engineers to repair the railway between the two countries and the supply of anti-aircraft batteries, as well as some infantry weapons. On several occasions, the Soviet Union accused China of obstructing the flow of Soviet aid. An initial transit agreement had been signed in 1965, after some hesitation on the part of China, but later China refused to allow Soviet officials to supervise shipments through China. Although Hanoi denied the Soviet accusations, they appear to have had some substance, since a new transit agreement was signed with North Viet-Nam in 1967, allowing Viet-Namese officials to go to the Sino–Soviet border and escort the material.

A letter from the Soviet Communist Party to other East European parties on 14 February 1966, quoted in *Die Welt* on 22 March 1966, throws further light on the Chinese refusal to co-operate with the Soviet Union in aiding Viet-Nam: 'The CPSU has proposed to the Chinese leaders more than once that joint action to support Viet-Nam be organized ... These proposals, which were received by the Politburo of the Viet-Namese Party of Labour with approval, were not accepted by the Chinese leaders.'

The controversy between Hanoi and Peking also concerned the proposed Chinese strategy for Viet-Nam. This amounted to a recommendation for prolonged guerilla warfare in the South and no peace negotiations until victory was finally achieved. Further, Viet-Namese theoreticians, according to *Asian Analyst* of July 1967, criticized the development of the cultural revolution in China, in particular the separation of the working class from 'its vanguard, the Communist Party' and the 'deification' of Mao Tse-Tung.

With the end of the cultural revolution and, in North Viet-Nam, with the death of Ho Chi Minh, Chinese relations with North Korea and North Viet-Nam were normalized. In May 1970, a new military aid agreement was signed between North Viet-Nam and China, covering military supplies on a grant basis for one year, and in July 1970 a Korean military delegation visited Peking. Both countries continued to receive Soviet military aid but after the bombing halt of 1968 and the opening of the Paris peace talks, major weapons supplies to North Viet-Nam declined. This decline, however, was only temporary; Soviet aid increased again during 1971, while Chinese military aid appears to have fallen slightly. After the resumption of US bombing late in 1971 both countries pledged to increase their aid to North Viet-Nam. After the mining of North Viet-Nam's coastal waters in May 1972, Soviet supplies were channelled mainly through China, and despite US attempts to cut off all land supplies as well, considerable quantities of equipment appear to have come through. Again, the build-up has mainly concerned the air-defence system and, for the first time, US B-52 bombers were brought down in 1972.

INTERNAL POLARIZATION – LAOS AND CAMBODIA

Laos and Cambodia can perhaps be said to epitomize the process of polarization, which has dominated the story of their arms imports. The two countries have been pulled apart, as it were, by the intensity of the East–West struggle in the region. Any attempts to remain immune from that struggle, through the establishment of neutral governments, have proved at best precarious, as in Cambodia, which managed to pursue a non-aligned policy for fifteen years, and at worst impossible, as in Laos, where the neutral government established by the Geneva Agreements of 1962 lasted less than a year. Both countries are currently divided between government forces, supported by the United States, and liberation forces, supported by North Viet-Nam and China.

The preconditions for polarization in Laos existed long before the arrival of the French and the creation of the state of Laos. Laos is geographically divided into a valley and a mountain region; the plains have been mainly inhabited by the Lao, the largest ethnic group, and the mountains by a variety of peoples, under the general domination of the Lao. (It is illustrative that the name of the largest of these groups, the Kha, means 'slave' in Laotian.) Further, the two empires, which now comprise

Thailand and Viet-Nam, have fought for suzerainty over Laos for centuries. The present alignment of Thailand and Viet-Nam with the US and socialist camps, respectively, and their support for the Lao and non-Lao groups in Laos complete the picture. An additional complication, however, is the Ho Chi Minh trail, by which supplies are brought down from North to South Viet-Nam, creating an area of engagement between North Viet-Nam and the United States.

There are essentially three political groupings in Laos today: the right (which includes the greater part of the army), the left (the Pathet Lao) and the neutralists (led by Souvanna Phouma). Their sources for arms have been determined by their role in the polarized conflict. Thus the right has relied mainly on the US and the left on the socialist countries. The neutralists have attempted to preserve a position between the two groups, which has proved impossible throughout the period, and therefore their arms supplies have been determined by their temporary align-ments with the other two groups. For example, in 1960 the Prime Minister, Souvanna Phouma, was leading a coalition of the left and the neutralists, equipped with Soviet weapons. Ten years later, he was leading a coalition of the right and the neutralists equipped with US weapons.

Laos was the product of the 1954 Geneva Agreements, which ended the Indo-China War. These Agreements prohibited the introduction of outside troops into Laos, with the exception of a small French military mission, and limited the amounts of mili-tary equipment to be supplied to Laos. In addition to the French military mission, which trained the army and established an Army Aviation Unit in 1955, the Americans announced their intention to provide aid in September 1954. Laos was also expli-citly offered protection in the SEATO treaty, signed in 1956. US military aid in 1956 and 1957 was probably of the order of $40 million a year (including a good deal of budgetary support), the weapons supplied consisting primarily of small, unsophisti-cated weapons – communications equipment, trucks, rifles and ammunition – designed for use by relatively untrained troops. Army Aviation, up to 1958, received twenty Cessna L-19 Bird

Dog monoplanes, four Aero Commanders, and Beaver and C-47 transports.

In 1956, Souvanna Phouma came to power. He rejected SEATO protection and, in 1957, reached an agreement which brought the political arm of the Pathet Lao – the Neo Lao Hak Sat – into the government. In 1958, the army of the Pathet Lao and the Royal Lao army began to integrate and elections took place, which proved a great success for the Neo Lao Hak Sat Party.

US aid was suspended after the election, until Souvanna Phouma and his Neo Lao Hak Sat ministers were ousted by a right-wing coup. The new government renounced the Geneva Agreements and, alleging that there had been a massive North Viet-Namese invasion, obtained substantial increases in US military aid. (A UN investigation in the autumn, however, failed to find evidence of this North Viet-Namese invasion.)

In August 1960, a neutralist parachute captain, Kong Le, seized power and reinstated Souvanna Phouma as Premier. Peace talks were offered with the Pathet Lao and diplomatic relations established with the Soviet Union. The United States declared that no further aid would be provided if negotiations with the Pathet Lao were begun and the right-wing general Phoumi Nosavan turned down an offer to be Vice-Premier. Instead, he went to Southern Laos and raised an army, equipped with US weapons.

Souvanna Phouma made his first request to the Soviet Union for aid in November 1960, and military aid, via North Viet-Nam, began in December. However, General Nosavan's troops captured Vientiane the same month and formed a new right-wing government, which was immediately recognized by the United States. Large amounts of arms were supplied, including T-6 Texan trainers for counter-insurgency operations, and a regular military assistance advisory group of 300 men was provided, instead of the 'civilian' Programs Evaluation Office (250 men) which had previously handled the matter of aid. By the end of October 1961, twenty-four US Special Forces teams were reported to be conducting combat and tactical training.

Soviet aid was directed towards the Pathet Lao on the request of Souvanna Phouma, then in exile in Cambodia, and on the condition that they co-operate with the neutralists under Kong Le. Soviet equipment, furnished in 1960 and early 1961, was provided on a grant basis and included 105-mm. howitzers, 85-mm. artillery pieces, 90-mm. anti-aircraft guns and other *matériel*. Members of the Pathet Lao were sent to the Soviet Union for training and North Viet-Nam provided military advisers. Together with the neutralists, the Pathet Lao eventually occupied more than two thirds of Laos.

The success of the Pathet Lao led the United States to move troops into Thailand and fears of escalation caused both the United States and the Soviet Union to impel the parties towards negotiation. The fourteen-nation Geneva Conference took place between May 1961 and July 1962. Despite the cease-fire, fighting continued. Soviet supplies to the Pathet Lao included ten Po-2 liaison and six Il-12 transport aircraft as well as a number of PT-76 tanks. The inflow of North Viet-Namese advisers also increased. On the other side, the United States supported the build-up of Nosavan's army to 70,000 men and provided substantial quantities of equipment including forty T-28 trainers for ground attack and army support. After a year of haggling, a co-alition government was formed in June 1962; it included the right and the left and was headed by Souvanna Phouma.

The declaration and protocol on the neutrality of Laos, signed in Geneva on 23 July 1962 by fourteen nations, including China, bound them to observe the neutrality of Laos. Also, like the agreements of 1954, it prohibited the introduction of foreign troops, except for a small French military mission, and limited the introduction of war material. The Laotian coalition did not last long: the Pathet Lao left the government in April 1963 after the assassination of a Patriotic Front Minister.

The Geneva Agreements were observed by the Soviet Union, which withdrew all its advisers (believed to number about 500) and halted supplies to the Pathet Lao. They were not, however, observed by either North Viet-Nam or the United States. North Viet-Namese forces were not withdrawn and, together with

China, North Viet-Nam has equipped the Pathet Lao. The USA maintained substantial numbers of military advisers in Laos, and the US air strikes over Laos were undoubtedly a violation of the Agreements.

The rightist and neutralist forces were merged in the spring of 1963 and equipped by the United States. From that time on, it is difficult to disentangle US military assistance to Laos from direct US intervention. From 1962, military assistance was classified and in 1968 it was included in the regular defence budget. In 1969, military assistance was valued at $90 million but, in addition, Senator Fulbright stated in October that the USA was spending $150 million a year 'to supply, arm, train and transport a clandestine army of 36,000 Meo [neutralist] soldiers'.

Moreover US expenditure on air strikes over the Ho Chi Minh trail and in the north, where the Pathet Lao operates, was very much greater than expenditure on military assistance. US intervention also took another form: in the spring of 1971, Laos was invaded by South Viet-Namese troops with US air support. On 21 February 1972, a cease-fire agreement was signed in Laos and negotiations are being held on a political solution to the conflict. In a broader sense, the solution of the problem in Laos is obviously linked to the settlement of the entire Indo-China conflict.

The story of Cambodian arms imports is much less complex. Unlike Laos, where the East–West struggle absorbed long-standing internal conflicts, the present divisions within Cambodia are largely the creation of outside intervention. The policy followed by Prince Sihanouk from Cambodian independence in 1954 until his overthrow in 1970 can be regarded as an attempt to avoid this fate. Aimed at preserving a balance in international affairs, it was a policy which grew from a recognition of China's future importance and the consequent need to come to terms with China, and from the historical position of Cambodia caught between the competitive struggles of Thailand and Viet-Nam.

In the first few years of independence, Cambodia's arms procurement policy was essentially Western-orientated. The substantial military aid provided at that time by the United

States – some $45 million in financial year 1957 – must be viewed in the context of Cambodian attempts to reduce the influence of the French. However, Cambodia avoided outright alignment with the West, particularly after the Bandung Conference of 1955, when Chou En-lai, on China's behalf, gave Cambodia assurances of non-intervention and recognized Cambodia's right to organize its internal defence and acquire foreign military assistance. Cambodia, in turn, assured China that it would not allow foreign bases on its territory and, the same year, renounced the protection extended by SEATO.

US aid and supplies began to decline from 1958. That year, Cambodia recognized China, and in 1960 the two countries signed a treaty of friendship and non-aggression. During this period, the local and traditional enmity towards Thailand and South Viet-Nam was giving rise to a further deterioration in Cambodia's relations with these two countries. Since the United States was pursuing a 'containment of China' policy and was developing very close relations with Thailand and South Viet-Nam, it became increasingly difficult to maintain friendly relations with the USA and in November 1963 Cambodia cancelled the US economic and military-aid agreements.

There was no dearth of alternative suppliers. As Prince Sihanouk said (quoted in *Keesing's Contemporary Archives*, 27 February–6 March 1965): 'China, the Soviet Union, France and Yugoslavia . . . hastened to grant us unconditional military aid after our rejection of US aid.' France became Cambodia's main supplier. Earlier, French aid had provided a balance to assistance from the USA but now it provided a similar balance to assistance from the socialist countries. Prince Sihanouk said, in an interview with *Le Monde* in June 1964: 'It is thanks to France that Cambodia has not swung into the socialist camp and can still call herself neutral.' For France, it provided an opportunity to reassert its influence in the area, and prove French independence from the USA. The French Minister of Defence, Pierre Messmer, visited Phnom Penh in January 1964 and announced a considerable gift of arms, including a squadron of AMX-13 tanks, complete with supporting transport and communications equipment,

100 lorries, twelve MS-733 Alcyon trainers, and six MD-315 Flamant reconnaissance planes. In a double rebuff to the United States, the French also released to Cambodia thirty Douglas A-1H Skyraiders, which it had refused to sell back to the United States. In accepting these planes, Sihanouk said that de Gaulle 'is to our people, to all the Indo-Chinese peoples, to all the peoples of Asia, Africa and Latin America the sole consolation which comes from the West'.

In receiving aid from socialist countries, Cambodia succeeded in maintaining a degree of independence and non-alignment. This is well illustrated by the choice of suppliers in the socialist camp – the Soviet Union, China and Yugoslavia. Cambodia had already secured Soviet aid before it rejected US aid in November 1963. In September, Prince Sihanouk announced a personal gift from the Soviet Union of four MiG fighters and twenty-four anti-aircraft batteries which would be operated by troops directly responsible to him and not by ordinary units. Additional Soviet supplies arrived in November 1964 and in May 1967. A new military-aid agreement was signed in 1968 for the delivery of some $6 million worth of arms.

The first military aid from China, consisting of 100 military lorries, a number of 75-mm. guns, and equipment for three battalions, was announced in January 1964. Later, anti-aircraft guns, bazookas and MiG-15s and 17s were supplied, a Chinese military mission arrived to train the air force and military experts were attached to the army.

In March 1970, during the absence of Prince Sihanouk, a group of officers took power in a military coup. This was followed by an invasion by US and South Viet-Namese troops. Since then, internal and external polarization which had previously been avoided was introduced in Cambodia. The new government now depends entirely on US supplies – received either directly or through South Viet-Nam. Up to December 1970, the Lon Nol government had already received $100 million in US aid and the US Congress appropriated a further $85 million in military and $75 million in economic aid. On the other side, Prince Sihanouk went into exile in Peking, from where he has proclaimed a new government and a Liberation Army which receives training and military supplies from China, and perhaps to some extent from North Viet-Nam. The Soviet Union has not extended any formal recognition of Sihanouk as head of state, and there is no evidence of Soviet arms to the guerillas.

OTHER RECIPIENTS

The supply of weapons to Malaysia, Indonesia and Burma follows a different pattern from that in most of the Far East. Competitive great-power penetration has, for most of the period, been limited and the conflicts in which these countries are involved have remained local and relatively minor. Malaysia, as a former British colony, has depended on Britain for arms supplies and British troops have been stationed in the country. Burma and Indonesia have pursued non-aligned policies, both veering towards the West, except during 1958–65, when Indonesia received substantial quantities of arms from the Soviet Union. On only two occasions did the development of polarized conflicts appear imminent, and both were connected with the introduction of arms from socialist countries. One was during the cultural revolution, when China extended aid to the rebels in Burma and US military aid to the government increased considerably. The other was during the Indonesian confrontation with Malaysia, in 1963–5. However, the fall of Sukarno in 1965 brought an end to the conflict: Western troops were withdrawn from Malaysia and Soviet supplies to Indonesia ceased.

Arms supplies to Malaysia and Burma have been relatively low. In Malaysia, this stems largely from the presence of British and Commonwealth troops. In the first two years after independence in 1957, Malayan forces, which had already existed for a long time, were engaged in a struggle against insurgents in the jungle, during which they received considerable British support, both in the form of troops and of arms. By 1960 the emergency was declared over and the number of Malayan troops was reduced from 20,000 to 8,000.

The Federation of Malaysia was created in 1963 and a limited military build-up occurred at that time, with British and Canadian help, both for the purpose of improving liaison between the component islands of the Federation and to cope with the guerilla-type war being waged by Indonesia in Borneo. The military equipment then acquired largely consisted of transport aircraft and COIN *matériel*. However, the presence of large numbers of British, Australian and New Zealand troops limited the necessity for arms imports and they fell after 1965. They rose again in anticipation of the British withdrawal from Malaysia, which was announced in 1967. But the need for more arms became less pressing when British proposals for withdrawal were modified and when arrangements were made for Australia and New Zealand to take over some of Britain's defence duties in the area. In particular, Australia is providing $22 million in military aid each year and has delivered sixteen CA-27 Avon-Sabre fighters. Malaysia is also to receive two squadrons of the new F-5E fighter from the USA. From 1969, Singapore has been rapidly expanding its military potential with purchases of fighters and missiles.

The low level of Burmese arms imports must be explained somewhat differently. The Burmese government has been engaged in various internal conflicts, involving a multiplicity of minority groups, such as the Karens, Kachins, Chins, Arakanese, Mons, White and Red Flag Communists and remnants of the Kuomintang troops. (The Kuomintang troops were the remnants of Chiang Kai-Shek's army which escaped to Thailand and northern Burma in 1949. They made border raids into China and were believed to be receiving support from Taiwan.) Consequently, Burma's weapons requirements have been mainly for COIN equipment. Further, Burma has not had the resources to purchase large quantities of arms and, for most of the period, has refused military aid, in accordance with its non-aligned policy.

In the first few years of independence, Burma was tied to Britain under a defence agreement which essentially provided for a monopoly of British or Commonwealth military aid. During this period, Burma received substantial US economic aid and, in 1950–51, some coastguard patrol vessels under MDAP (the Mutual Defense Assistance Program). However, in the early fifties, Burma moved towards a more neutral position, partly to avoid the development of a polarized situation within the country. Identification with the Western camp was alien to the socialist views of the leading Burmese political party, would have antagonized China and could have resulted in the unification of resistance groups in an anti-imperialist cause, with Chinese support. Burma refused to comply with eligibility requirements of the US Mutual Security Act and terminated the defence agreement with Britain. Although Burma continued to purchase most of its equipment from Britain and the United States, it did attempt a limited amount of diversification. Twenty Spitfire fighters were purchased from Israel in the mid-fifties, Japanese helicopters were delivered as war reparations and Yugoslavia equipped an army brigade in return for rice.

Throughout this period, Burma remained on good terms with socialist countries. Economic aid was provided by the Soviet Union, and in 1960 a border agreement was concluded with China. However, relations with China rapidly deteriorated during the cultural revolution. China began to provide assistance to rebel groups, particularly the Karens and White Flag Communists (BCP), who were said to use Chinese territory as a refuge, to have Chinese instructors and to be equipped with Chinese weapons, including the AK-47 assault rifles and possibly also mortars, light artillery, recoilless rifles and various crew-served weapons. Anti-Chinese riots, in June 1967, led to a break with China and, thereafter, China officially endorsed the Burmese Communist Party's aim of overthrowing the Ne Win government.

As a result of these developments, the Burmese government turned to the United States for support. For the first time since 1951, Burma received military aid, deliveries including twelve F-86 fighters, helicopters, trainers, trucks, patrol boats, small arms and supporting equipment. It was the largest military build-up in the period.

But the process of polarization appears to have been halted

by rapprochement with China; in 1970, the two countries began to exchange diplomats again. Further, Burma has, once more, rejected US military aid, although it continues to purchase US weapons.

Unlike Malaysia and Burma, Indonesia has been one of the largest importers of arms in the Far East. Its heavy military build-up – quite out of proportion to its economic resources – was concentrated in a seven-year period, 1958–65. This build-up has to be explained as much in terms of internal political factors as in the military contingencies which Indonesia faced. Like many Middle Eastern countries, the military contingencies were associated with the growth of radical nationalism, which in itself was largely centred on the armed forces.

It was nationalism that led Indonesia first into the conflict over West Irian (West New Guinea) and then into the confrontation with Malaysia, which, like the Dutch presence in West Irian, was regarded as an expression of imperialism. The foreign policy of the Sukarno government aimed at the establishment of a Greater Indonesia, which would assume the leadership of all the Malay peoples and become the big independent power in the region.

Weapons were demanded not merely for use in the conflicts, but also because the armed forces, created during the revolution against the Dutch, represented a symbol of nationalism and played an important role in the struggle for independence. This also explains their demands for political participation. They were opposed to parliamentary democracy up to 1957, and to Sukarno's reliance on the Communist Party after 1957. They were not, however, unified: there was constant rivalry between the three services not only to get the largest share of the military budget but also for political power. The army was Sukarno's most pronounced enemy and it is significant that it was the army which finally overthrew him in 1965. So the appeasement of the armed forces, especially the air force, which was at least partly loyal to Sukarno, also proved expensive.

In the first few years of independence, Indonesia relied mainly on Dutch military aid. In addition, the US provided about $5 million worth of military aid, mainly for internal security. But, like Burma, Indonesia, in the early fifties, moved increasingly towards a neutral position. Indeed, the conclusion of a military-aid agreement with the United States in February 1952 led to a political crisis in which the government was forced to resign and, thereafter, Indonesia paid for US weapons. In 1955, Indonesia was host to the Afro-Asian Conference at Bandung, in which the dominant tone was anti-Western and anti-American, and in 1956 the first trade agreement was signed with the Soviet Union.

By 1957, the Indonesian government found itself in great need of arms both to confront the Dutch in West Irian and to cope with the growing threat by rebels to the authority of the central government. Sukarno's proclamation of 'guided democracy' had led to the outbreak of revolts in the outer islands, in which supporters of parliamentary democracy, Sumatran separatists, Muslim groups and some sections of the army joined forces. The US was unsympathetic to Indonesian requests for arms and, although its official position was one of 'strict neutrality', there was some evidence of covert US support to the rebels.

A limited US agreement for the supply of light military equipment did not prevent Indonesia from seeking other sources of supply. On 16 May 1958, it was announced that a variety of aircraft, ranging from gliders to jet fighters and bombers, had been ordered from Yugoslavia, Czechoslovakia and Poland. The same year, Indonesia also purchased military equipment from the Soviet Union, Italy, the Federal Republic of Germany, India and Egypt.

These purchases led Britain and the United States to view requests for arms more favourably. Britain granted export licences for six Gannet naval aircraft, as part of an order for eighteen such aircraft placed before the outbreak of the Sumatra rebellions, and the US agreed to the sale of fifty combat aircraft and ten transports. But as the clash with the Netherlands intensified in the second half of 1960, these two countries became increasingly unwilling to authorize further deliveries of military equipment. Indonesia approached the Soviet Union again and, in 1961, acquired a $450 million credit, covering the delivery of MiG-19 fighters, An-12 transport planes and as many as twenty-five Tu-16 medium bombers, as well as submarines and torpedo boats. A further agreement was signed with the Soviet Union in May 1962.

The long history of Indonesian 'confrontation' against the Netherlands ended in 1963 and, on 1 May, West New Guinea, as West Irian, was finally absorbed into Indonesia. However, as soon as this confrontation was ended, a new one was initiated, this time against the new state of Malaysia, on the grounds that it perpetuated British imperialism in South East Asia. Britain, the United States and later Canada all imposed embargoes on Indonesia. Although Soviet support for this new confrontation was hesitant, the Soviet Union agreed to continue its military aid and, in both 1963 and 1964, granted moratoria on Indonesian arms debts. Deliveries included, among other things, MiG-21 fighters equipped with air-to-air missiles.

The continuance of Soviet supplies was largely the result of the need to counter growing Chinese influence, in Indonesia in general, and in the increasingly powerful Indonesian Communist Party (the PKI) in particular. By 1965, arrangements were being made for the supply of Chinese arms and military equipment. Indeed, with the presence of British troops in Malaysia, it looked as if the confrontation was rapidly developing into another manifestation of the East–West struggle.

The whole situation changed abruptly with the abortive airforce coup in October 1965 which led to the army takeover. The Communist Party was brutally suppressed, the Indonesian Ambassador to China was recalled, and President Sukarno was reduced to the position of nominal head of state. Indonesian–Soviet relations cooled, and Indonesia's relations with the United States, Britain and the Netherlands improved. Indonesia's economic situation was such that no further purchases of arms could be considered, and no other country was interested in providing substantial military aid. By 1968, the size of Indonesia's foreign debt had reached $3·1 billion, of which $880 million was owed to the Soviet Union. Although the Soviet Union was virtually forced to consent once more to a rescheduling of Indonesia's arms debts, it was certainly not prepared to increase them. A minor military-assistance agreement was signed with the United States in April 1967. After 1970 military aid from the United States has increased, and Indonesia has also intensified co-operation in military matters with its neighbours, in particular with Australia, Malaysia and the Philippines.

8   The Indian Sub-Continent

Supplies of major weapons to South Asia have shown much the same rising trends as supplies to the Third World as a whole; they increased four and a half times between 1950–54 and 1968–72, with a peak in 1958 of $330 million, and another one of $345 million ten years later. Throughout the period, India has accounted for around three quarters of the total supplies.

The demand for weapons in the region has been dominated by the tensions arising from the process of decolonization. Most important was the partition of British India, which formalized and brought into the open the historical conflict between Hindus and Muslims. But in the wake of the British withdrawal there have been other conflicts as well. There has been the conflict between Afghanistan, whose ruling group is Pathan, and Pakistan, over the future of those Pathans who live in the border areas of Pakistan. The conflict between China and India concerned the border between the two countries, which had been drawn by the British. The arms races accompanying these conflicts have been fuelled by the interests of the two great powers.

The Soviet Union has had a virtual monopoly of weapon supplies to Afghanistan during the past twenty years. Between 1960 and 1972, imports of major weapons totalled some $135 million. The US has supplied economic aid, including some defence support aid, and a little military training. Ceylon's arms purchases have been small, and have come almost entirely from Britain. However, in 1971, in the face of insurgency, arms have been supplied by the UK, USA, USSR, Pakistan and India. Neither Afghanistan nor Ceylon are further dealt with in this book.

INDIA

From independence in 1947 India's military planners were preoccupied with the possibility of war with Pakistan. In 1954,
Pakistan signed a military assistance pact with the United States
including modern sophisticated aircraft, tanks and other equipment on the understanding that it would join both SEATO and
the Baghdad Pact, and the Indian purchases of major weapons

Table 11 Indian Sub-continent: supplies of major weapons, by supplier
US $ mn, at constant (1968) *prices*

Supplier:	USA	UK	France	USSR	China	Other	Total[a]
1950–54							
$ mn annual							
average	8	22	12	–	–	0·4	**42**
per cent	19·0	51·7	28·3	0·0	0·0	1·1	**100·0**
1955–9							
$ mn annual							
average	24	102	22	5	–	5	**158**
per cent	15·2	64·7	13·8	3·4	0·0	3·1	**100·0**
1960–64							
$ mn annual							
average	39	46	4	31	–	14	**134**
per cent	29·4	34·4	2·9	22·8	0·0	10·6	**100·0**
1965–9							
$ mn annual							
average	1	25	14	136	6	18	**200**
per cent	0·7	12·3	7·2	67·9	3·0	8·9	**100·0**
1970–72							
$ mn annual							
average	1	22	10	103	32	7	**175**
per cent	0·5	12·6	5·7	58·9	18·6	3·7	**100·0**
1950–72							
$ mn total[a]	365	1,040	290	1,168	127	206	3,197
Per cent of							
total	*11·4*	*32·5*	*9·1*	*36·5*	*4·0*	*6·5*	***100·0***

[a] Figures may not add up to totals owing to rounding.
Source: SIPRI worksheets.

between 1954 and 1958 were primarily a reaction to this. Although the orders for Canberras, Gnats and Mystères placed in 1954 were part of the planned expansion of the Indian air force envisaged at independence, later orders for Hunters, additional Canberras and Ouragans were not envisaged at the time of independence and closely followed reports that Pakistan was to receive F-86 Sabre fighters and B-57 Canberra bombers from the United States. A MX-13 light tanks were ordered from France after Pakistan had received M-41 Bulldogs from the United States. The order for MiG-21s, signed with the Soviet Union in the summer of 1962, was invariably referred to in connection with the United States' promise to supply two squadrons of F-104 Starfighters to Pakistan.

There are, however, reasons to suppose that Indian purchases of major weapons were also influenced by factors other than the possibility of a war with Pakistan. It can be argued that India's attempts to match Pakistani weapons were made more with an eye to public opinion than through contemplation of their use. First of all, in the fifties, India chose to acquire largely prestige weapons – modern jet aircraft, an aircraft carrier and anti-submarine frigates – but neglected the acquisition of smaller types of weapons. For example, there was no attempt to acquire modern infantry weapons – the army still possessed Second World War mortars, artillery and howitzers and its standard rifle was the First World War ·303 Lee-Enfield – and the only small vessels acquired during this period were six minesweepers and an oiler. Furthermore, there was a gross neglect of the backing required for such sophisticated weapons, such as radar, spares and repair facilities, and many were inoperable.

Towards the end of the fifties, the Indian government began to recognize the possibility of a border conflict with China. In the belief that China did not want war and would be deterred by a demonstration that the Indians were prepared to use force if necessary, the Indian government made motions towards establishing some kind of defence in the area, including the deployment of troops and the purchase of transport planes and helicopters from the Soviet Union for use in the Himalayas.

The conflict erupted on 20 October 1962. And as soon as the magnitude of the defeat of the Indian Army was realized, India appealed for help to Britain, the United States and all friendly Western countries, as well as to the Soviet Union. The response of the Western nations was immediate. Under the Nassau Agreement the United States and Britain agreed to make gifts of military equipment to India of $60 million each. Commonwealth countries would contribute to the British share. In addition, the United States was to supply a further $50 million of equipment, and France, Canada and Australia jointly contributed some $10 million worth of supplies.

All this aid was specifically requested to meet the Chinese threat. In a letter to President Ayub Khan on 12 November 1962, Nehru made it quite clear that the military help given by friendly countries would be utilized 'solely' for defence against China and 'cannot and will not' be used for any other purpose. He further added that the idea of any conflict with Pakistan was repugnant to India and 'we on our part will never initiate it'. In November 1962 the government of India gave assurances to both the USA and to Britain that any military assistance received would be used only to repel China.

There is no doubt that in the first two years or so after the conflict the expansion of the armed forces was primarily directed towards China. The army, which before the conflict amounted to ten or eleven divisions, was expanded to twenty-one divisions, ten of which were mountain units with 14,000 men and 300 vehicles. The Himalayan Warfare School set up in March 1962 was also expanded, and a mobile army headquarters training team was set up to give instruction in jungle warfare. The biggest problem, however, was equipment. The replacement of the ·303 Lee-Enfield rifle by the semi-automatic Ishapore rifle, which had been decided upon before the Chinese invasion, was speeded up, the French supplied a number of Hotchkiss-Brandt heavy mortars which are now being produced in India, the ordnance factories undertook to develop a mountain howitzer, and the production of Japanese Nissan trucks was also accelerated. The emergency airlifts by Britain and the United States during the conflict had included automatic rifles, anti-personnel mines, 81-mm. mortars, mountain artillery and communications equipment.

For the air force, the immediate requirements were for transport planes, helicopters and communications equipment in order to be able to provide logistical support. The aircraft needed to have short- and rough-field capability and also a high-altitude capability. The United States supplied twenty-four C-119 packets, in addition to twenty-six which had been supplied in 1954, and three Caribous as emergency aid. The C-119s were adapted for high-altitude conditions by the addition of supplementary engines called 'Jet-Paks'. Canada also provided suitable aircraft on an emergency basis, and in 1963 India acquired sixteen Caribous under a loan agreement. The helicopter requirement was met by purchasing and deciding to produce under licence the Alouette III. Finally, the United States agreed to set up an early-warning system and, in 1963, delivered mobile radar units to India. India also made massive investments in the building of roads and airfields in the border area.

After 1964 it is less clear that the weapons acquired were directed against China. The Defence Plan for 1964–9 envisaged the build-up of the air force to forty-five squadrons, including the replacement of older aircraft such as Vampires, Toofanis (Ouragans) and Mystères with modern fighters and the acquisition of a sophisticated air defence system. In September 1962 an agreement was signed with the Soviet Union for the purchase and manufacture of MiG-21s. In September 1964 it was announced that the Soviet Union had agreed to supply thirty-eight MiG-21s in addition to those ordered in 1962, thus enabling India to re-equip three of its twelve existing fighter squadrons with MiG-21s, as well as SA-2 Guideline missiles. Neither the air-defence system nor the huge number of fighters appear to have been necessary in view of the limited air capabilities of both China and Pakistan. In 1966, the most sophisticated aircraft reported to be possessed by China were ten to fourteen Tu-4 long-range bombers, perhaps 400 to 500 Il-28 light bombers and thirty-five MiG-21s. Most of China's air force was concentrated in the eastern areas of China.

Table 12 India and Pakistan: comparison of the introduction of sophisticated weapons

	Aircraft and missiles[a]		Tanks and anti-tank missiles		Naval vessels	
	India	Pakistan	India	Pakistan	India	Pakistan
1950		Sea Fury (fighter)			Destroyer, 'R' class	
1951		Vickers Attacker (bomber)				Destroyer, 'O' class
1952	Ouragan (fighter bomber)					
1953	Vampire (fighter)		Sherman		Destroyer, 'Hunt' class	
1954				Chaffee Sherman Bulldog Patton		
1955						
1956		F-86 Sabre (fighter)	Centurion			Destroyer, 'Battle' class Cruiser, 'Dido' class
1957	Hunter (fighter)		AMX-13			
1958	Canberra (bomber)[b] Mystère (fighter) Short Seacat (SA missile)	Canberra (bomber)[c]			Cruiser, 'Colony' class Frigate, 'Leopard' class Frigate, 'Backwood' class	Destroyer, 'CV' and 'Ch' class
1959	Gnat (fighter)					
1960	Seahawk (fighter)				Frigate, 'Whitby' class Aircraft carrier, 'Majestic' class	
1961						

Table 12 – contd

	Aircraft and missiles[a]		Tanks and anti-tank missiles		Naval vessels	
	India	Pakistan	India	Pakistan	India	Pakistan
1962		F-104 Starfighter (fighter)				
1963	MiG-21 (fighter) Atoll (AA missile) HF-24 (fighter) Guideline (SA missile)					
1964		Sidewinder (AA missile)	PT-76			Submarine, 'Tench' class
1965			Vickers 'Vijayanta'	T-59 Cobra (missile)		
1966		MiG-19 (fighter) Il-28 (bomber)				
1967			T-54			
1968	Su-7 (fighter)	Mirage III (fighter)			Submarine, 'F' class	
1969			Entac (missile) SS-11 (missile)		Frigate, 'Petya' class	
1970						Submarine, 'Daphne' class
1971	Styx (SS missile)	F-5 Freedom Fighter (fighter)			Missile boat 'Osa' class	
1972	Tigercat (SA missile)	Mirage 5 (fighter)			Frigate 'Leander' class	

[a] Excluding anti-tank missiles.
[b] India bought English Electric Canberra bombers from the U.K.
[c] Pakistan received Martin Canberra bombers from the USA.
Source: SIPRI country registers.

In any case, the Indian purchases of MiGs were exclusively connected in official Indian statements with Pakistan's F-104s.

Similarly, the expansion of the navy after 1964 cannot be attributed to the threat from China. In 1964, a programme for the expansion and modernization of the Magazon Docks in Bombay was launched, and three 'Leander' class frigates were to be constructed there with the help of a $1·3 million British defence credit. Also, in 1965, India signed an agreement for the purchase of four submarines and some frigates from the Soviet Union after negotiations with Britain and the United States had fallen through. It is clear that the Indian military planners did not conceive of a Chinese invasion by sea. Indeed, the purchase of submarines was officially explained by the US delivery of a submarine to Pakistan in 1964. It is possible, though, that the naval expansion also had some connection with the deterioration of relations between Indonesia and India after Indonesia raised the question of Indian sovereignty over the Andaman and Nicobar Islands in the Indian Ocean. And, more recently, Indian naval policy may have been concerned with the impending British withdrawal from the Far East, announced in July 1967.

By 1966, Pakistan had received twelve F-104s and a submarine from the USA and forty MiG-19s and eight Il-28s from China. These supplies were continually mentioned when India decided to acquire up to 200 MiG-21s, 150 Su-7s and a number of submarines. Although India's politicians continued to express serious concern about Pakistan's intentions, it is doubtful whether they believed that they needed such massive quantities of weapons to fend off an attack from Pakistan. The encounter in September 1965 was evidence against this view, since the Indian position was maintained quite satisfactorily without these sophisticated weapons, and in the December 1971 war the greatest losses were claimed among the Su-7s and MiG-21s. The relatively unsophisticated Gnat fighter, produced in India, proved a great success in both wars and on both occasions this led to decisions to resume production.

On the other hand, the possibility of Sino-Pakistan military co-operation against India may have been of greater concern to the Indian government. China and Pakistan agreed on a border demarcation in 1963, and there were renewed hostilities on the Sino-Indian border in January and February 1965. Then, in May of the same year, there were serious armed clashes between India and Pakistan in the Rann of Kutch, and the crisis reached its height in September 1965, when war broke out between the two countries. China gave verbal support to Pakistan during the war, and within a year began to supply military equipment to Pakistan. But there was also the concern, especially after the 1962 defeat, to demonstrate to the Indian public India's superiority over its neighbours, and to demonstrate to the world at large that India is a worthy rival to China in Asia.

In 1971 tensions were again increasing between India and Pakistan; the breakaway of the eastern wing of Pakistan and the ensuing civil war, together with natural disasters and famine, brought more than nine million refugees to India. This placed a heavy strain on India's economy and created social tensions, especially in the provinces directly affected. The first Indian objective in this situation was to halt the stream of refugees and repatriate those who were already in India as soon as possible, and steps were taken to speed up the resolution of the crisis. Troops were sent to the borders and aid was also provided to the Bengali insurgents – the Mukti Bahini – in the form of sanctuary, arms and training. On 3 and 4 December war broke out on the western and eastern front. On 16 December the Pakistani army in East Pakistan surrendered unconditionally to the Indian army, and a ceasefire on the western front was declared the following day.

The new state of Bangla Desh is, for obvious reasons, very close to India. This has eliminated one cause of conflict and could have a negative effect on India's arms requirements. This effect may well, however, be offset by the other pressures dealt with above, for instance continued tensions with Pakistan.

The role of the suppliers

India's policy of non-alignment, which essentially involved a refusal to join any military alliance, was formulated at independence. Before 1962, India refused to receive any military aid, preferring to pay for all weapons imports, although it was ready to accept large amounts of economic aid. India also avoided purchases of arms from either of the two great powers. For example, when India was considering the purchase of Hunters and Canberras from Britain during the mid-fifties, an offer of bargain-price MiG-17s and Il-28s from the Soviet Union was turned down. Indeed, apart from the gift of two transport planes from the Soviet Union in 1955, India did not purchase any Soviet equipment until 1960. Similarly, the only major transactions with the United States during the fifties were the purchase of Sherman tanks in 1951 and of C-119 transports in 1954. When, in 1959–60, India was considering the replacement of the ·303 Lee-Enfield rifle, certain army circles were known to favour the Colt A.R.15, a US rifle, but it was decided to pursue the development of the indigenous Ishapore rifle instead of acquiring a foreign rifle.

But although India avoided the purchase of equipment from the United States and the Soviet Union, it did not attempt to avoid reliance on a single source of supply. In the 1950s, nearly two thirds of India's supplies of major weapons came from Britain, its traditional supplier, and up until 1962 India remained only marginally less dependent on Britain than it had been before independence. Even the purchases of French aircraft and tanks do not seem to have been made with the object of reducing dependence on Britain, as the Ouragans purchased from France in 1953 were ordered only after India had first considered buying Meteors from Britain. A bias in the armed forces, given their training and equipment, towards British hardware was inevitable. But even when the Indian air force actually expressed a preference for the Mirage, Krishna Menon chose to buy Hunters; in this case, the Hunters were the cheaper planes.

A change became apparent in early 1962. In 1961, it was reported that the United States had promised two squadrons of F-104s to Pakistan. Twelve were received in 1962. India began expressing interest in a similar acquisition, but no deal was negotiated with the United States. On 23 May, Menon told the Lok Sabha that India was considering the purchase of Soviet jet aircraft, listing price, ease of maintenance and other advantages of the MiG over comparable Western types. And in September 1962, after the Lightning (offered at a cut-rate price of $750,000, that is, less than half the market price), the Mirage and Swedish Draken had been considered, an agreement was signed with the Soviet Union providing for the purchase of twelve MiG-21s and Soviet technical assistance in building facilities to produce them. This deal represented the first serious sign that India was reducing its military dependence on the West and, in particular, on Britain. The determining factor, however, seems to have been price and terms. The price of the MiG-21 was $830,000, and, as with other Soviet transactions, long-term credit was offered, payable in rupees.

The Sino-Indian conflict was followed by two important changes which affected India's arms procurement policy. First, India requested military aid from whoever was willing to grant it. And secondly, although this was only an indirect consequence of the war with China, India came to rely militarily on one of the great powers, the Soviet Union.

During and in the immediate aftermath of the 1962 Sino-Indian conflict, the Western powers rushed to the aid of India with everything from woollen socks to guns. But no emergency aid was received from the Soviet Union and, despite official assurances that it would fulfil its obligations under the agreement of September 1962, rumours were rife that the Soviet Union would not continue to supply arms to India. The rumours continued until the first six MiGs scheduled for December 1962 arrived in mid-1963. The political significance of their delivery was considerable: it indicated that the Soviet Union did not accept China's argument that India had become a capitalist satellite.

After the first flush of the invasion, the Western powers soon became disillusioned with the new India. Quite apart from the fact that it continued to receive military equipment from the Soviet Union, it also refused to accept a US and British commitment for air defence in case of attack. The Indian government made it quite clear that it would prefer to purchase its own air-defence system. But the Western powers were unwilling to supply such a system.

The Soviet Union, on the other hand, was willing to extend support to India and increase both economic and military aid, and in 1963 promised to provide air-to-air missiles for the MiG fighters and to establish in India a $42 million SA-2 anti-aircraft missile complex with a missile technology school to serve it. Then, in September 1964, India signed an agreement with the Soviet Union for an additional direct purchase of MiG-21s. The value of the deal was put at $142 million. The Soviet Union also agreed to provide twenty Mi-4 helicopters and about seventy light tanks with associated equipment. The Soviet credit of $142 million included technical assistance and machinery for three factories to be built in India to assemble and manufacture more MiGs – altogether a total of about 200. The new agreement revised and enlarged the original one signed in 1962. Reportedly, the credit was repayable in rupees, for over ten years at 2 per cent interest, which the Soviet Union could use to buy Indian products, such as tea, jute and cashew nuts.

The story of India's naval purchases is very similar. During the visit of Chavan, the Defence Minister, to London in November 1964 to negotiate the defence credit for the building of the 'Leander' class frigates, he requested the loan of three fully operational 'Daring' class destroyers from Britain. Britain offered the loan of three very old 'Weapon' class destroyers instead, which India declined. The United States also proved unresponsive, and in 1965 India accepted a Soviet offer of 'Petya' class frigates. In 1964, also, India began looking for a submarine. Britain offered an obsolete Second World War model which India turned down. Britain also appears to have offered facilities for the construction of an 'Oberon' class submarine, but the terms were not favourable. On 6 September 1965, Chavan told the Lok Sabha that an agreement had been signed for the provision of four Soviet submarines. All were delivered by 1970.

In September 1965, during the Indo-Pakistani conflict, the UK and USA went a stage further by imposing an embargo on both participants. The US embargo was lifted for cash or credit purchases of non-lethal equipment in February 1966 and for cash or credit purchases of spares for lethal equipment in April 1967. The British embargo was lifted for purchases of equipment in early 1966.

The Soviet Union imposed no embargo. In March 1966 an agreement was concluded for the purchase of forty Soviet Mi-4 helicopters at a cost of $4·5 million. And at the time of the Soviet–Pakistan negotiations in 1968, India concluded successful negotiations with the Soviet Union for the purchase of about 100 Su-7 ground-attack fighters, including a few Su-7 conversion trainers, and later for additional Su-7s. There were further orders of naval vessels in 1969, including an order for six motor torpedo boats.

After the partial lifting of the US embargo in April 1967, the USA made an attempt to limit India's purchases from the Soviet Union by agreeing to provide India with a $17 million loan to complete the air-warning system project which had been started after 1962. The agreement provided for a limitation on India's total defence spending. However, the concern of the Western powers with the predominance of the Soviet Union as an arms supplier to South Asia had not been sufficient to increase their willingness to provide military aid to India. And during the 1971 war between Pakistan and India the United States renewed its embargo. India had then already formalized its relationship with the Soviet Union in a Treaty of Friendship and Co-operation signed on 9 August 1971. This treaty also has military implications: it forbids the parties to join any military alliance directed against the other party. In addition, Article 9 states that 'Each High Contracting Party undertakes to refrain from any assistance to any third party that engages in armed conflict with the other party. In the event of either party being subjected to attack or threat thereof, the High Contracting Parties shall immediately enter into mutual consultation with a view to eliminating this threat and taking appropriate effective measures to ensure the peace and security of their countries.'

These provisions could be directly applied to Pakistan, whose arms deal with the Soviet Union in 1968 had caused worry in

India, and Article 9 was indeed invoked during the December 1971 war with Pakistan. During that war the Soviet Union extended considerable verbal and material support to India.

Soviet aid has later been extended to India's ally Bangla Desh, which was promised a squadron of MiG-21s.

The bulk of India's front-line air force and naval equipment will be from Soviet sources for at least the next few years. In the short run, therefore, India has become fairly heavily reliant on one of the two great powers, a policy which goes against that followed in the 1950s.

In the long run India is working towards greater independence through the expansion of its domestic defence industry. Some diversification exists in the choice of sources for the licensed production of arms, where both France and Britain are increasing their participation from 1970. However, the most important project is still the production of the MiG-21.

PAKISTAN

Pakistan's defence policy has been preoccupied with maintaining a military balance *vis-à-vis* India. Because it could not hope to mobilize the same manpower resources as India, Pakistan attempted to offset India's manpower superiority with firepower superiority. For this reason, the quest for arms has assumed great importance. When India's rearmament after 1962 threatened to remove Pakistan's superiority in firepower, a conflict erupted.

The preoccupation with the Indian military threat also dominated Pakistan's foreign policy stance. This was at least partly because of the political role of the military in Pakistan, where the armed forces have had complete independence in military policy-making since Ayub Khan became commander-in-chief of the Pakistani armed forces in 1951. Indeed, the military ruled Pakistan from 1958 to 1971. The independent position of the military in Pakistan has tended to subordinate political questions to military questions. Thus, whereas in India decisions on arms purchases depended on political and financial considerations, at any rate up to 1962, in Pakistan it was military decisions, and in particular the quest for arms, which to a large extent determined Pakistan's political alignments.

Pakistan's relations with the United States

Ever since independence, Pakistan's defence policy has been preoccupied with the danger from India. Pakistanis believed that the Hindus never accepted partition and that some day they would take military action to re-incorporate Pakistan into India. Pakistan's geographical division into Eastern and Western wings, and its more limited land and manpower resources, added to its sense of insecurity. Consequently Pakistan's preoccupation with acquiring arms for a possible conflict with India was a determining factor in its foreign policy. In May 1954, Pakistan signed a military-aid agreement with the United States, one part of which was the understanding that Pakistan would co-operate in regional defence. In September 1955, Pakistan joined the Baghdad Pact and SEATO. In February 1957 the Pakistani Prime Minister, Suhrawardy, told the Pakistan National Assembly that the alliance with the United States was the only way in which Pakistan could receive aid against the threat from India.

US aid to the Pakistani armed forces between 1954 and 1965 totalled well over $1 billion (including supporting assistance). The broad objective of the military assistance was to create a multi-service capability to resist external attack, the major emphasis being on the development of the air force. Pakistan received 120 F-86s, twenty-six B-57 Canberras and twelve F-104s as well as Sidewinder AA missiles. By 1963, the last British aircraft were being phased out and the Pakistan air force became completely dependent on the United States, as did the army, which, in addition to heavy artillery and Patton tanks, received M-24, M-4 and M-41 tanks. The navy continued to receive British ships, financed under the US Military Assistance Program. In 1964, Pakistan received a submarine on loan from the United States, the first submarine to be received by either Pakistan or India.

In 1956, the US government claimed it had in Pakistan 'a very

fine loyal and anti-communist ally', but after 1962 the relationship began to show signs of strain. When the United States and
Britain sent emergency aid to India, Pakistan was offended and
urged that settlement of the Kashmir issue should be a precondition for India to receive any military aid. In a meeting with
the US Ambassador on 29 October 1962, the Foreign Minister
of Pakistan indicated that if the United States insisted on supplying arms to India, Pakistan might have to do some rethinking
about its membership in the Western military pacts and reassess
its alignments. At first, the United States did what it could to
preserve Pakistan's 'free-world orientation', making repeated
assertions of continued aid and even programming increased
assistance for the financial year 1965. But by the summer of 1965,
US–Pakistani relations were approaching a crisis.

In early August, the United States decided to postpone some
of its aid commitments to Pakistan in view of Pakistan's increasingly militant tone towards India. And when the conflict with
India broke out the following month, and the United States
placed an embargo on both parties, it was Pakistan which was
most affected, because Pakistan depended almost entirely on the
United States for military equipment. The United States also
decided to terminate all military grant assistance, except training
programmes, and to withdraw military advisory groups.

Kashmir and Indian rearmament

Indian rearmament after the 1962 Sino-Indian conflict threatened
to remove Pakistan's superiority in firepower and was certainly
one of the important factors in determining the outbreak of
hostilities over Kashmir in September 1965. Pakistani leaders
were deeply disturbed by the supply of Anglo-US arms to India,
despite Nehru's assurances that the military aid would be used
solely for defence against China. In November and December
1962, Pakistani leaders alleged that Nehru was creating a 'war
hysteria to receive massive arms assistance from the West'.
Bhutto, then Foreign Minister, described the Sino-Indian conflict
as a 'phantom war' and a 'phoney war'.

In the various negotiations which followed in the next two years, no agreement was reached about Kashmir, as Pakistan's minimum demands were far above the maximum that India was willing to concede. Further, as the first round of the negotiations was about to begin, it was announced that China and Pakistan had agreed on a demarcation of their boundaries. The improvement in Sino-Pakistani relations diminished the mutual confidence between India and Pakistan necessary for successful negotiations over Kashmir.

At the end of 1964, the Indian government took certain measures which tied Kashmir more closely into the Indian Federation. And by 1965, when the manpower advantage to the Indians in terms of regular forces was roughly 4:1 (somewhat less than 2:1 if Pakistan's militia and Azad Kashmir forces, which were used in the fighting, are included) and India was attempting to match Pakistan's firepower, it is reasonable to assume that Ayub had despaired of a negotiated settlement. Large and powerful groups in Pakistan had been pressing for an invasion of Kashmir, and many Indians believed that the military junta in Pakistan, 'preening itself on US equipment and training, has for long been confident that an armed collision between India and Pakistan would yield dividends. This confidence was further strengthened by India's poor showing in 1962.'

These factors, by themselves, may not have been sufficient to lead Pakistan to war. The determining factor in Pakistan's guerilla attack on Kashmir in August 1965 seems to have been its acute awareness that any advantages in firepower which its armed forces possessed over India were being whittled away, and that victory would be difficult in a few years.

In the actual conflict, the more sophisticated equipment possessed by Pakistan did not give it a great advantage. The Pakistanis reportedly proved unable to operate the automatic control needed to fire the guns of the Patton tanks and thus their offensive was considerably hampered. Pakistan's missile-equipped F-104s also proved of little value in the conflict, in which airpower had only a marginal role. India's much less sophisticated subsonic interceptor, the Gnat, was probably more useful.

Western arms supplies after 1965

Pakistan's search for arms after September 1965 was not confined to one supplier. Immediately after the conflict, the country received arms and ammunition from Turkey and was also reported to have acquired NATO equipment from Portugal, arms and ammunition from Iran, and financial help for arms purchases from Saudi Arabia. There were two main sources of arms in the West. First, Pakistan began to purchase weapons from France, and secondly it made a determined effort to acquire surplus US equipment from Europe.

From France, Pakistan ordered submarines in 1966 and received Mirage IIIs in 1968. In 1967 it ordered three 'Daphne' class submarines, and in 1970 thirty Mirage 5s and ten Alouettes, for assembly under licence.

The supply of surplus US equipment in Europe to Pakistan was another matter: it aroused intense controversy in the United States, in Europe and in India. The most celebrated example was the supply of ninety F-86 Sabre fighters, built in Canada under US licence, from the Federal Republic of Germany to Iran and hence to Pakistan. In order to sell these planes the Federal Republic of Germany required US approval.

The planes were flown to Iran by Luftwaffe pilots between March and November 1966. They were then flown to Pakistan, allegedly for repairs, but this reason seems to have been rather thin, since Pakistan did not even have the necessary repair facilities for its own F-86s. The planes cost Iran $87,000 each – approximately 10 per cent of their original price. In reply to Indian protests, the West German government told the Indian government on 8 September 1966 that all but a few of these aircraft had been returned to Iran. Since the delivery of the planes was not completed until November 1966, the West German reassurance does not seem very convincing. In fact, according to the US Department of Defense, the planes were being moved back and forth between the two countries.

In September 1967, it was reported that, according to US sources, the planes now formed part of the Pakistani air force and the US government had accepted the situation. The Indian government maintained that the planes had been returned to Iran, presumably for the sake of public opinion. However, they reportedly took part in the air war with India in December 1971. There has also been a controversy over Pakistan's attempt to purchase surplus Patton tanks from Belgium, Italy and Turkey.

In the meantime, the US government gradually eased the arms embargo imposed in the course of the 1965 war. First, in February 1966, when it became clear that Pakistan was buying arms from China, the United States partially lifted the arms suspension by permitting both countries to purchase for cash or credit, subject to case-by-case review, non-lethal spare parts and end items. And in April 1967 the United States expressed its willingness to consider, on a case-by-case basis, the cash sale of spare parts for previously supplied lethal equipment.

Perhaps as a result of a State Department study indicating that the withholding of military aid had 'not been successful in any instance', the US Administration announced, in response to queries by Indian journalists in October 1970, that the USA would supply six F-104 Starfighters, seven B-57 bombers, 200 armoured personnel carriers and four maritime patrol craft. It was stressed that this was a 'one-time exception'. However, the equipment was not transferred, and on 25 March 1971 a new ban was imposed. This ban did not affect equipment for which export licences had already been granted. According to a survey conducted by the General Accounting Office in Washington, the US air force airlifted $3·8 million worth of military equipment to Pakistan on a priority basis in July 1971. This equipment included spares for F-104s. Pakistan also acquired US equipment from other sources: ten F-104s were supplied by Jordan and some Libyan F-5s may also have been supplied. The US embargo on Pakistan was lifted in the spring of 1973.

Pakistan's relations with China and the Soviet Union

Until 1960, Pakistan's attitude to China was ambivalent. Pakistan recognized China early in 1950, and at Bandung in 1955 both countries assured each other of the absence of aggressive intentions. In 1956, Chou En-lai visited Pakistan and a joint communiqué on peaceful coexistence was signed. On the other hand, Pakistan accepted US bases on its territory despite assurances to the contrary at Bandung, and voted against China's admission to the UN. In April 1959, Ayub suggested that, following the Chinese takeover in Tibet, India and Pakistan should settle their differences and come together in case of external attack.

The proposed defence pact was contingent upon settlement of the Kashmir issue and was to be directed against the USSR, Afghanistan and China. India was suspicious of Pakistan's motives and the move produced no tangible results; two years later Ayub Khan was ridiculing the suggestion of a Chinese threat.

Already by the end of 1959, Pakistan had begun to make approaches to China on the demarcation of the border between Sinkiang and Azad Kashmir. In December 1961, at a meeting between the Chinese Ambassador and Ayub Khan, Ayub suggested that if China would agree to the demarcation of its border with Pakistan, Pakistan would support China's admission to the UN. The Chinese then indicated interest in this proposal. In 1963 Pakistan and China signed the Kashmir border demarcation agreement.

Pakistan does not appear to have received Chinese military aid until after the US embargo of September 1965. Although Pakistani army officers were reportedly training in China, Bhutto was only warning the big powers that if they did not stop military aid to India, Pakistan would seek a remedy from other sources.

During the Indo-Pakistani War of September 1965, equipment with Chinese markings was found on captured Pakistani army personnel. But this in all probability came from Indonesia, which had reportedly agreed to supply Pakistan with surplus military equipment under a kind of lend-lease arrangement.

On 23 March 1966, during the Republic Day Military Parade, the Pakistan army displayed three Chinese T-59 tanks, and the fly-past was led by four Chinese MiG-19s flown by Pakistani pilots, who had been undergoing conversion courses on MiG-19s since January 1966. The agreement appears to have been negotiated during a visit of a Pakistani delegation to China in October 1965. During this period, Pakistan received forty MiG-19s, eight Il-28s and approximately eighty T-59 tanks. But it is not clear how great was the Chinese commitment to aid Pakistan. There were only Indian reports of Chinese deliveries from 1966, and the fact that Pakistan has been seeking Soviet, French and surplus European equipment suggests that it was not altogether satisfied with what it had received. A deal with the Soviet Union in 1968 included spares for MiG aircraft; during this period it had been reported that the MiG-19s were grounded through lack of spares.

Pakistan's relationship with the Soviet Union became closer during the early 1960s as Pakistan and the United States became disenchanted with each other. In 1961 and again in 1965, the USSR pledged to aid a number of developmental projects in Pakistan's third five-year plan. Nevertheless, it was not until 1968 that the Soviet Union agreed to supply arms to Pakistan.

Pakistan appears to have asked for weapons earlier than this. It threatened to seek aircraft from the Soviet Union in 1965, and in 1966 an air-force delegation headed by Air Marshal Nur Khan, Commander-in-Chief of the Pakistani air force, visited the Soviet Union. But his mission does not seem to have been successful. In 1967, it was rumoured that Pakistan had requested Su-7s, and Pakistan did purchase a limited number of Mi-6s in that year. In reply to Indian protests, the Soviet Union explained that these helicopters were for civil use only.

In June 1968, a military delegation visited Moscow and an agreement to supply arms was signed, although the content of the arms deal with the Soviet Union was not made known. Western newspapers reported that the Soviet Union was seeking refuelling facilities in East Pakistan after India had turned down a similar request. So far, Pakistan has received T-54/55 tanks, 130-mm. artillery guns, spares for MiG aircraft, ammunition and other miscellaneous military stores.

The treaty of friendship and co-operation signed between the

Soviet Union and India in August 1971 undermined the foundations for Pakistani reliance on the USSR in military matters. One of its stipulations, that neither party should provide assistance to a third party that engages in armed conflict with the other, meant that continued Soviet supplies would be impossible in the case of war with India. Indeed, when war broke out in December 1971, the Soviet Union supported India and condemned Pakistan.

Instead, China came to the aid of Pakistan. Relations between Pakistan and China had improved after the cultural revolution and arms supplies probably continued, although on a limited scale. In February 1971 a $300 million economic and military aid agreement was signed, and from mid-1971 there were reports of the impending supply of large numbers of MiG-19 fighters and T-59 tanks. President Yahya Khan disclosed in November that, although China would not intervene physically in case of war between India and Pakistan, it would provide all necessary arms and ammunition. He further said that Pakistan would be expected to pay for some of its equipment, but China provided twenty-five-year interest-free credit. After the war in December, President Bhutto and Air Marshal Rahim Khan visited Peking, where they were promised unlimited military aid, and in March and April 1972 Pakistan reportedly received sixty MiG-19s and 100 T-54 and T-59 tanks, plus six small coastal patrol boats. This delivery seems designed to make up for the Pakistani losses in the December war, rather than to provide an offensive capability.

9 The Middle East and North Africa

Military expenditures and arms imports have risen more rapidly in the Middle East than anywhere else in the world. In the early 1950s the inflow of major weapons averaged about $40 million per year; at the time of the Suez crisis in 1956 it was stepped up to around $200 million per year; at the time of the June War of 1967 it increased to about $600 million per year. An all-time peak of $900 million was reached in 1971.

Inevitably, the Arab–Israeli conflict has dominated the Middle East arms race. The pattern of arms supplies to Egypt and Israel has been remarkably similar, in that they have followed each other in acquiring successively more sophisticated weapon systems. Jordan, Syria and Iraq have also been heavily involved. But arms races in the region have been infectious and have spread out from the countries immediately bordering Israel – eastwards to the Persian Gulf and Arabian peninsula and westwards to the four North African countries. And in recent years the inflow of major weapons has been rising as fast in the countries bordering the Persian Gulf as in the countries directly involved in the Arab–Israeli conflict. Since the middle 1960s Kuwait, Iran and Saudi Arabia have all been acquiring air-defence systems (in addition to tanks and other equipment) which have given them a level of sophistication in armaments comparable with Egypt and Israel.

Although Israel is the main reason for the arms races, there are many others. The Kurdish minority fighting for autonomy in Iraq, the Yemeni civil war between the Royalists supported by Saudi Arabia and the republicans supported by Egypt, tribal revolts in Iran, various border disputes involving most of the countries in the Arabian peninsula, Iran and Iraq, and local insurgencies, particularly in the peninsula, have all played a part in swelling stocks of weapons. In addition, the Arab world has always been infected with rivalries – rivalries for leadership,

Table 13 Middle East: supplies of major weapons, by supplier
US $ mn, at constant (1968) *prices*

Supplier:	USA	UK	France	USSR	Other	Total[a]
1950–54						
$ mn annual average	7	20	4	–	6	37
per cent	17·4	54·7	10·4	0·0	17·4	100·0
1955–9						
$ mn annual average	35	15	40	78	31	199
per cent	17·8	7·5	19·9	39·1	15·7	100·0
1960–64						
$ mn annual average	22	14	36	104	4	180
per cent	12·0	7·9	20·2	57·8	2·1	100·0
1965–9						
$ mn annual average	137	58	21	219	26	462
per cent	29·6	12·7	4·6	47·5	5·7	100·0
1970–72						
$ mn annual average	280	89	17	301	35	721
per cent	38·7	12·3	2·4	41·8	4·8	100·0
1950–72						
$ mn total[a]	**1,838**	**807**	**554**	**2,908**	**443**	**6,550**
Per cent of total	*28·1*	*12·3*	*8·5*	*44·4*	*6·8*	*100·0*

[a] Figures may not add up to totals owing to rounding.
Source: SIPRI worksheets.

dynastic quarrels between monarchies, rivalry in Islamic holiness,
rivalry in the commitment to Arab unity and, above all, rivalry
and ambitions over oil.

These conflicts and the growth of armaments are closely related
to the internal stability or instability of many Middle Eastern
countries. In particular, internal pressures from growing urban
classes are associated with the demands of Arab nationalism for
Arab unity and opposition to colonialism and to Israel. These
demands in turn are related to the role of the armed forces. All
the Middle East armies were created or organized by Europeans
and in consequence are or were Westernized in style and inspira-
tion, but they are often 'anti-imperialist', that is, anti-British or

anti-French or anti-American (and possibly, now, anti-Soviet), in their political stance. Indeed, the resistance to foreign penetration stems directly from the European notion of a nation state. Most Middle Eastern regimes, moreover, depend on the support of a military establishment.

INTERNAL PRESSURES FOR ACQUIRING ARMS

The acquisition of arms, especially of modern major weapons, helps to reduce internal pressures and problems in two ways: it serves to satisfy popular demands through a demonstrable commitment to Arab nationalism and to modernization, and it serves to build up support for the regime among the armed forces.

The role of the army in establishing independence was most explicit in Egypt. The preferential alliance signed with Britain in 1936 on the transfer of domestic sovereignty to Egypt specified that British troops would remain at Suez until Egyptian forces were strong enough to take over their function. The treaty also specified that Britain would be responsible for the supply of weapons and instruction to the Egyptian army. The fact that Britain was unwilling or unable to meet Egyptian demands for weapons reinforced the prevalent belief that the British were determined to stay in Egypt and prevent the emergence of a strong independent Egypt astride the Suez Canal. Strengthening the army, buying equipment for it, was necessarily therefore seen as a part of establishing Egyptian independence, the need for which was confirmed by the Suez crisis of 1956 and the association of Israel with Britain and France. At the same time, the officer corps was recruited from the increasingly vociferous urban middle classes, where the demand for Arab nationalism was strong.

In Syria, Iraq (after 1958) and Algeria, the acquisition of arms, particularly from socialist countries, has also been associated with the notion of independence. In Algeria, this stemmed directly from the struggle for independence in 1954–62, despite the fact that the core of the Algerian army comprised the Algerian

Table 14 Israel and the UAR: comparison of the introduction of sophisticated weapons

	Aircraft and missiles[a]		Tanks and anti-tank missiles		Naval vessels and ship-to-ship missiles	
	Israel	UAR	Israel	UAR	Israel	UAR
1950		Meteor (fighter)	Cromwell			
1951	Mustang (fighter)					
1952	Meteor (fighter)			Charioteer		
1953		Vampire (fighter)				
1954			AMX-13	Centurion Valentine Sherman AMX-13		
1955	Ouragan (bomber) Mystère (fighter)	MiG-15 (fighter) Il-28 (bomber)				Destroyer, 'Z' class
1956	Vautour (fighter)		Nord SS-10 (missile) Super Sherman	T-34 T-54/55	Destroyer, 'Z' class	Destroyer, 'Skoryi' class
1957		MiG-17 (fighter)		JS-III		Submarine, 'W' class Submarine, 'MV' class
1958						
1959	Super Mystère (fighter)				Submarine, 'S' class	
1960						
1961		MiG-19 (fighter) Tu-16 (bomber) Kennel (missile)				

Table 14 – contd

	Aircraft and missiles[a]		Tanks and anti-tank missiles		Naval vessels and ship-to-ship missiles	
	Israel	UAR	Israel	UAR	Israel	UAR
1962	Mirage III (fighter) Nord A.S. 30 (missile)	MiG-21 (fighter) Atoll (missile)				Patrol boat, 'Komar' class, armed with Styx missiles
1963	Hawk (missile)	Guideline (missile)	Nord SS-11 (missile) Entac (missile) Patton Isherman	Snapper (missile)		
1964						
1965						
1966	Matra R-530 (missile)					Submarine, 'R' class
1967		Su-7 (fighter)			Submarine, 'T' class	
1968	A-4 Skyhawk (fighter bomber)	Frog 3 (missile) Samlet (missile)			Gunboat, 'Saar' class, armed with Gabriel missiles	
1969	F-4 Phantom (fighter) Bullpup (missile) Sparrow (missile) Shrike (missile)			PT-76		
1970			M-60			
1971						
1972		SA-6 (missile)		T-62		

[a] Excluding anti-tank missiles and ship-to-ship missiles.
Source: SIPRI country registers.

troops from the French army, which were stationed in Morocco and Tunisia during the war. Arms have also been acquired to ensure the support of the armed forces; there was a rapid military build-up after the military coup in 1965.

The need to satisfy the military establishment by means of substantial purchases of arms has been of crucial importance in Syria and Iraq – two countries characterized by chronic instability. Syria's internal politics have been the most confused and turbulent of any in the Middle East, and since independence in 1946, when subordination to France ended, there have been eight successful *coups d'état* and numerous attempted coups, as well as peaceful changes of government. The army and the principal political party, the Ba'ath (founded during the Second World War, with aims of socialism, independence and Arab unity), are both rent with factions, and the acquisition of arms has been a prime objective of the one and a principal weapon of persuasion for the other. Iraq's arms-procurement policy has been similarly affected by *coups d'état* and the differing complexions of the factions that executed them.

The role of the army in demonstrating the regime's strength and commitment to modernization is most clearly seen in the monarchies. Oil-rich Iran, Kuwait, Saudi Arabia and Libya have chosen to buy expensive and sophisticated air-defence systems. In countries where pilots and technicians are scarce, such weapons have limited military value, but they do provide excellent spectacles. In all these countries the expansion of the oil industry and associated investments created new and vociferous urban classes who resented their continued exclusion from politics.

Libya and Saudi Arabia offer parallel examples of the process. In both countries the ruling class for many years distrusted the regular armed forces created by Britain and the USA, preferring to rely on traditional Bedouin levies. In both countries concessions to the growing urban populations in terms of increased participation in politics were associated with the expansion of the regular armed forces. In Libya this led to the formation of a government based on a coalition of traditional elements and young technocrats in the autumn of 1967. The new government initiated a $1,100 million defence programme in February 1968, but it was too late: the monarchy was overthrown by the army in September 1969. In Saudi Arabia the same modernizing pressures, aggravated by the despotism and extravagance of the ruling family and by the excitements of the Yemeni civil war which broke out in 1962, culminated in the deposition of King Saud by his brother, Faisal, supported by the army, in 1964. A programme of military expansion was then initiated.

In Kuwait, Morocco and Jordan, the armed forces are recruited from non-urban sections of the population, loyal to the monarchy. Eighty per cent of the officers and men of the Moroccan army are Berber, while the radical urban opposition is mainly Arab. In Kuwait the armed forces are dominated by the Sabah ruling clan, while the urban population has largely comprised immigrants from other Arab countries. Arms are important to ensure the continued loyalty of the groups from which the armed forces are recruited. The Kuwaiti armed forces, for example, are the best paid and, per capita, the most lavishly equipped in the Middle East. And arms are also important to appease the opposition. In Morocco, arms requirements often stemmed from irredentist claims, pressed by the opposition. Jordan has its own special problems resulting from its proximity to Israel, and from the fact that the urban classes consist mostly of Palestinians. The regime has been under constant pressure from the Palestinians to strengthen the armed forces and to increase the commitment to the Palestinian cause. Owing to the national scarcity of resources, Jordan has depended on the willingness of supplying countries to provide weapons as aid. These problems came to a head in the fighting in 1970 between King Hussein's army and the Palestinian guerillas. Although the King has on several occasions made concessions to the Palestinians, American airlifts of supplies have proved necessary to underline the West's sincerity in helping the King to defend Jordan against Israel.

Lebanon, Tunisia and Israel are exceptions to the Middle East pattern. In Lebanon and Tunisia, the political role of the armed forces has been minor, and for most of the period their arms imports have remained low. The Lebanese population is composed of numerous minority groups of Christians and Muslims, and the constitution ensures that the major political offices and seats in the Chamber of Deputies are shared between the various communities. This has made for compromise politics both internally and externally, and the role of the armed forces, and hence arms imports, has been important only when the compromise threatened to break down. This occurred first in 1957–8, when Lebanon endorsed the Eisenhower Doctrine against Muslim opposition, and, more recently, as the growth of Palestinian guerilla movements on Lebanese territory, and the consequent Israeli raids, has drawn Lebanon more directly into the Arab–Israeli conflict.

In Tunisia, a homogeneous, relatively non-urbanized society, the army plays an insignificant political role. It is noteworthy that Tunisia has purchased the least weapons and has been the most moderate on the Palestinian issue of any country in the region. Further, the border disputes in which it is involved have never flared into open conflict.

The Israeli armed forces are very different from those in Arab countries. Whereas the Arab armed forces were largely established and trained by foreign powers, the Israeli forces were initially based on the various guerilla units that came into existence under the mandate. Today, the integration of the Israeli armed forces into Israeli society has meant that the political power of the military is at once diffuse and more pervasive. Further, as an industrialized country, the internal need to demonstrate a commitment to modernization is much less important; political disputes about arms procurement have tended to concern alternative military strategies rather than the position of different social groups. Thus, Israeli arms-procurement policy has been governed primarily by its perceptions of the military requirements.

Another distinctive feature of the Israeli situation is the development of an indigenous armaments base. Israel is self-sufficient in small arms and claims to be capable of producing most of its ammunition and spares requirements. In addition it can overhaul, maintain and repair most of its weapons, and Israeli engineers have been very successful in modifying weapons purchased or captured from abroad. Nevertheless, Israel has been dependent on imports for major items of equipment.

THE PATTERN OF SUPPLIES

The large-scale acquisition of arms by Middle Eastern and North African countries has been facilitated by the wealth accruing from oil, but it has also been promoted by the interests of outside powers. More than 90 per cent of the major weapons supplied to Middle Eastern countries have come from four suppliers: the Soviet Union, the United States, Britain and France. However, the pattern of supplies has changed considerably during the period. In the first half of the fifties, the Western powers had a monopoly over arms supplies; Britain alone was supplying over half the total. But by the 1960s the Soviet Union had become the most important supplier, and now accounts for over 40 per cent of the total. Also, the share of the United States has tripled over the past decade.

The pattern of supplies has reflected the differing regimes in Middle Eastern and North African countries. The monarchies have relied on Western countries, mainly Britain and the United States, while for radical Arab nationalist groups the acquisition of weapons from the Soviet Union has been regarded as a means of reducing dependence on the West. Thus Egypt, Iraq, Syria, the Yemen (since 1962) and Algeria have all relied mainly on the Soviet Union for arms. In Jordan, the Palestinian demands for strengthening Jordan's military capabilities have been associated with demands for Soviet weapons. In order to appease the urban population, the Moroccan King has, from time to time, also acquired arms from socialist countries. And in a similar fashion the Shah of Iran chose to buy Soviet weapons in 1966, at a time when he was involved in a dispute with the United States over oil and arms supplies and when he required radical support for a land-reform programme.

France was Israel's primary supplier, and has also sold weapons to Lebanon and its former North African colonies. After the 1967 embargo, republics, such as Iraq and Libya, began to see France as an alternative to the Soviet Union, and monarchies, such as Saudi Arabia, began to see France as an alternative to Britain and the United States.

THE ARAB COUNTRIES AND ISRAEL

The first post-war decade was characterized by the withdrawal of the colonial powers and the increased influence of the United States. In the early fifties, the Western powers had a monopoly over arms supplies and were thus able to use them as a lever to persuade countries to join a Western military alliance. Under the Tripartite Declaration of 1950, Britain, France and the United States announced that they would restrain arms supplies to countries involved in the Arab–Israeli conflict, except for the purpose of internal security or for the defence of the region as a whole, that is to say, except for the consolidation of the Western-orientated alliances. In October 1951, the United States, Britain and Turkey invited Egypt to join such an alliance – the Allied Middle Eastern Command – under whose provisions Egypt would receive sufficient arms supplies. But the proposal was rejected by the Waf'd government because a policy of alignment with the West was inconsistent with Arab nationalism. (The Waf'd party was originally formed as a popular protest movement against the British.) And although it was reactivated after the military coup in 1952, the new leaders, General Naguib and Colonel Nasser, proved no more compliant.

During this period, both Egypt and Israel managed, to some extent, to circumvent the ban on arms supplies. Egypt imported Vampire fighters from Italy, via Syria, and British Valentine tanks which had been exported demilitarized to Belgium for use as agricultural tractors. Israel managed to acquire surplus Sherman tanks in 1951–2, Swedish Mustangs in 1952–3, and British Mosquitoes sold to France for scrap. Both countries, also, received matching supplies of aircraft and tanks from Britain and France in 1953–4; for example, together with Syria, they both received Meteor fighters.

The restraint broke down in 1954, the year that France agreed to sell a substantial number of aircraft to Israel. The deal was financed by a US subsidy and, although it is clear that this was part of American assistance to France for the development of its defence industry, it is not unreasonable to suppose that the USA was anxious to calm Israeli fears concerning US negotiations for military-assistance agreements with Iraq and Egypt, without involving itself directly. There was strong internal French opposition to the deal until the outbreak of the Algerian War at the end of 1954.

The same year, Iraq signed a military-assistance agreement with the United States, on the understanding that it would join a regional defence system. There was much internal unrest in Iraq at the time and arms were urgently needed. The Iraqi delegate told a meeting of Arab heads in Cairo in early 1955: 'The West will not supply these arms for the sake of our black coloured eyes, but only if we come to an understanding with it. We cannot obtain arms from the West without agreements.' The formation of the Baghdad Pact was announced in February 1955.

In response to these deals, to mounting tensions between Israel and Egypt, and to the US refusal to supply arms without conditions, Egypt turned to the Soviet Union. On 27 September 1955, a deal with Czechoslovakia for the supply of equipment was announced. The terms of the deal appear to have been very favourable; prices were low and payment was in cotton. According to President Nasser, the arms were entirely unconditional, and Egypt simply had to pay the cost.

The arms deal with Czechoslovakia marked the end of any Western monopoly and any pretence at restraint. Indeed, Soviet proposals for an international embargo on arms supplies to the Middle East in 1956 and 1957 were rejected by the Western powers because they linked an embargo to the withdrawal of foreign troops and foreign bases. In the months leading up to the Suez crisis, Egypt received MiG fighters, Il-28 bombers, tanks, command cars, self-propelled anti-aircraft guns, light anti-tank guns, machine-guns, bazookas and other weapons. The Soviet Union also agreed to supply arms to Syria and Yemen. The Syrian deal with Czechoslovakia covered MiG-15 fighters and trainers, as well as a number of tanks, anti-aircraft guns, ammunition and small arms. French supplies to Israel also increased rapidly, as part of their joint preparation for the Suez campaign. On the eve of the war, Israel received thirty-six Mystère fighters.

The Soviet Union emerged from the Suez crisis as an entrenched Middle East power. Virtually all the supplies to Egypt and Syria were destroyed. (It is thought that something like 250 aircraft, including the Syrian MiG-15s, were destroyed on the ground on Egyptian airfields.) Negotiations for their replacement were started immediately, and by 1957 Nasser declared that Egyptian military equipment had been restored and even improved. The most important weapons Egypt received from the USSR at the time were eighty MiG-17s and thirty Il-28s, as well as five submarines. Syria also received considerable quantities of arms, including sixty MiG-17s, some torpedo boats and light and medium tanks. This was the period of closest Soviet–Syrian relations; the Communist Party was then the strongest single political force in Syria.

The Western powers, on the other hand, emerged from Suez somewhat battered. To restore its position, the United States announced a new political offensive in January 1957. This was the Eisenhower Doctrine, under which the US offered to increase economic and military assistance and to use US troops to protect any nation threatened by 'international communism'. Outside the Baghdad Pact, Lebanon was the only country to endorse the doctrine. But, although this brought Lebanon economic aid and arms supplies, it also led to the outbreak of civil war in 1958. The Muslim groups in Lebanon, where the commitment to Arab nationalism was strong, opposed the doctrine and were supported by other Arab countries.

King Hussein of Jordan welcomed the doctrine, in contradiction to his radical government. This government had been elected on the wave of anti-British feeling following the Suez crisis. It terminated the Anglo-Jordanian treaty, under which Britain retained the responsibility for equipping and training the Jordanian army, which it subsidized to the tune of $25 million per year. The last British troops left Jordan in July 1957. The government attempted to increase ties with radical Arab states and to reduce Jordan's dependence on the West, and so the British subsidy was to have been replaced by one provided by Egypt, Syria and Saudi Arabia. However, in April 1957 King Hussein dismissed his government, and the US promised $30 million in economic and military aid.

On 14 July 1958, the Iraqi monarchy was overthrown. US troops were moved to Lebanon and British troops returned briefly to Jordan. The Lebanese civil war ended after the leader of the rebels was appointed Prime Minister and US troops were withdrawn, marking the end of Lebanon's brief flirtation with the Western camp. The new Iraqi government adopted a policy of non-alignment and established close relations with the Communist Party. The first shipload of Soviet weapons arrived on 27 November 1958 and included a number of planes – MiG-17, Yak-11 and Il-28 – motor torpedo boats, and light and heavy tanks. At the same time, military relations with the West were broken off.

This was a period of strained relations between Egypt and the Soviet Union. There had always been rivalry between Iraq and Egypt for leadership of the Arab world. After the revolution the nationalists in Iraq had turned against the local supporters of President Nasser and entered into a close alliance with the Communist Party. The Soviet Union began to indicate that it considered that the Iraqi revolution, rather than the Egyptian, represented a more advanced political development. The Communist Party was banned in Egypt, and the formation of the United Arab Republic (UAR), a union of Egypt, Syria and Yemen in February 1958, substantially reduced the power of the Communist Party in Syria. Egypt began to reduce its dependence on the Soviet Union, by accepting economic aid from the United States and by building a domestic defence industry with Western help. The Soviet Union responded by temporarily slowing down arms supplies.

Nevertheless, Soviet military aid did not cease and when, in November 1959, the Soviet Union expressed its willingness to resume arms supplies, the UAR immediately accepted the offer. The period 1960–66 was one of intense competition between Israel and Egypt. In 1961, Egypt received its first Tu-16 bombers and in 1962 MiG-21s armed with Atoll missiles, in response to the Israel purchase of Mirage fighters armed with Nord AS-30 missiles. Both countries received surface-to-air missiles in 1962. This was also a period of close co-operation between Israel and France, particularly in the industrial sphere. Israel undertook development contracts with French firms for new weapons, the most notable example being the MD-660 medium-range surface-to-air missile developed by Dassault, and suggested commercially profitable modifications to French weapons. France also placed contracts in Israel; in particular, Israel undertakes the overhaul of French air force Mystères and Super-Mystères.

During this period, Jordan relied almost entirely on Britain for arms, and received, among other things, more than twenty Hawker Hunters.

Syria broke away from the UAR after a *coup d'état* in 1961. And from then until 1966, when the left wing of the Ba'ath party assumed power and came to terms with the Communist Party, Soviet arms supplies were very moderate. In 1966, a new military agreement was signed, reported to be worth $200 million and to include MiG-21s and Guideline surface-to-air missiles.

From 1960, there was some swing back towards the West in Iraq. A series of coups, assassinations and accidents caused Iraq to veer between rivalry and co-operation with Egypt and between Britain and the Soviet Union as favoured arms suppliers. The choice of suppliers largely depended on the attitude of successive governments towards the Kurdish demands for self-determination, which the Soviet Union supported, and the Communist Party.

During this period, the US, with the exception of a deal for Hawk missiles with Israel in 1962, was very restrained in its arms supplies to Western-orientated regimes. In an attempt to improve its standing with the radical Arab states, it supplied supporting assistance to Egypt, Syria, Iraq and Yemen. However, by 1966, Nasser's 'undesirable political adventures', as in the Congo and the Yemen, and his outspoken attacks on the West, had led to a halt in US aid to Egypt. At the same time, there was pressure on the Jordanian regime from Palestinians, as well as other Arab states, to strengthen Jordan's defence against Israel. At the Arab summit meeting in September 1965, Jordan was given two months in which to acquire jet aircraft from the West, or to accept Soviet offers of the MiG-21. This finally led the US to agree to the supply of F-104 Starfighters. The Sub-Committee on Disarmament of the Senate Foreign Relations Committee was told in 1967:

> In the end, when it appeared that Jordan would be forced to accept MiG-21s and thus open its country to a large Soviet training mission [deleted] – a move which we regarded as inimical to the integrity of Jordan and a grave threat to the stability of the Middle East – we agreed to sell Jordan a small number of F-104s from our MAP inventory.

In order to avoid offending Israel, which had put pressure on the United States to prevent earlier deals, the US also agreed to supply A-4 Skyhawks to Israel. Arms supplies to Jordan were speeded up after heavy Israeli raids led to increased internal tensions in November 1966.

The June War of 1967 sharply polarized the conflict in the Middle East. The Arab republics, particularly Egypt, found themselves more than ever dependent on the Soviet Union, while Jordan and its regime emerged so weak from the war that continued British and US support was more than ever necessary. Finally, the French imposed a total embargo on the area. Although it was selectively lifted for certain countries and certain types of equipment, it left the United States as the main supplier to Israel. Earlier, the United States had restrained arms supplies to Israel for fear of jeopardizing relations with Arab states. As the Senate Foreign Relations Committee was told by Paul C. Warnke, Assistant Secretary of Defense for International

Security Affairs, in June 1968: 'We think it would be desirable for France to continue as a major supplier to Israel, so that we avoid a polarization of the area between those who are customers of the Soviet Union alone and those who are customers of the United States alone.'

The countries with the most immediate requirements for weapons were Egypt, Syria and Jordan – they had lost the bulk of their front-line equipment. Most of the Syrian and Egyptian losses were replaced by the second half of 1968, but the Soviet deliveries mostly comprised defensive equipment; the Soviet Union did not, for example, replace Egypt's Tu-16 bombers. In Syria, dissatisfaction with the level of Soviet arms supplies and with Soviet attempts to persuade Syria to moderate its position towards Israel led to the signing of an arms deal with China in May 1969. North Korea also agreed to provide 'material aid'. These deals were followed by a new $200 million military agreement with the Soviet Union in July 1969. Deliveries included MiG and Su-7 fighters, helicopters, tanks, self-propelled guns, armoured personnel carriers and artillery rockets.

The United States and Britain were initially unwilling to replace Jordanian losses. But repeated threats to turn to the Soviet Union for arms, combined with increased internal pressures from senior officers of the armed forces, as well as Palestinians, finally led to substantial British and American arms supplies. The US finally delivered the long-awaited F-104s in 1969–70, together with Patton tanks and other equipment, while Britain delivered additional Hunter aircraft and Centurion tanks. Britain also agreed to supply Tigercat surface-to-air missiles, in a $36 million deal financed by Saudi Arabia. British and US support was, however, insufficient to prevent the outbreak, in 1970, of civil war between the army and the Palestinians. The US response followed the pattern of its behaviour in previous Jordanian crises. The Sixth Fleet was deployed off Jordan and troops in Germany were flown to Turkey. After the conflict, the USA agreed to an additional $30 million in aid for the financial year 1971 and a $200 million military-aid package for the next five years.

Iraq had the smallest losses of all the Arab countries, and

Soviet supplies after the war were minimal. It turned to France to acquire arms, although negotiations for the Mirage were suspended after Iraq failed to grant an oil concession to French companies. A new Ba'athist regime, which came to power in 1968, appointed a number of communists in the government and came to a settlement with the Kurds. A military-aid agreement with the Soviet Union was probably signed in May 1969.

Throughout 1968 and 1969, fighting across the Suez Canal, which had never completely stopped, intensified. In October 1968, a few weeks before the US elections, the USA agreed to supply F-4 Phantoms and additional Skyhawks to Israel, and additional Su-7s, MiG-21s and SA-2 missiles were supplied by the Soviet Union to Egypt in 1969. From March 1969, the situation in the Canal Zone became virtually one of open war. In July, Israel resumed, for the first time since the war, large-scale air attacks on Egyptian territory, and in the autumn destroyed more than half the SA-2 missile sites.

In January 1970, the Soviet Union agreed to supply new defensive equipment, including the SA-3 anti-aircraft missiles, to Egypt, in response to heavy Israeli air raids. The operation of new missile sites was supervised by Soviet military personnel. The effectiveness of the air-defence system (six Phantom fighter-bombers were shot down in June and July) brought a halt to deep penetration raids in the Nile Valley, but raids across the Suez Canal continued until the cease-fire began on 7 August 1970. It later emerged that the US government had agreed on a $500 million aid package to persuade Israel to accept a cease-fire. This aid package was authorized by Congress in January 1971 and was followed by the re-opening of the Jarring peace talks, which had broken down in March 1969. The talks broke down again in June 1971 and the United States suspended further deliveries of military aircraft – Skyhawks and Phantoms – to Israel.

Although Soviet equipment continued to be delivered to Egypt during this period, there were no reports of new military aid agreements. But on 27 May 1971 the Soviet Union formalized its relations with Egypt with the signing of the Soviet–Egyptian Treaty of Friendship, and it has later been reported that, on this occasion, Egypt was promised the type of weapons – long-range fighter-bombers or surface-to-surface missiles – that would make it possible for Egypt to launch a major offensive against Israel.

Although the stocks of Soviet-operated defensive equipment were increased, the Soviet Union still withheld the supply of offensive weapons. Further meetings between Soviet and Egyptian officials in October 1971 and February and April 1972 were probably mainly concerned with the Soviet supply of weapons. Nevertheless, there was no immediate increase in arms supplies to Egypt. It is likely that the MiG-25 fighters and Tu-16 bombers, which appeared in Egypt during the autumn of 1971, were exclusively operated by Soviet military personnel, on reconnaissance missions.

Sadat's visit to Moscow in October 1971 led to renewed Israeli demands for additional military aircraft. On 15 October 1971, a resolution was passed by seventy-eight US Senators calling on the Administration to resume deliveries of Phantom fighter-bombers. It was reported that the US government had offered increased military aid if Israel would accept an interim agreement to re-open the Suez Canal, but the terms for such an agreement were emphatically rejected by Prime Minister Meir in a speech in the Knesset on 26 October: 'Israel is not prepared to agree to political conditions that harm our security even in return for promises of vital military aid.'

On 15 November 1971, the US Administration declared that the Middle East balance was unchanged. It was not until Prime Minister Meir's visit to the United States in December that the US agreed to resume deliveries of Skyhawk aircraft and, a few weeks later, of Phantoms. The agreement was followed by the Israeli decision to resume talks.

Thus the polarization of the Middle East conflict has led to a complicated relationship of mutual dependence between the participants and their suppliers. For different reasons, both the US and Soviet governments have had to find compromises between their mutual interests in preventing the outbreak of war and their conflicting interests in ensuring that their clients appear well-defended. The compromises have not been symmetrical. For

the Soviet Union, the outbreak of war is likely to lead to a defeat
for the Arab nations and consequently a political defeat for the
Soviet Union, or Soviet military intervention entailing the possibility of direct confrontation with the United States. Yet withholding arms supplies to minimize the risk of war could lead to
loss of political support among Arab states. The Soviet solution
has been to allow only defensive weapons to be operated by the
Egyptians and to extend its supervision over Egyptian military
activities. For the United States, the outbreak of war could lead
to a further deterioration in its relations with Arab countries
and/or the possibility of direct confrontation with the Soviet
Union. At the same time, Israel is able to exert considerable
domestic pressure on the US government to ensure that US
arms continue to flow into the country. The US solution has
been to provide, after some delays, all the weapons demanded by
Israel in return for limited progress towards a political solution.

In similar situations, the dependence of the client state on the
supplier is very great, both for military and political reasons.
However, the difference between the Soviet desire to prevent the
outbreak of war and the pressures on Egypt to reach a 'decision'
with Israel proved too great. When continued Egyptian demands
for weapons which could be used to launch a decisive campaign
against Israel did not yield results President Sadat took the drastic
step of terminating the mission of the Soviet advisers and experts
in Egypt. In his speech to the central committee of the Arab
Socialist Union on 18 July 1972 he reportedly said:

We do not ignore the fact that the Soviet Union, being a great Power,
has its own role to play on the international scene and its own strategy.
As for ourselves, part of our territory is occupied and our goal is to
liberate it. Moreover we are convinced, in face of the intransigence of
Israel and the permanent support she enjoys from the United States,
that the Middle East crisis can only be resolved by a decisive battle.

He added further,

The principal difference has always been with regard to the nature of
these armaments to be supplied by the Soviet Union and the date of
their delivery to Egypt.

The withdrawal of Soviet personnel was virtually complete. Some of the equipment previously reported to have been operated by Soviet personnel was turned over to Egypt. The Egyptian move has not been followed by any spectacular changes in the Middle East situation. The Soviet Union has increased its aid to Syria, in particular, and Iraq whereas Egypt has looked for new sources of arms, mainly in Western Europe. The Soviet Union has also supplied Egypt with limited quantities of spares as well as a batch of surface-to-air missiles.

THE PERSIAN GULF AND ARABIAN PENINSULA

From 1965, arms supplied to this area have increased very rapidly. The Yemen civil war introduced the Soviet Union as an important supplier, and this was followed by increasing competition from the Western powers. In 1967, Britain announced its intention to withdraw from the Persian Gulf and a number of armed forces were expanded in anticipation of taking over the British functions. In the wake of the British withdrawal came also the resurgence of latent conflicts in the area. Finally, by 1965, oil revenues had become very large indeed, which increased the pressure to acquire arms and facilitated their purchase.

The Yemen civil war broke out in September 1962, when the monarchy was overthrown. The republican regime, recognized by the United States and the Soviet Union, but not by Britain, was entirely dependent on the UAR, not only for troops and arms, but also for administrative and technical assistance. Soviet aid was fairly substantial, but until the withdrawal of Egyptian troops in 1967 it was largely channelled through Egypt. Indeed, it is said that the UAR objected to the direct delivery of arms from the Soviet Union to Yemen as negotiated in an agreement in 1964.

The Royalists received their arms from Saudi Arabia, which in turn acquired arms from Britain and the United States. The Yemen civil war coincided with the growing strength of the modernizing factors in Saudi Arabia. In the Middle East, a typical way of demonstrating the government's commitment to modernization is through the expansion and re-equipping of the armed forces, particularly with prestige weapons. Some time in 1963, Saudi Arabia expressed the need for a sophisticated air-defence system to protect the supply lines to the Royalists in the Yemen, and after intricate negotiations lasting two years the Saudi Arabians agreed upon the British Lightning fighter and the American Hawk missile. The British deal was part of the offset arrangement with the United States for the purchase of F-111. The total deal was worth around $300 million and was facilitated by easy credit terms. It has taken several years to deliver and install the equipment and to train Saudi Arabians to operate it, but in 1966 the British agreed to an interim deal, known as Operation Magic Carpet, consisting of second-hand aircraft and missiles operated unofficially by British personnel.

Modernizing pressures in Kuwait and Iran were also increasing; Kuwait followed Saudi Arabia's example in acquiring Lightning fighters, while Iran received considerable numbers of F-5 fighters and Hawk missiles from the United States. Up to this time, only Iran had been a sizable military power. As a 'forward defence area' and member of CENTO, Iran has been accorded high priority for US aid; over the period as a whole, the country received nearly $1 billion in US military aid and its arms imports have been exceeded only in the Middle East by Egypt. However, during the fifties, the army had a primarily internal function, being responsible for controlling tribal rebellions and for helping the police maintain law and order in the cities.

During the sixties, the Shah initiated a number of social and economic reforms, and, as in Kuwait and Saudi Arabia, the purchase of sophisticated weapons formed part of a policy of modernization. US aid has dwindled since 1967, when Iran was declared a developed country, but substantial oil revenues enabled it to continue arms purchases at an even higher level. Since 1965, major arms imports have averaged $130 million per year. In 1966, the need to acquire radical support for the internal reforms, acrimonious negotiations over oil and dissatisfaction with the level of US arms supplied led Iran to sign a $110 million deal for the purchase of 'non-sensitive' equipment – armoured troop carriers, trucks and anti-aircraft guns – from the Soviet Union. This deal was followed by new arms supplies from the United States, as well as large purchases from Britain and Italy. When the United States agreed to sell the Phantom, the most sophisticated aircraft in the region, the head of the US International Logistics Negotiations office told the Senate Foreign Relations Committee: 'He [the Shah] has made it abundantly clear also that if the United States is unwilling or unable to meet his major military requirements, he is determined to go elsewhere to acquire what he needs.'

Early in 1973 it was announced in Washington that an arms deal had been concluded between the USA and Iran, worth more than $2,000 million. The deal included Phantoms, F-5Es and a total of 580 helicopters. A year earlier, Iran purchased 800 of the sophisticated Chieftain tanks from Britain.

The rapid increase in arms supplied to Kuwait, Saudi Arabia and Iran must also be attributed to the prospect of British withdrawal. The Anglo-Kuwait agreement signed on independence in 1961, under which Britain 'undertook to assist the Government of Kuwait if the latter request such assistance', was terminated in 1968, following the British announcement of withdrawal. This led to new arms purchases, including patrol boats, anti-tank missiles and helicopters.

Both Saudi Arabia and Iran have expressed an interest in playing a more active role in the Persian Gulf area and both have laid down plans for the expansion of their navies (the Iranian plans are much the more grandiose). Iran, in particular, has been involved in a number of disputes over territorial rights in the region, both with Iraq and with Britain. In addition, the Arabs claim the Arab-populated Khuzistan, the source of Iran's richest oil resources. In an interview with the *Washington Post* in 1969, the Shah explained that it was necessary for Iran to build up a defence capability to match all potential trouble-makers in the area combined:

We have to develop such a potential to keep this area secure after the British leave. Iran can do it because we have no territorial or colonial designs. Iran's role in the Persian Gulf is to present the image of strength, wisdom, and absolutely altruistic purposes and, yet, without any thought of trying to play Big Daddy.

The British withdrawal has also led to smaller build-ups in other states. There is a proposal to establish a joint defence force among the Trucial states, Bahrein and Qatar. However, there are a number of conflicting interests in the area involving oil, ill-defined borders, dynastic quarrels and the possibility of insurgency. These conflicts involve outside powers (such as Saudi Arabia and Iran) as well and have recently come into the open. Consequently, some of the Persian Gulf states, notably oil-rich Abu Dhabi, Bahrein and Qatar, have established their own armed forces, mainly with British and Pakistani help.

Although the end of the civil war in the Yemen led to a slow-down in Soviet arms deliveries and signs of rapprochement with the West, the independence of Southern Yemen under a radical regime has been followed by an influx of Soviet arms, including T-34 tanks and some MiG-17s. The left-wing coup in 1969 enabled China to gain a toe-hold in the peninsula, through the establishment of a military mission. China has also been supplying small arms to the Dhofar guerillas in Muscat and Oman. The intensification of the conflict in Oman has led to a rapid increase in arms supplies to the government, including British transports and trainers and Italian helicopters.

NORTH AFRICA

Just as in the Middle East – and for much the same reasons – there has been a rapid build-up of arms in the four North African states, Morocco, Algeria, Tunisia and Libya, since 1960. The whole area did not buy more than $3 million of major arms per year up to 1960, but since then the average has been over $40 million per year, which may be small by Egyptian or Iranian standards, but which brings these countries into the group of modern well-armed nations.

The pressures for acquiring arms have been much the same as

in the Middle East. All four countries have been concerned to free themselves from foreign domination and in particular to rid themselves of foreign troops and bases. All four are members of the Arab League and pledged, in varying degrees, to the Arab

Table 15 North Africa: supplies of major weapons, by supplier
US $ mn, at constant (1968) *prices*

Supplier:	USA	UK	France	USSR	Other	Total [a]
1950–54						
$ mn annual average	–	–	–	–	–	–
per cent	0·0	0·0	0·0	0·0	0·0	**0·0**
1955–9						
$ mn annual average	0·1	0·1	5·1	–	0·01	**5·3**
per cent	2·1	1·9	95·8	0·0	0·1	**100·0**
1960–64						
$ mn annual average	1·5	0·3	2·3	7·3	1·6	**13·1**
per cent	11·3	2·7	17·7	56·0	12·3	**100·0**
1965–9						
$ mn annual average	9·2	7·2	2·6	24·6	3·9	**47·5**
per cent	19·4	15·1	5·5	51·7	8·2	**100·0**
1970–72						
$ mn annual average	9·6	5·7	56·9	6·9	4·5	**83·0**
per cent	10·8	6·8	68·6	8·4	5·4	**100·0**
1950–72						
$ mn total [a]	81·1	55·2	220·8	180·3	41·1	**578·6**
Per cent of total	*14·0*	*9·5*	*38·2*	*31·2*	*7·1*	*100·0*

[a] Figures may not add up to totals owing to rounding.
Source: SIPRI worksheets.

cause, including the war with Israel. All of them have border disputes with their neighbours. And, as in the Middle East, these conflicts are related to internal pressures stemming from the nationalistic demands of urban groups, which have affected the role of the armed forces and determined their build-up.

All the major powers have active interests in the area which they endeavour to promote through the supply of arms. The Western powers are particularly interested in North African oil, and they have, or have had, military bases on North African territory. The Soviet Union has refuelling facilities for its Mediterranean fleet in Algeria. President Pompidou's new policy of re-establishing the French presence in the Mediterranean has led to increased French supplies of arms to all four North African countries since January 1970.

For most of the period, Algeria has depended on the Soviet Union for arms. The first military-aid agreement was signed in December 1960, but until independence in 1962 all shipments, mostly of weapons suitable for guerilla warfare, were channelled through the UAR, Morocco and Tunisia, in order to avoid direct confrontation with France. A few major weapons were delivered directly to Algeria in 1962–3, including Il-14 transports, Mi-4 helicopters, several motor torpedo boats and tanks for mine-clearing operations on the Tunisian and Moroccan frontiers.

However, it soon became clear that increased arms supplies were going to be necessary. The task of absorbing guerilla units into the regular army met with considerable opposition and guerilla resistance was not finally overcome until 1964. Further, a border war with Morocco broke out in 1963, in which the Algerian army proved ill-equipped and ill-trained for regular combat operations; equipment from Egypt, Cuba and the USSR was received only after the conflict had erupted. The process of transforming the armed forces from a still heterogeneous guerilla force into a strong conventional army was speeded up by various organizational measures as well as by measures to improve the armed forces in training and equipment. A new arms-trade agreement was concluded with the Soviet Union for 100 T-34 tanks, thirty self-propelled guns, light anti-aircraft weapons and several hundred trucks, as well as eighteen Yak-11 trainers from Czechoslovakia.

In July 1964, the Ben Bella government announced the formation of a people's militia, under direct control of the President, to deal with anti-government outbreaks. This decision was part of a policy to reduce the political power of the army and it is noteworthy that an agreement was concluded with China, in February 1965, for the supply of 'some material' to the militia.

However, in June 1965, the government was overthrown by Boumédienne, Chief of Staff of the Army and Minister of Defence, in a bloodless coup.

The armed forces remained the basis of Boumédienne's power and this perhaps explains the unexpected military build-up in the following few months. The Chinese-equipped militia was disbanded and the armed forces were strengthened by sophisticated Soviet equipment. Between 1965 and 1967, total major weapons imports amounted to $116 million, and included Il-28 bombers, MiG-21s, 'Komar' class patrol boats equipped with missiles, SA-2 anti-aircraft missiles and T-54/55 tanks.

Algeria sent two MiG squadrons to Egypt during the June War, and, more recently, with Soviet and Egyptian assistance, has been improving its airfields and air defence to provide dispersal facilities for Egypt in case of Israeli attack. Nevertheless, relations with the Soviet Union have deteriorated; it was felt that Soviet support for Arab states was insufficient and Algerians were dismayed by the excessive dependence of the UAR on the Soviet Union. Apart from a few patrol boats, no further deliveries of major weapons have been reported since 1967. Instead, French military assistance, which was extremely small up to 1967 and concentrated on the gendarmerie, has increased substantially. In 1969, 341 officers and NCOs were serving in Algeria. The same year, Algeria purchased twenty-eight Fouga Magisters. The agreement included the provision of training facilities in France and the setting-up of a flying school at Bou Sfer. Algeria has also taken delivery of some Puma helicopters.

Morocco and Tunisia have, for the most part, purchased arms from Western countries. Tunisia's arms imports have been extremely small and have come mainly from the United States and France. US military aid, which began in 1957 after France had turned down a request for arms and after President Bourguiba threatened to turn to the Soviet Union, has included twelve Patton tanks, purchased on favourable credit terms. And recently it has been expanded somewhat. Military co-operation between France and Tunisia intensified in the late sixties and substantial deliveries were made to Tunisia in 1969–70 under the

French military-aid programme. Tunisia has also purchased aircraft from Sweden and Italy.

French weapons supplies and military assistance to Morocco were concentrated in the period immediately after independence in 1956. At the time, Morocco's arms build-up was directed towards freeing that part of Morocco which was still under the Spanish protectorate – a task completed in 1958.

In 1959, an agreement was reached with the United States concerning the withdrawal of US troops from bases acquired from the French. About 1,700 US military personnel were, however, to remain at the airbase in Kenitra to assist the Moroccans in training in telecommunications and base operations and to use the communications facilities there. US military aid to Morocco began in 1960.

The opposition daily, *Rai el Amm*, strongly protested against the delivery of US equipment and this may be one reason why on 15 November 1960 the government announced that it had decided to accept Soviet military aid, including MiGs and Il-28s. Another reason may have been Morocco's claim to Mauritania, which received little sympathy from the Western powers. However, relations with the Soviet Union cooled after the border war with Algeria.

Morocco made no real attempt to maintain parity with Algerian equipment, although the Algerian build-up provided the justification for Morocco to order twelve F-5s, among other items of equipment, from the United States in 1965. A further arms deal worth $14 million was negotiated in February 1967 but its implementation was delayed by Congressional opposition stemming from the June War. After the June War, relations with Algeria, and hence socialist countries, improved, and in 1967 and 1968 Morocco received thirty reconditioned tanks from Czechoslovakia in return for primary products. In addition, it signed an agreement with Sud Aviation in 1968 for the supply of twenty-four former Luftwaffe Magisters. These deals may have provided a lever to persuade the United States to increase its supply of arms; by July 1970, Morocco had received 21 F-5s and a further three were delivered in 1971.

Until 1969, Libya relied entirely on the United States and Britain. Libya signed treaties with both countries in 1953 and 1954, under which they provided military aid in return for base facilities. The growth of radical Arab Nationalist forces led to pressure for increased arms supplies and, at the same time, for reduced dependence on the West. Already in the late fifties, the United States was providing military aid to Libya in response, according to hearings before the Senate Foreign Relations Committee, to requests from the Libyan government 'as a result of the vulnerability of the Libyan internal situation demonstrated during the Suez war of 1956 and in order to enable the Libyans to refuse Soviet offers of military assistance'. This 'vulnerability' became more marked in the sixties. Both in 1964 and 1967, the Libyan government requested US and British withdrawal, after violent anti-Western riots. The main response was to increase arms supplies. From 1964 to 1969, US grant aid amounted to $9·4 million and the US also sold $50·2 million worth of military equipment; total military aid up to 1964 had only amounted to $8 million. During this period, Libya ordered eighteen F-5 fighters.

In 1967, a new government, including members of the radical opposition, was formed and defence spending increased rapidly. Libya signed an air-defence deal for Rapier and Thunderbird missiles from Britain, and in 1969 ordered a considerable number of British tanks. It also appears that Soviet military aid began during this period.

In September 1969, the monarchy was overthrown in a military *coup d'état*. The new government negotiated the withdrawal of British and American troops and turned to France and the Soviet Union for arms supplies. The British air-defence deal was cancelled, according to the Libyans because it was designed 'to serve the interests of imperialism in Libya', and according to the British because Libya had failed to continue payments. The British tanks were never delivered, because of British insistence on a guarantee that they should not be used against Israel.

In January 1970, Libya ordered 110 Mirages from France, including at least fifty Mirage 5 and fifty Mirage III, worth $144 million. Libyan pilots and technicians are trained in France and the planes are being delivered in 1971–4. The same year it was reported that Libya was receiving 200 tanks, about seventy-five field guns and anti-aircraft artillery, at least thirty-six amphibious vehicles and associated field equipment from the Soviet Union. However, the Libyan purchase of French arms indicates the Libyan interest in avoiding a dependence on the Soviet Union similar to that which has developed among other Arab republics. Indeed, the Egyptian decision to expel its Soviet advisers is widely attributed to Libyan influence.

10 Sub-Saharan Africa and South Africa

SUB-SAHARAN AFRICA

Major weapons imports to the thirty-five Sub-Saharan African countries have been extremely low, amounting to less than 3 per cent of the total for the ninety-six Third World countries (including Viet-Nam). In fact only thirty-one of the thirty-five countries in the area have imported major arms. (Sub-Saharan Africa, as discussed here, does not include South Africa, which is dealt with separately at the end of this chapter.) Moreover the weapons have generally been very unsophisticated: only thirteen air forces possess combat aircraft with jet engines (Congo (Zaire), Ethiopia, Ghana, Guinea, Kenya, Mali, Nigeria, Rhodesia, Somalia, Sudan, Tanzania, Uganda and Zambia), and only nine of them have tanks (Congo (Zaire), Ethiopia, Guinea, Ivory Coast, Mali, Somalia, Sudan, Tanzania and Uganda). Zambia is the only Black African country to possess missiles.

Major weapons imports amounted to a mere $8 million per year for the whole of Sub-Saharan Africa until 1959, when they suddenly rose to a yearly average of $30 million in the early sixties. This was due mainly to the establishment of armed forces in the twenty-eight nations which became independent between 1955 and 1965. After a peak of $80 million in 1966 arms imports fell back again to only a third of this figure between 1965 and 1969, but a new $70 million peak was reached in 1971. Most of these countries have not acquired much more than the initial batch of equipment and the average expenditure of each nation on major weapons has been only $1·4 million per year since 1965.

One reason for this is that the pressures to import arms have been much weaker in Sub-Saharan Africa than in other regions: the countries which differ from the pattern are those where there have been serious armed conflicts, such as the Congo (Zaire),

Table 16 Sub-Saharan Africa: supplies of major weapons, by supplier
US $ mn, at constant (1968) *prices*

Supplier:	USA	UK	France	USSR	Other	Total
1950–54						
$ mn annual average	2	5	–	–	*	7
per cent	26·4	70·7	0·0	0·0	2·9	100·0
1955–9						
$ mn annual average	1	8	–	–	1	10
per cent	6·6	85·8	0·0	0·0	7·6	100·0
1960–64						
$ mn annual average	7	7	4	5	9	31
per cent	21·3	22·7	12·1	14·5	29·3	100·0
1965–9						
$ mn annual average	6	6	7	8	20	47
per cent	12·8	11·9	14·6	17·5	43·1	100·0
1970–72						
$ mn annual average	7	8	8	14	17	54
per cent	12·4	15·4	14·4	25·5	32·2	100·0
1950–72						
$ mn total	95	153	77	105	204	634
Per cent of total	*15·1*	*24·1*	*12·1*	*16·6*	*32·2*	*1·000*

* = less than 1.
Source: SIPRI worksheets.

Nigeria, the Horn of Africa and the Sudan, or those which have
been threatened with conflicts or have adjoined them, such as
Rhodesia and Ghana. Thus for instance Nigerian imports of
major weapons rose from 7 per cent of the total for the area
before the 1967–70 conflict to 37 per cent during the conflict.
The equivalent increase in the Horn was from 2 per cent to 38
per cent. Another, and probably more important, reason for the
low arms imports is the lack of resources: most of the countries
in the region are poor and non-urbanized. In some cases the
two great powers have been willing to overcome this by providing
military aid, which has gone mainly to those countries which
have also been involved in serious armed conflicts.

Apart from the conflicts, other factors have also influenced the demand for weapons. One is simply the creation of armed forces as an attribute of independence. In the words of President Hamani Diori of the Niger, at the inauguration of his new state's army: 'Henceforth, in the eyes of the world and of the whole of our people, you are the visible sign of our political independence and of our proclaimed will to defend it against all aggression.'

Many African leaders, however, devoted little attention to the role of their armed forces after independence. The new states had other important priorities for their limited funds. Also it was usually the politicians who had played the main part in the drama of independence and not the military, particularly in those countries – mainly British but also sometimes French – where economically and educationally backward areas had been made the main recruiting grounds for the army, thereby inseminating opposition between the military and the politically conscious élite. Where armed forces were inherited from colonial days, they were generally maintained and enlarged, particularly because the army might be more reliable in the event of internal dissent than a locally recruited police force which might identify with the dissident population, especially if the country was ethnically divided.

The possession of an army served both as a mark of nationhood and as a symbol of national unity above ethnic allegiances. Moreover, for many African leaders the goal of 'true independence', that is to say independence for all of Africa and independence to settle African affairs without outside interference, became a very important concept. It was felt that armed forces were required to protect their own state's integrity and that of their neighbours and also to help liberation movements in countries still struggling for independence. For example, the role, and perhaps more importantly the potential role, of African armies in the Congo crisis and similar situations was a significant factor in the establishment of armed forces in several countries. In addition, the need to aid liberation movements is increasingly felt as an obligation, and guerilla training camps have been permitted and even encouraged in a number of states bordering

South Africa, Rhodesia and Portuguese territories, in spite of the risks for these states of making themselves vulnerable to the much greater armed strength of those territories. Hence the recent increase in arms-buying by, for instance, Zambia and Tanzania. The struggle for political power within the new states has sometimes had a bearing on the demand for weapons. In Kenya, for example, a rift between the radical followers of Vice-President Oginga Odinga and the more conservative members of the government in 1964–6 led to an unofficial influx of military assistance from socialist countries which was only halted after the deposition of Odinga in March 1966.

This, however, is an exceptional case, and generally political rivalries affect the flow of arms only when the army is directly involved. Initially such involvement concerned the role of armed forces inherited from colonial days and, in the case of former French colonies, of veterans from the metropolitan armies as well. Neither of these groups allowed the political leaders to neglect them. The mutiny of the Force Publique in the Congo (Zaire) five days after independence and the East African mutinies in January 1964 were all related to low pay and to slowness in the africanization of the officer corps. In Togo, President Olympio was assassinated in January 1963 after having refused to enlarge the 250-man army to find place for about 300 returning veterans of the French Army.

The africanization of the officer corps has in many African countries been the crucial factor in the transition from the essentially feudal army of the colonial era to a modern army in a modern state. The need for certain educational standards limited officer training in a number of countries to those groups which had been educationally favoured during the colonial era, and, as these were often the same groups as had provided the political leaders, the differences which tended to beset the earliest days of independence have often faded away.

There is an interesting contrast here with the Middle East. In the Middle East the transition to a modern army reflected the increasing power of an emerging middle class, and a state of opposition between the army and the traditional ruling class has been one factor contributing both to the frequency of military coups and to the high level of arms imports. In Africa this pattern is rare: the army was generally a conservative tradition-building force in colonial days, and the modernizing groups on the side of nationalism and radicalism were normally civilians.

On the other hand the army's monopoly of force and its firm organization under the leadership of an educated élite gave it a basis for political power. The army often felt competent to intervene in politics when it considered political leaders incompetent, hence the increasingly frequent military coups of the past ten years (more than twenty successful coups in fifteen states in the 1960s) and hence also, in part, the increase in arms imports of the past ten years designed to satisfy the army's demands in the hope of averting a coup or to maintain its position after a coup. In Ethiopia, for instance, an attempted coup in December 1960 caused the Emperor not only to increase the army's pay at the expense of the civil service but also to arrange for a substantial increase in American military assistance.

Some countries have adopted a policy of 'demilitarizing' the army by integrating it into the political structure, giving it a role in economic development and in educating the masses. Sometimes this policy has been combined with the creation of large politicized para-military forces to share the maintenance of law and order with the army and to reduce its power as the sole armed force. Guinea, Mali and Tanzania, for instance, have adopted these methods, with varying success.

The role of the suppliers

The pattern of arms supplies to Sub-Saharan Africa has been markedly different from the general world pattern. The two great powers together account for only 32 per cent of supplies, compared with 67 per cent for the Third World as a whole, while the former colonial powers, France and Britain, account for more than 35 per cent of the supplies as compared with 20 per cent in the Third World generally.

More than two thirds of all the major weapons supplied to

Sub-Saharan Africa have gone to one seventh of the states in the area – Congo (Zaire), Ethiopia, Ghana, Nigeria, Rhodesia, Somalia and the Sudan. These countries (with the exception of Rhodesia) are at the same time the main recipients of great-power military aid and those where the most serious armed conflicts have taken place. Anywhere else this would be an indication that the USA and the USSR were engaged in another bout of competitive arming and that the conflicts were polarized into East–West rivalry. But in Sub-Saharan Africa it is an open question whether the increased arms requirements generated by the conflicts proved to be most easily met by recourse to the two great powers (which are generally the cheapest source of arms) or whether the interests of the great powers exacerbated the conflicts and created the demand for more weapons. In the case of the conflicts in the Horn of Africa and in the Congo the latter could be argued, but probably the former is more appropriate in the cases of the Sudan and Nigeria. It is also significant that there are many conflicts in Sub-Saharan Africa which have not developed into war, and one explanation may be economic constraints which the great powers are not interested in removing by more extensive provision of military aid.

The United States has provided more major weapons to Sub-Saharan Africa than the Soviet Union, but the Soviet Union has supplied sophisticated weapons to a larger number of countries. Except in Ethiopia and the Congo (Zaire), US military, assistance programmes have been confined to internal security, training and civic action, and economic aid has generally been preferred as a more appropriate method of achieving the 'emergence of stable democratic nations' less likely 'to turn to extremist solutions for their problems', in the official American phraseology. These American interests coincided to a large extent with those of the former colonial powers and were therefore well served by the latter's arms supplies and military aid. The Soviet Union, unlike the USA, has not laid down any rules about 'appropriate' recipients or types of arms and, in at least two known instances, recipients have found it difficult to absorb the types delivered. Ghana found Soviet heavy transports too costly to operate, while Somalia received fighters and tanks which were of little use in its border wars. Nevertheless, Soviet supplies have been very moderate, and so limited have been supplies from the great powers that there have even been speculations of a tacit understanding between them.

Britain is in fact the largest supplier of weapons to Sub-Saharan Africa, and in the 1960s – the period of heaviest arms acquisition – provided 17 per cent of the total. France comes next with 14 per cent, spread over nearly twice the number of countries. This gap is a symptom of the differences between these two and their respective ex-colonies.

Former French dependencies

When all the French dependencies became independent in 1960, France undertook far-reaching responsibilities for their defence. They each had to create their own military institutions and training centres, but about two thirds of all the officers and virtually all the non-commissioned officers required for their armies already existed in the French forces and became available, as did large numbers of soldiers – 200,000 in Upper Volta, for example. France signed technical-assistance agreements with the new states, including the equipment of the new armed forces. Multilateral and bilateral defence pacts gave France various obligations for the internal and external defence of the territories, in return for which it was accorded the right to use various military facilities. Under special unpublished agreements there have been a number of French interventions to help maintain public order, as for instance in Cameroun, Congo (Brazzaville), Chad (twice), Niger, Mauritania, Gabon and the Central African Republic. Up to the early 1960s, French forces stationed in Sub-Saharan Africa amounted to around 40,000, but since the independence of Algeria in 1962 and the restructuring of French defence these have dwindled to 6,000 or less, and instead, a '*force d'intervention*' is maintained in France to help out if required. There are now only two major French installations in Black Africa: a naval base in Senegal and a base in the Ivory Coast.

French withdrawal from its naval base in Malagasy has been negotiated.

France has continued to train large numbers of military personnel for the new states – 2,600 per year during the early 1960s, 1,000 to 1,500 per year in the mid-sixties, and 800 per year at the end of the sixties. The bulk of French expenditure on military assistance overseas goes on this training – something like $40 million a year in the early 1960s and $19 million in 1970. About 1,400 French military personnel were said to be with the armed forces of the ex-colonies in 1970, chiefly in training centres. At independence, the ex-dependencies also received gifts from France of a first supply of military *matériel* and equipment amounting, in the first two years, to about $80 million, as well as the equipment and installations already on the ground. The weapons in this initial supply normally comprised two or three Broussard liaison monoplanes, a C-47 transport, an Alouette helicopter, some armoured vehicles and patrol boats, and a quantity of army equipment. Additional quantities of the same material were supplied later, also as free gifts. Senegal, the Ivory Coast, Malagasy and Mauritania have been more lavishly equipped than the rest, all getting more aircraft and helicopters. In the case of Mauritania this was to ensure its defence against Morocco, while the other three countries are sites of French bases. In return for this equipment the new states have undertaken to obtain spares and replacements from France and to place re-equipment orders there.

The former French dependencies have also received small amounts of military aid from the United States, Israel and the Federal Republic of Germany, and the Republic of Mali and Congo (Brazzaville) have received aid both from the Soviet Union and from China.

Guinea, the only French dependency to cut itself off from France at independence, has received arms mainly from the Soviet Union. Soviet supplies were concentrated in the early sixties, when Guinea was a member of the Union of African States together with Ghana and Mali. This aid was largely replaced by West German in the mid-sixties, but Guinea's proximity to Portuguese Guinea-Bissau and its support for the PAIGC have recently brought it closer to the socialist camp again. In 1970 alleged West German participation in the Portuguese invasion of Guinea led to the severance of diplomatic ties.

Former British dependencies

Former British dependencies have bought many more arms from Britain than the former French dependencies have from France, partly because the British have not maintained close military associations with them, or provided aid or troops as the French have done, and partly because the ex-British territories are on the whole much larger and better off economically than the ex-French. At independence the British ex-dependencies were generally granted fairly substantial quantities of equipment, but Britain has on the whole been reluctant to continue giving hardware except when compelled by special needs. They have, however, been encouraged to come to Britain for supplies by the provision of intensive training in the use of British equipment.

The explanation for these differences must be sought in the historical differences in the colonial concepts of the two powers. For instance, in military matters the British kept their colonial forces quite separate from the metropolitan army. The officers of the local forces were almost all British, and very few Africans served in the British army. In consequence, the ex-dependencies had few veterans with experience as officers (only three each, for example, in Tanganyika and Uganda).

Intervention has been rare. The United Kingdom has a general obligation under the terms of British Commonwealth membership to help 'by all appropriate action' any other member which is a victim of aggression, but Kenya is the only country in Sub-Saharan Africa where there has been a substantial British contribution of troops.

Diversification has been a characteristic of the ex-British colonial countries. In particular they have turned to small or medium-sized powers, because dealing with them has the advantage, for newly independent states, of not carrying the same political implications as dealing with the greater powers. Thus they have tended to turn to British Commonwealth countries such as Canada, which in fact has become the fifth largest supplier of weapons to Sub-Saharan Africa, providing 5 per cent of the total.

For African nations, diversification of military assistance helps not only to reduce military dependence, but also to avoid some of the problems connected with the role of the armed forces, that is to say, to avoid the development of a unified officer corps with an alien tradition. Training assistance from other Third World countries with experience in these problems and with closer political identification is especially useful in this respect, although it is not the only objective of such co-operation. They have, for instance, a common experience in handling the types of equipment they receive and in the difficulties posed by climatic conditions and by the generally low technical and educational level in the Third World. In addition to military co-operation between neighbouring states – for instance, Zambia and Tanzania – India, Pakistan, Nigeria, Ethiopia, Israel and Egypt have all provided military assistance. This aid has emphasized training and advice, while equipment grants have been rare.

Kenya has maintained the closest association of all the ex-dependencies with Britain and has received $44 million out of the total of $65 million of British aid to African countries. But Kenya's arms imports have been low, and one reason for this is the air, logistical and technical support given by Britain for the operations against the Somali population on Kenya's north-eastern frontier. A temporary divergence from the British connection during 1964–6, when a quantity of Soviet arms and *matériel* entered the country, has already been mentioned. Uganda's arms have come from a variety of sources, including Britain, Israel, Czechoslovakia, the Soviet Union, the Federal Republic of Germany, Canada and the USA. In the war against Tanzania, in September 1972, General Amin of Uganda also received aid from Libya.

Tanzania is anti-militarist by tradition and its arms purchases have been kept low. Diversification has also been very important in this country, and weapons and training have been received from the Federal Republic of Germany, Canada and the Soviet Union. In recent years it has had to make considerable expenditure on defence projects on its borders with Rhodesia and Mozambique because of the guerilla camps in its territory, which are the object of hostile action from across the borders. Tanzania's air defence will be strengthened by the supply of MiG fighters from China, which are due for delivery in 1973.

Zambia has similar problems with air incursions by Portuguese and Rhodesian aircraft. In 1969 it severed long-standing military training arrangements with Britain because of dissatisfaction with British policy over Rhodesia. In particular, Zambia requested that Britain supply the Rapier air-defence system as aid, arguing that Britain was responsible for the situation in Rhodesia and should, consequently, ensure Zambia's defence. Although Britain refused to do this and Zambia terminated the training agreement, it nevertheless went ahead and purchased the missiles at a cost of $15 million. Italy has replaced Britain in providing training assistance and has also supplied some major weapons. And, most recently, Yugoslavia has joined Italy as a supplier to Zambia with the delivery of similar equipment – trainers and light attack aircraft.

Ghana is another country which broke away from its old connections with Britain. It seemed about to become, in Nkrumah's own phrase, the 'vanguard force' in a socialist-oriented pan-African independence struggle, and acquired arms from both the Soviet Union and China. But after the fall of Nkrumah it changed track again and is once more importing arms from Britain and the West.

Ghana also provides a good example of a traditionalist Western-oriented military élite at variance with radical civilian politicians who try to politicize the army but merely succeed in getting themselves thrown out.

From independence in 1957, Ghana relied mainly on Britain for arms and military training. However, the Congo crisis provided a touchstone in Ghana's foreign policy. Nkrumah was convinced that the Western powers played a critical role in deposing Lumumba. Ghana's attempts to help (at Lumumba's request) in the early stages of the conflict were not only undermined, but presented in the West as the most flagrant interference in the internal affairs of the Congo. Nkrumah therefore turned to the Soviet Union, and an arms deal was signed in 1961. At the same time an attempt was made to reduce dependence on Britain by a drastic africanization of the officer corps. About 200 British officers and NCOs were replaced. However, by the end of 1961 many of the dismissed British officers were called back, and the next year a new training agreement was signed with Britain. The reason for this is that the organization, training and equipment of the army was entirely British and any major changes would have required enormous financial expense which Ghana could not afford.

Nkrumah tried to adjust the bias by setting up a countervailing military force, the 1,200-strong Presidential Guard, to be armed and equipped by the Soviet Union, and by signing an agreement with China for the equipment and training of the Freedom Fighters – guerillas with bases in Ghana. This and his offer to send troops to fight the Smith regime in Rhodesia were among the decisive factors in turning the army against him and in his overthrow in February 1966. Since that date the army has ruled Ghana in a spirit of cautious conservatism and has bought a modest amount of major weapons from Britain, Canada, the United States and Italy.

Rhodesia has had its own armed forces since 1923. Its air force was set up in 1936 and was expanded during the Second World War, receiving its first fighter aircraft, nineteen Spitfires, in 1951–2. In the ten years 1953–63, when Rhodesia was joined with Zambia (then Northern Rhodesia) and Malawi (then Nyasaland) in the Central African Federation, the armed forces of the three territories were amalgamated and greatly expanded. Indeed, during the period of its existence, the Federation received the bulk of major weapons imported into Sub-Saharan Africa, nearly $60 million worth. These included thirty-two Vampire fighters and trainers, thirty Canberra light bombers and, just before it broke up, twelve Hunter fighters. Eight Alouette helicopters were also acquired from France. When the Federation broke up in 1963, the greater part of these armed forces – half the Federal army and all the air force except for some transport aircraft – went to Rhodesia rather than to its other partners.

Since UDI two years later Rhodesia has officially received no further major weapon supplies, but the Rhodesian air force has shown itself quite adequate for COIN operations, which suggests that there must remain some sources of supply. The main source is undoubtedly South Africa, although there have been some reports of both French and Italian aircraft being introduced, possibly via South Africa.

The remaining former British territories, the Sudan and Nigeria, show quite different patterns of arms acquisition because, as already mentioned, they have been the locations of two of the four major conflicts in post-war Africa. These conflicts are reviewed in the following section.

Conflict areas

The internal and external conflicts in Sub-Saharan Africa have for the most part been caused by artificiality in the colonial borders which split or united ethnic and cultural groups in a random fashion. Differences in the treatment of different groups by the colonial powers have also been a cause of internal difficulties. There have been two major armed conflicts – in the Congo (Zaire) and in Nigeria – border clashes and something like an arms race between Ethiopia and Somalia with Kenya also involved, and a prolonged civil war in the Sudan. All these have influenced major arms supplies. Other conflicts, such as those between Mauritania and Morocco, those in Chad between Arab northerners and other inhabitants, and those in Burundi between Hutu and Watusi, have had little or no effect on supplies of major weapons, though they may have affected imports of other arms.

The Democratic Republic of the Congo – Congo (Kinshasa) or Zaire – where the earliest of the major conflicts began in 1960, is perhaps the area in Africa where the super-powers have come nearest to direct confrontation, and imports of major weapons were at one time substantial. Since 1960, when the civil war began immediately after the departure of the Belgians, the Congo has accounted for more than 10 per cent of Sub-Saharan Africa's major weapons imports, the largest proportion coming from the United States.

During the initial phase of the Congo crisis – when Lumumba was still head of the central government in Kinshasa – the Soviet Union provided military assistance in the form of transport aircraft and lorries. Little Soviet assistance appears, however, to have been provided to Lumumba's followers when they were in opposition six months later. By then the central government was relying on the UN troops and some assistance was also forthcoming from Belgium, which, together with France, was also the main source of arms and mercenaries for Katanga, the secessionist state.

From late 1962 the USA has been the main supplier of arms to Congo (Zaire) and the level of US supplies has been closely connected to the intensity of the fighting in the country. Thus, supplies increased drastically in 1964 and 1967 when the central government was involved in combatting first the radical followers of Gizenga, armed with weapons from the Soviet Union, China and some radical African states, and then an uprising of foreign mercenaries joined by local forces. Other sources of aid have been Italy, Israel, Belgium and Britain.

The Sudan first became a major importer of arms during the same period as the Congo (Zaire), in 1962–4, when the southern (pagan and Christian) peoples began their efforts to escape from domination by the Muslim Arab north. This struggle has not led to large imports of major weapons – the weapons mainly needed for the war in the south were small arms, armoured cars and transport aircraft – but the number of men under arms, apart from the insurgents in the south, rose from 5,000 in 1957 just after independence to 18,500 ten years later and to 27,450 by 1970. Already by 1965 three quarters of the army were employed in combatting the insurgency in the south. However, in February 1972 the south was granted regional autonomy and a new southern command was to be set up in the army, integrating the forces of the southern Anya Nya with the regular army.

Perhaps a more important determinant of the size of major weapons imports is the fact that from the late 1960s the Sudan has increasingly identified itself with the Arab cause in the Middle East war with Israel. Some time after the 1967 June War an agreement was signed with the Soviet Union providing for the supply of heavy tanks and supersonic fighters, a type of weapon not appropriate for the war in the south.

The unsuccessful military coup in July 1971 and the communist purge that followed it has had a serious impact on Sudan's relations with the Soviet Union. Instead, relations with China have improved and China has supplied tanks and jet aircraft. Sudan's stand on the Middle Eastern issue also appears to have softened somewhat.

In the Horn of Africa, a sort of arms race developed during the 1960s between two neighbouring African states, Ethiopia and Somalia. In part this competitive build-up was promoted by the competing interests of the two great powers in the area. Because Ethiopia and Somalia both guard the passage from the Indian Ocean to the Red Sea, as well as being near the storm centre of the Middle East, both the United States and the Soviet Union have made possible, and even encouraged, the build-up of armaments. Yet the arms race never developed into a 'cold war' issue between the great powers; the conflict was never polarized into a direct confrontation between East and West.

Both the USA and the USSR supplied unusually large amounts of aid to Ethiopia; it received the largest military aid grant by the United States to any country in Africa and also received Soviet economic aid equalled in value in Africa only by that provided to Ghana. In 1971, it also received $60 million in Chinese economic aid.

Ethiopia has been a major importer of weapons for longer than any other Sub-Saharan nation and is overall the largest importer of major weapons, having received nearly 12 per cent of the total supplied since 1950. Immediately after the Second World War the air force was trained and equipped by Sweden, the small navy by Norway and the army by Britain, which also provided Ethiopia's first fighter aircraft. American aid began in 1953, and between then and 1971 Ethiopia received $152 million worth of US military aid. One of the principal American communications bases was set up in Eritrea on a twenty-five-year lease. Ethiopia has also continued to obtain some supplies of arms, by purchase or through loans, from Britain and from other sources including the Federal Republic of Germany, Israel and Yugoslavia.

The origin of Somalia's arms procurement is its commitment, assumed at independence in July 1960 when the former British Somaliland and Italian Somalia were united, to unite all Somalis. As 80 per cent of Somalis are nomads or semi-nomads, who from time immemorial have moved across the borders of what are now Ethiopia and Kenya as well as over their own territory, this 'Greater Somalia' aspiration inevitably caused the new Somalia to clash with its neighbours. Armed skirmishes built up from early 1961 to 1963, the period when the Somali armed forces were being trained and equipped jointly by the former colonial powers, Britain and Italy, and also by Somalia's old friend Egypt.

In 1963 Somalia's relations with the West deteriorated. Britain showed that no support would be given to Somali efforts to incorporate the large population of Somalis in Northern Kenya, and the United States, the Federal Republic of Germany and Italy tried to limit their supplies of arms to Somalia to weapons which would not threaten or alarm Ethiopia and would be appropriate only for internal security. They were supplied on the condition that Somalia would not procure arms from other sources. In October Somalia accepted an unconditional Soviet offer of a $30 million long-term credit to be used to expand the army from 4,000 to 10,000 men and to strengthen the air force. MiG-15 and MiG-17 fighters and trainers were delivered as well as a large number of tanks. However, by 1956–6, it became apparent that the Somali economy could not in fact stand the strain of armaments on this scale; the infrastructure was not strong enough to absorb the aid. Also many of the weapons were too sophisticated for the border fighting. By the latter part of 1966 shipments of arms were being left to rust in port, and thereafter Somalia settled down with its neighbours and Western aid was briefly resumed. No major weapons have been imported for several years.

The latest and fiercest of the conflicts, that in Nigeria between 1967 and 1970, provides a good illustration of the difficulties of diversification in times of war. Before the war Nigeria had a far-reaching policy of diversification. Its relatively modest imports of major weapons, averaging $2·4 million a year, came from no fewer than twenty countries. When civil war began as a result of the secession of the eastern region – Biafra – Nigeria was able to get arms from only one of these twenty, namely Britain, and from a wholly new supplier, the Soviet Union: all the others imposed embargoes. Biafra had even more difficulty and was forced to buy arms privately at inflated prices, mainly through Portugal and France.

During the three years of war, Nigeria imported an average of $8·8 million worth of major weapons per year – 30 per cent of all arms coming into Sub-Saharan Africa during those years. Although the British supplies were limited to types of weapons previously supplied – for example Saladin armoured cars, artillery, small arms, ammunition and so on, but no air-force equipment – the quantity of arms supplied rose drastically. According to Nigerian trade statistics they increased by a factor of 110 between 1966 and 1969 while the growth of the Nigerian army during the same period was from 11,500 to 160,000, a factor of 14.

As usual, the Soviet Union was willing to supply the types of weapon required. Imports from the Soviet Union and its allies included MiG-17 and Il-28 bombers, and possibly MiG-19 fighters, together with armoured cars, and there were also reports of the delivery of Su-7 fighters. Nigeria also managed to buy, from various countries, some helicopters and a number of Dakotas for transport and for conversion into bombers.

Biafra bought surplus weapons from private dealers, mostly Second World War bombers and early post-war civil aircraft. It also possessed a few Alouette helicopters, and some Swedish trainers armed with machine-guns were smuggled to Biafra and flown by Swedish volunteers. The war was kept going by a substantial influx of small arms to Biafra, coming originally from France by way of Gabon and the Ivory Coast, and the Federal forces needed fairly large supplies of major arms from Britain and the Soviet Union before they achieved decisive successes.

Liberation movements

Small amounts of weapons are provided to the African liberation movements, mainly by the Soviet Union and its allies in Eastern Europe. An alternative source is China, and at least one of the groups – FRELIMO, the one most active in Mozambique – has been receiving substantial and regular supplies from China as well as from the Soviet Union, but either as a result of positive Chinese policy or as a result of Soviet attempts to keep China away from favoured recipients, Chinese aid has generally gone to small rival movements. Some help has also been given by North Korea, North Viet-Nam and Cuba. The host countries where the groups are based do not often have any spare weapons to give: in many cases their own armies are smaller than those of their revolutionary guests. Instead the host countries assist the movements by providing sanctuary and in securing aid from foreign suppliers. Some Middle East and North African states have also given help, including Algeria, Egypt and Libya.

A major source of arms is the Western weapons captured from the Portuguese, such as the West German automatic G-3 guns.

Portugal

As the biggest user of weapons in Sub-Saharan Africa at the present time, Portugal and its involvement in the continent may be worth a note.

The war which Portugal has been waging since the early 1960s against liberation movements in its overseas territories puts a very heavy burden on its economy, which it would not be able to meet were it not for a steady inflow of arms and aid from its partners in NATO. Between 40 and 50 per cent of the Portuguese national budget has been devoted to defence, and of that more than three quarters has gone in military expenditures on the forces in Africa. Portugal admits to having more than 130,000 troops in Africa, but unofficial estimates put the figure nearer 200,000.

The Portuguese economy could not support military activity on this scale if outside sources did not provide most of the necessary weapons. Theoretically, the NATO countries supply Portugal with weapons in order to enhance Portugal's contribution to NATO, and they insist that the weapons shall be used only in 'metropolitan' Portugal. But although the Portuguese contribution to NATO is so small that weapons on the scale provided cannot possibly be used for that purpose, both for commercial reasons and in return for military facilities on Portuguese territory, the supply goes on.

The USA provided large amounts of aid to Portugal in the 1950s, including a large number of fighter and training aircraft, several frigates and other warships, a considerable number of tanks and probably 155-mm. howitzers. Since 1961 military aid from the USA has been on a much smaller scale, not above $5 million a year, but there has been substantial economic aid, and many of the pre-1961 weapons still turn up in the overseas territories (for example napalm canisters marked 'Property of the US Air Force' have been found in African villages bombed by the Portuguese).

At present, the main supplier of arms to Portugal is France, and the weapons are all of the type mainly suitable for COIN action. For instance, the helicopter units are exclusively equipped with Alouettes, some of them armed with air-to-surface missiles. Reports mention the use of AML-60 armoured cars, mortars, hand-grenades, machine-guns and sub-machine-guns.

Apart from the United States and France, the biggest source of Portuguese weapons has been the Federal Republic of Germany, which *inter alia* sold forty G.91R fighters to Portugal in 1966 (which were at once transferred to Guinea-Bissau and later to Beira), eight patrol boats in 1961–2 (three of which were sent to

Guinea and the other five to Angola) and three corvettes in 1970 (one of which is certainly in Angolan waters and the others may be), fifteen Nord 2051 D transport aircraft in 1968 (now operating as paratroop carriers in Angola and Mozambique), as well as Transall C-160 and Do-27 aircraft.

SOUTH AFRICA

South Africa is, by far, the largest military spender in Africa. Its defence expenditures are twenty times greater than those of the average Black African nation, and its major weapon imports since 1965 have been 96 per cent of the total major weapon imports to the rest of Sub-Saharan Africa.

During the sixties, there was a major arms build-up in South Africa. Between 1961 and 1966, defence expenditures rose by 500 per cent but since then the annual rate of growth has been only 5 per cent. Major weapon imports, which during the fifties averaged only $13 million per year, reached a peak of $120 million in 1965. Since then they have fallen, and the average for the five years 1968–72 was $43 million. The major period of equipment had been completed and South Africa is now developing its own defence industry.

Two main factors have determined South Africa's arms imports and its choice of suppliers: its position in the Western strategic calculus and the opposition caused by its policy of apartheid.

Historically, South Africa has been closely aligned with the West, in particular with Britain. Guardian of the alternative route to the Indian Ocean, South Africa has occupied a special place in the British and later Western defence systems. It fought alongside the Western powers in both world wars and in Korea, so that during the fifties it was assured of a steady flow of weapons from the West, including Sabre fighters from Canada and Sikorsky helicopters from the USA.

Traditionally, there had been close co-operation with Britain in military matters. South Africa's army, navy and air force were

Table 17 Main Southern African liberation movements

Country	Movement	Base
Guinea-Bissau and Cape Verdes	African Independence Party of Guinea and the Cape Verdes (PAIGC)	Conakry and liberated territories
Mozambique	Mozambique Liberation Front (FRELIMO)	Dar Es Salaam
Angola	(i) Revolutionary Government of Angola in Exile (GRAE)[a]	Kinshasa
	(ii) Popular Movement for the Liberation of Angola (MPLA)[a]	Brazzaville, Lusaka, Dar Es Salaam
	(iii) National Union for the Total Independence of Angola (UNITA)	Inside Eastern Angola, formerly Lusaka
South West Africa	South West Africa People's Organization (SWAPO)	Dar Es Salaam, Lusaka
Zimbabwe (Rhodesia)	(i) Zimbabwe African People's Union (ZAPU)	Lusaka
	(ii) Zimbabwe African National Union (ZANU)	Lusaka
South Africa	(i) Pan Africanist Congress (PAC)	Banned in Zambia and Botswana at end of 1968
	(ii) African National Congress (ANC)	Lusaka, Dar Es Salaam

[a] GRAE and MPLA agreed to join forces on 13 December 1972.

created with British assistance and patterned on the British model, and the equipment was almost entirely of British origin. Under the Simonstown Agreement, concluded between the two countries in 1955, Britain supplied $50 million of naval vessels, and in 1957 eight Avro Shackleton maritime reconnaissance aircraft, incorporating special design features to facilitate their additional use as tactical bombers and transports, were delivered.

From around 1960 South Africa's international position became threatened. A wave of independence was sweeping over

Africa, creating a large number of new states with a 'say' in world politics, especially in the UN. The first two of these new states in Sub-Saharan Africa, Ghana and Guinea, followed a radical militant policy and sharply criticized South Africa. At the same time, the Sharpeville massacre, the gradual annexation of South West Africa and the increasingly rigid enforcement of apartheid lowered South Africa's prestige in world opinion. The exclusion of South Africa from the Commonwealth in 1961 confirmed this development.

South Africa responded with a heavy military build-up. Between 1961 and 1967, both the Permanent Force of the South African armed forces and the voluntary Citizen Force were increased spectacularly and by 1970 it was possible for South Africa to mobilize, in case of emergency, 120,000 fully armed and trained men within two days.

Large quantities of new equipment were also purchased. For the first time France was approached as a source of major weapons, and the Mirage III with Nord and Matra missiles became South Africa's new fighter, Alouette II the general helicopter, and Alouette III was also ordered in large numbers. In the USA, orders were placed for thirty-seven Cessna 185 liaison planes and seven C-130B Hercules transports. Most of these items were delivered between 1962 and 1964. In 1961, the Simonstown Agreement was renewed, taking into account South Africa's arms requirements, and purchases from the UK included an order for Buccaneer marine bombers with six Canberras for interim training and six Wasp helicopters.

Within South Africa, the build-up of sophisticated equipment probably had two functions – to provide a show of strength to the local population, and to provide a deterrent against any contemplated attack from independent African states to the north. But the strategic considerations which have dominated so many discussions in Western Europe of South Africa's defence appear to have received fairly low priority. As early as 1963, Defence Minister Fouché explained that 'the first task of the defence forces is to help the police maintain law and order'.

Table 18 South Africa: supplies of major weapons, by supplier
US $ mn, at constant (1968) *prices*

Supplier:	USA	UK	France	Other	Total [a]
1950–54					
$ mn annual average	0·5	7·6	–	–	**8·1**
per cent	5·7	94·3	0·0	0·0	**100·0**
1955–9					
$ mn annual average	1·1	10·6	–	5·6	**17·4**
per cent	6·3	61·3	0·0	32·3	**100·0**
1960–64					
$ mn annual average	4·8	7·1	10·8	0·3	**23·1**
per cent	21·1	30·8	46·9	1·2	**100·0**
1965–9					
$ mn annual average	4·4	17·1	25·7	7·6	**54·8**
per cent	8·0	31·2	46·9	13·9	**100·0**
1970–72					
$ mn annual average	–	4·2	27·3	3·9	**35·3**
per cent	0·0	11·8	77·2	11·1	**100·0**
1950–72					
$ mn total [a]	**54·1**	**224·8**	**264·4**	**79·2**	**622·5**
Per cent of total	*8·7*	*36·1*	*42·5*	*12·7*	*100·0*

[a] Figures may not add up to totals owing to rounding.
Source: SIPRI worksheets.

The UN embargo

In August and December 1963 the United Nations passed resolutions which banned the sale of arms, and equipment to produce arms, to South Africa. Britain and France, however, reserved their right to supply equipment for external defence.

A series of national embargoes were announced during 1963 and 1964. When announcing its embargo in August 1963, the United States said that existing contracts would be fulfilled. Similarly, when the new British Labour government announced its embargo in November 1964, 'firm contracts' were excluded. When the Conservative government came to power in June 1970, it announced its intention to resume arms supplies for maritime defence. However, a legal inquiry into the obligations under the Simonstown Agreement determined that Britain was obliged only to supply spares for the vessels originally purchased under the agreement and Wasp helicopters for use on the three anti-submarine frigates supplied under the original agreement.

For a number of reasons, the UN resolutions have not been universally observed, and South Africa has continued its heavy military build-up. First of all, a number of the embargoes contained important loopholes.

The first of these allowed several countries to continue to supply spare parts and ammunition. Britain supplied spares for Canberra bombers, Buccaneer bombers and Shackleton maritime reconnaissance aircraft, and the Canadian government did not stop the supply of spares until July 1970. The United States, on the other hand, has pursued a more restrictive policy on the supply of spares, one result of which was that the Sikorsky helicopters had to be replaced owing to the shortage of spares.

By means of another loophole, Britain and, explicitly, the United States do not embargo equipment and raw materials that can be used for both civil and military purposes. The United States fulfilled a contract from 1962 for twelve Cessna 185s and has sold South Africa six C-130E Hercules transports which have a limited civil use. Britain also agreed to supply eighteen Beagle 206 light planes, but these were vetoed by the United States because they had US engines. Britain did, however, sell a total of six HS-125 transports, in place of the French Fan Jet Falcons vetoed by the United States. During 1970 it became known that a $70–80 million sale of military radar had been authorized under the Labour government. The equipment is said to have been used for a radar defence system to safeguard against an attack from the north, but according to the Foreign Office this sale did not constitute a breach of the embargo since it concerned electronics and communications equipment not covered in the embargo. Britain, the US, the Federal Republic of Germany, France and

Italy have also made contributions to the South African defence industry.

A third loophole in the embargo is the failure to veto all supplies of equipment with US or British designed or produced components. While the USA has vetoed some French and British equipment, it has not shown the same vigilance with respect to Italy. Thus, the Piaggio P.166, which South Africa chose in preference to the vetoed Beagle, also has a US engine, and Italy has exported about twenty Aermacchi-Lockheed 60 transports, built under US licence. Britain does not have the legal power to prevent the re-export of British-designed equipment, nor has it made any attempt to introduce such a law. Transall, the French military transport sold to South Africa, has a Rolls Royce engine. The Impala has a British-designed engine sub-licensed from Italy.

Another reason why South Africa has been able to continue its military build-up, despite the UN resolutions, is that some suppliers refused to restrict arms sales. In particular France was the main beneficiary of the arms embargoes. South Africa is now the third largest client of the French aerospace industry, and between 1961 and 1970 has imported $280 million worth of French military aeronautical equipment. A general arms deal was concluded in 1964 in which South Africa received a further squadron of Mirages; a new peak in French arms supplies occurred in the late 1960s with the delivery of sixteen Super Frelon heavy-lift helicopters, additional Alouette IIIs, Puma helicopters, nine Transall C-160 transports, and three 'Daphne' submarines.

The South African contribution to French weapon technology is particularly interesting. On 2 May 1969, the South African Minister of Defence, Piet Botha, announced that a low-level all-weather surface-to-air weapon system was under development by French companies according to specifications by South African experts for the South African government, which was financing the programme with some help from the French government. The system, called Cactus/Crotale, is made by Matra/Thomson Houston Hotchkiss Brandt, and its initial value is estimated at

$100 million. The first two batteries were delivered in 1971–2, with the third due to arrive during 1973.

In October 1970 it was announced that no French contracts for the sale of helicopters to South Africa would be renewed and that the export of arms and light armoured vehicles which could be used against guerillas should be reviewed. The announcement was greeted with calm in South African statements, which emphasized that South Africa had reached self-sufficiency in the field of armoured vehicles and small arms. And, indeed, military co-operation between France and South Africa was in no way broken. In June 1971 an agreement was signed for the licensed production of the Mirage III and the advanced fighter Mirage F-1 in South Africa.

Italy's main contribution to South Africa's defence was the permission to produce the M.B.326 under licence, with the accompanying parts and assistance. The M.B. 326 is an armed trainer, known in South Africa as Impala, and it is particularly suitable for counter-guerilla activities.

But perhaps the most important consequence of the embargo has been the development of an indigenous arms industry in South Africa, developed with great assistance from outside. In May 1965 Minister of Defence Botha announced that he had acquired 127 licences for local manufacture. In March 1966 Commandant-General Hienestra said that South Africa would shortly be manufacturing 140 different types of ammunition and bombs and was capable of manufacturing a whole range of infantry weapons and armoured plating equal to the best quality produced overseas. The FN 7·62 automatic rifle, and an improved version of the Mark R 1, with ammunition, have been manufactured in South Africa under Belgian licence. In March 1968, Botha told the Senate that South Africa had achieved self-sufficiency in rifles, mortars, grenades, small arms and ammunition. He also said that South Africa had developed napalm bombs, aerial bombs, smoke bombs, two types of cheap, highly effective shrapnel mines, and an anti-armour mine. Several hundred Panhard armoured cars have also been manufactured in South Africa under French licence. In 1972, Botha said that the Republic could no longer be isolated by arms boycotts but was absolutely self-sufficient with regard to its internal needs. South Africa also claims considerable progress in exporting arms.

The most important development in the aircraft field has been the production of the Atlas Impala, which began in 1967. Eventually about 70 per cent of the airframe and engine were to be built in South Africa. The Atlas factory was set up with French assistance from Sud Aviation, at a cost of $42 million. By the spring of 1969 an estimated 60 per cent of the initially planned 300 planes had been produced and assembled in South Africa. By 1972, the manufacture of a more advanced strike version was being planned. The agreement with France for the production of the Mirage under licence will, of course, further enhance South Africa's competence in the field of aircraft production.

South Africa appears also to have made some advances in the field of rocketry. The Rocket Research and Development Institute was established in 1963 and was reported to be developing a rocket-propelled surface-to-air missile. In December 1968, South Africa's first locally produced short-range rocket was successfully test-fired; it has a maximum range of four miles. On 2 May 1969, Botha announced that, in addition to the Cactus/Crotale surface-to-air missile system, an air-to-air missile, which has already been successfully tested, was under development.

Conclusion

It is clear that the arms embargo on South Africa has been ineffective in reducing South African armament, and has, instead, promoted the build-up of an indigenous defence industry. However, this is not to say that if it were possible to institute a complete embargo it would have no effect on South Africa's military strength.

South Africa has two types of weapon requirements: for COIN and for external defence. South Africa probably considers COIN requirements most urgent; they are militarily most important and this is also the field where its self-sufficiency is greatest. It is, however, far from complete. The only aircraft so far produced in South Africa is the Impala, which is excellent for COIN. But the maximum share of domestic production planned for the Impala is 70 per cent and an effective embargo on the remaining 30 per cent would cause great difficulties for South Africa. In addition, South Africa has no production capability in the field of helicopters, transport and reconnaissance aircraft, although the development of a light transport is considered. Its capability in the field of armoured cars can be disputed. It has been manufacturing the Panhard armoured car under licence from France, and, according to Piet Botha, a second generation of armoured cars, but reportedly South Africa bought 250 Panhard engines from France in March 1968 at a value of $850,000. The degree of self-sufficiency in small arms and infantry weapons is more complete and at the same time more difficult to assess. However, a number of these weapons are produced under foreign licence and it is possible that their production would be disturbed by an embargo on machinery and parts.

As an industrialized country it would probably be possible for South Africa to build up a relatively self-sufficient armaments base. This would, however, take considerable time and would be extremely expensive, especially if an embargo on all equipment, spares, machinery and production rights were instituted, denying South Africa continued access to international know-how. It is unlikely that at any stage South Africa would be capable of producing sophisticated conventional equipment on a completely indigenous basis. Only the great powers and Britain and France do this. If Britain and the United States were willing to close their loopholes in the embargo this would affect deliveries from nearly all other Western countries as well (since most equipment in these countries incorporates parts from either the US or Britain). Only a few types of French equipment, notably the Mirage, would be available. If the trend towards more international collaboration in weapon production continues, then this will further reduce the number of items available to South Africa.

Since an important function of sophisticated equipment is its demonstration effect, a continued embargo from all other countries would have considerable significance. It has often been suggested, with reason, that a lifting of the embargo on equipment suitable for external defence would demonstrate to both the South African government and its opposition implicit support from Western countries for the present regime.

11   Latin America

Compared with those of Asia and the Middle East, military budgets in Latin American countries are relatively low, and the equipment supplied was relatively unsophisticated until the late sixties. Total military budgets averaged $1·5 billion yearly in the early sixties, of which only 10 per cent was devoted to arms purchases. By 1971 Latin American military expenditures were approaching $3 billion.

Six countries – Argentina, Brazil, Chile, Cuba, Peru and Venezuela – are responsible for 85 per cent of the total arms purchases of the region. Brazil is the largest recipient, accounting for 25 per cent of the total, followed by Cuba, which accounts for a further 15 per cent. Cuban arms imports, however, were concentrated in a four-year period, 1960–63, when Cuba received $265 million worth of major weapons, mainly from the Soviet Union. These were the most sophisticated weapons in the region, and included MiG-21s, Guideline and Atoll missiles, and 'Komar' class patrol boats armed with Styx missiles, although some of these were later returned to the Soviet Union.

Until Peru purchased the Mirage 5 in 1968, no Latin American country, apart from Cuba, possessed supersonic aircraft. By 1972, Argentina, Brazil, Colombia and Venezuela had bought Mirage fighters. In 1968, only three countries, Chile, Argentina and Brazil, possessed missiles – the British ship-to-air missile, Seacat. But since then, all the five major recipients, Argentina, Brazil, Chile, Peru and Venezuela, have embarked on a modernization of their armed forces, purchasing both missiles and naval vessels from Europe, and gradually phasing out their Second World War equipment. The same trend also applies to the smaller Latin American arms recipients, for instance Ecuador and Colombia.

Two main factors account for the low level of arms imports until the end of the 1960s. The first is the dominant position of the United States, which has minimized supplier competition in the region. The second is the absence – with a few exceptions – of armed conflicts. Since coping with internal insurgency is

Table 19 Latin America: supplies of major weapons, by supplier
US $ mn, at constant (1968) *prices*

Supplier:	USA	UK	France	USSR	Other	Total[a]
1950–54						
$ mn annual average	26·6	21·2	0·3	–	15·4	**63·5**
per cent	41·9	33·3	0·5	0·0	24·3	**100·0**
1955–9						
$ mn annual average	41·1	21·3	3·9	0·8	37·7	**103·8**
per cent	39·6	20·5	2·9	0·7	36·3	**100·0**
1960–64						
$ mn annual average	50·5	22·0	2·8	54·0	8·0	**137·5**
per cent	36·7	16·0	2·1	39·3	5·9	**100·0**
1965–9						
$ mn annual average	34·9	15·9	8·9	2·3	21·5	**83·5**
per cent	41·8	19·1	10·6	2·7	25·7	**100·0**
1970–72						
$ mn annual average	42·6	18·3	24·2	9·0	43·0	**136·6**
per cent	30·5	13·4	17·7	6·6	31·8	**100·0**
1950–72						
$ mn total	**891·0**	**456·8**	**147·6**	**312·4**	**543·2**	**2,351·0**
Per cent of total	*37·9*	*19·4*	*6·3*	*13·3*	*23·1*	*100·0*

[a] Figures may not add up to totals owing to rounding.
Source: SIPRI worksheets.

largely the task of the police forces, the military role of the armed forces is limited. The demand for weapons thus stems only from the political role of the armed forces, which is of considerable importance. The choice of weapons, however, has in the past been heavily influenced by US decisions.

THE DEMAND FOR WEAPONS

The justification for possessing a military establishment must always be strategic. Yet the strategic function of Latin American armed forces is extremely limited. Disputes between Latin American states have been few and shallow and, on the whole, the Organization of American States (OAS) has been remarkably successful in arbitration. Although there was an increase in internal insurgencies in the early sixties, Latin American armed forces regard their primary role as that of 'national defence', relegating counter-insurgency to the relatively large and well-equipped police forces.

Yet, although the strategic function of Latin American armed forces is minimal, the political function – the power to make and unmake governments – is of primary importance. Weapons are not so much instruments of war as symbols of the power of the military establishment. In fact, the role of the military establishment as 'guardians' of the political institution is explicitly recognized by the constitutions of some Latin American countries. Generally, the armed forces intervene in politics when civilian governments are paralysed or seem likely to take measures which might threaten the status quo, although on occasion the armed forces have intervened with the object of taking radical measures of reform. But the military establishments are not unified. Indeed, most of the combat experience since 1942 has been gained in battles fought between different branches of the armed services, generally over the issue of granting civilian rule. For example, in 1962 the Ecuadorean air force, which supported civilian rule, defeated the army, which supported military rule. In May of the same year, the Venezuelan marine corps was defeated in battle by a combination of the army and air force, after attempting to overthrow the civilian government.

Undoubtedly, there is a relationship between the political role of the armed forces and the level of military spending. In only two Latin American countries apart from Cuba – Mexico and Costa Rica – are the armed forces firmly under civilian control.

And these same two countries devote the lowest proportion of GNP to defence in Latin America – 0·7 per cent and 0·5 per cent respectively, compared with 1·8 per cent for Latin America as a whole, during the years 1960–64. Beyond this, however, the relationship is difficult to ascertain and there are several reasons why attempts to relate the frequency of military coups and degrees of autocracy to levels of defence spending or arms procurement are bound to fail.

First of all, long periods of civilian rule are not necessarily evidence of politically weak military establishments. Governments, whether civilian or military, remain in power on military sufferance, and in order to retain their support most governments will assure the armed forces a steady proportion of the budget and independence in military policy-making. In an examination of the parliamentary debates in Argentina, Brazil and Chile, undertaken by the Center for International Studies at the Massachusetts Institute of Technology, it was found that defence expenditures are rarely questioned. And this is true even in periods of financial stringency. For example, in 1967, despite Peru's considerable external debt and despite US pressures, President Belaúnde Terry went ahead with the purchase of the Mirage 5 from France and gave the armed forces authority to float a $120 million loan to purchase military equipment. The loan was to be repaid by the government over a period of five years. Belaúnde was reported to have admitted privately that any attempts to impede the purchase of supersonic aircraft would have ruptured his relations with the military beyond repair.

Two exceptions to this general rule are Perón in Argentina and Goulart in Brazil. Between 1948 and 1952, Perón attempted to reduce the power of the military by drastically reducing military expenditures and by 'peronizing' – making political appointments in the armed forces. At the same time he tried to build up support among organized labour. Although growing opposition led him to modify this policy somewhat after 1952, he was overthrown in 1955 and military expenditures increased by 30 per cent. Although his powers were severely limited by the military establishment, Goulart, who was Vice-President of Brazil from 1955 to 1961 and President from 1961 to 1964, tried to pursue a similar policy. And after his overthrow in 1964, military expenditures rose by 50 per cent.

A second reason for the difficulty in finding a relationship between military coups and military expenditures is the fact that political issues are likely to take priority over military issues. The armed forces rarely overthrow governments merely to secure an increase in military expenditures, just as civilian governments rarely risk losing power merely in order to reduce military expenditures. More important issues are at stake. Indeed, periods in which the armed forces are preoccupied with political problems are often periods in which their demand for weapons is relatively low. Both 1962 and 1963 were peak years for military coups and inter-service battles. Military coups took place in Argentina, Guatemala, Peru, Ecuador, Honduras and the Dominican Republic, and inter-service battles took place in Argentina, Guatemala, Ecuador and Venezuela. The coups were all directed at the prevention of populist governments, while the battles were over who should rule. Yet 1962 and 1963 were low years for major arms imports and were not noticeably high for military expenditures.

Thus any government, whether civilian or military, with the exception of the two examples given above, will meet the demands of the military establishment. This, in turn, will ensure the continuance of the political role of the military establishment. The function of weapons in reinforcing the position of the military establishment is reflected in two features of Latin American arms procurement.

The first and perhaps most important feature is inter-service rivalry. Military establishments are rarely unified, and generally the divisions between various services reflect recruitment from different sections of society. The navies are generally recruited from wealthy urban and land-owning families, and they tend to play a conservative role in Latin American politics, supporting military intervention whenever a government shows radical tendencies. In contrast, the armies generally have the lowest class composition of the three services and have, on occasion, been radical in their demands. Often, the armies have been divided in their political loyalties, with some factions supporting the navy and other factions supporting the air force. Air forces have tended to play a moderate role, supporting civilian rule where this does not seriously threaten the status quo.

The divisions are often reflected in the acquisition of similar types of weapons by different branches of the armed services. Several navies have marine corps. In Argentina, Brazil and Peru there are naval and army air arms in addition to the air force. In the Dominican Republic, the National Guard acquired tanks in order to offset the tanks possessed by the air force.

It is possible to trace the inter-service rivalry in Argentina since 1950 through an examination of Argentinian arms procurement. As in several other countries, the Argentinian navy has supported conservative army factions while the air force has supported moderate army factions, and so procurement has tended to concentrate on the air force in periods of civilian rule and on the navy during periods of military rule.

Perón was elected President of Argentina in 1945, after the Group of United Officers, a group of colonels of which he was one, had seized power from the ruling conservative government in 1943. In addition to cutting military expenditure, he reduced the size of the army by one third, progressively civilianized the cabinet, established a workers' militia and undertook a number of far-reaching economic and social reforms. The one service he did not neglect was the air force. As well as purchasing large quantities of aircraft in the late 1940s, including 100 Meteors, thereby making Argentina the first Latin American country to acquire jet fighters, he also expanded the aircraft industry, such that between 1945 and 1950 four different fighters reached prototype stage.

But by the early fifties, his support was becoming eroded. He lost the support of the peasants, the Church and above all the armed forces. Difficulties in the aircraft industry led to the cutback of the aircraft programme. The navy had always been strongly opposed to the regime – there had been two attempted naval coups in 1944 and 1945 – so, despite the purchase of two cruisers in 1951, it was the navy which enabled a divided army to overthrow Perón in September 1955.

The military junta which succeeded Perón was dominated by the army and the navy. The President was General Aramburu from the army, the Vice-President was Admiral Isaac Rojas of the navy, and only one member of the five-man junta came from the air force. During this period, the naval air arm was greatly expanded. Sixty F-4U Corsair naval fighter-bombers, six Lockheed Neptune reconnaissance aircraft, twelve F-9F Panthers and an aircraft carrier were purchased. A number of aircraft were also purchased for the army. But at the same time an order for Canadian Sabre fighters for the air force was cancelled, the aircraft production programme was further reduced, and all plans for indigenous fighter aircraft were abandoned.

By 1958 the process of 'deperonizing' the armed forces was sufficiently complete for elections to be held. They were won by a wing of the radical party, led by Frondizi, with the support of the Peronists, who were themselves barred from participating in the elections. The new government ordered twenty-eight Sabre fighters from the United States and various other air-force equipment. In 1960, a US air-force mission was established, and work on combat design projects was reinitiated. Argentina also received two submarines and destroyers on loan from the United States during this period, but this was a consequence of the US naval aid programme rather than any particular Argentinian demand.

Frondizi was re-elected in March 1962. But, two weeks after the election, the new government was overthrown in a military coup. After the coup, there emerged two factions in the armed forces: the Gorillas, centred in the navy, infantry and engineering units, believed that Argentina was not ready for democracy and demanded indefinite military rule; the Legalists, centred in the cavalry (which included the mechanized brigades) and the air force, believed that the military should stay out of politics unless the alternative is chaos or dictatorship. The acknowledged leader of the Legalists was the cavalry officer General Onganía. In April 1963 the issue was resolved in a pitched battle in which the air force destroyed the naval air arm.

Table 20 Five main Latin American recipients: supplies of sophisticated weapons[a]

	Argentina	Brazil	Chile	Peru	Venezuela
1950 1951	2 cruisers, 'Brooklyn' class	1 cruiser, 'St Louis' class 1 cruiser, 'Brooklyn' class	2 cruisers, 'Brooklyn' class		(24) Vampires
1952			17 F-47 D Thunderbolts	3 destroyer escorts, 'Bostwich' class	6 Canberras
1953 1954			32 B-26 Invaders	2 submarines, 'Abateo' class	2 destroyers
1955		25 F-47 D Thunderbolts 10 Corvettes	5 Vampires	14 F-86 F Sabres 8 B-26 Invaders	15 Venoms and Sea Venoms 22 F-26 Sabres (3) Vampires
1956	10 F-4U Corsairs			16 Hawker Hunters 8 Canberras	1 destroyer 3 frigates, 'Almirante' class 10 Canberras
1957	12 F-9F Panthers 52 F-4U Corsairs	24 B-26 Invaders 2 submarines, 'Gato' class		2 submarines, 'Abateo' class 60 Sherman M-4s	3 frigates, 'Almirante' class (15) AMX-13s
1958 1959	1 aircraft carrier	2 destroyers, 'Fletcher' class	20 F-80C Shooting Stars	1 Hawker Hunter 10 F-80C Shooting Stars	
1960	28 F-86 F Sabres 2 submarines, 'Balao' class	20 F-80C Shooting Stars	2 destroyers, 'Almirante' class	1 cruiser, 'Almirante' class 1 cruiser, 'Almirante' class 1 destroyer, 'Fletcher' class 2 corvettes	1 submarine, 'Balao' class
1961	3 destroyers, 'Fletcher' class	1 aircraft carrier 2 destroyers, 'Fletcher' class	2 submarines, 'Balao' class	1 destroyer, 'Fletcher' class 40 M-24 Chaffees	

Table 20 – contd

	Argentina	Brazil	Chile	Peru	Venezuela
1962					
1963		2 submarines, 'Balao' class	2 destroyers, 'Fletcher' class Seacat missiles		1 submarine, 'Balao' class (3) Canberras 74 Fiat F-86 Sabres
1964					
1965	Seacat missiles	Seacat missiles 55 M-41s			
1966	12 A-4 Skyhawks		4 escort destroyers	2 Canberras	
1967	13 A-4 Skyhawks 2 destroyers, 'Fletcher' class	1 destroyer, 'Fletcher' class			
1968	1 aircraft carrier	1 destroyer, 'Fletcher' class			
1969	60 AMX-13s Cobra missiles Nord AS 11, AS 12 missiles		21 Hawker Hunters	14 Mirage 5s 78 AMX-13s	Seacat missile
1970	25 A-4 Skyhawks 12 Canberras Tigercat missiles		4 Hawker Hunters	6 Canberras 1 destroyer, 'Terre' class 1 destroyer, 'Terre' class 10 Exocet missiles	
1971	2 submarines, 'Balao' class 2 destroyers, 'Fletcher' class	3 submarines, 'Guppy' type			
1972	16 A-4 Skyhawks		7 Hawker Hunters 1 cruiser	10 Exocet missiles	20 Canadian F-5s 100 Sidewinder missiles 1 submarine 142 AMX-30s
1972–3	14 Mirage IIIs R 530 missiles	16 Mirage IIIs R 530 missiles 3 submarines, 'Oberon' class			

[a] Sophisticated weapons include: jet combat aircraft, aircraft carriers, destroyers, frigates, corvettes, cruisers, submarines, tanks and missiles. Items in italics were purchased from Europe; all other items were supplied by the United States.
Source: SIPRI country registers. Figures in brackets are estimates.

As a result of the air force victory, elections were held the same month, and were won by Illia, leader of the other wing of the radicals. In 1965, the Argentina government persuaded the United States to supply fifty A-4 Skyhawks for the air force and M-41 tanks for the cavalry. But the regime depended on the support of the Legalists, and this support was not to last long. On 28 June 1966, after disagreement had arisen over Illia's refusal to send troops to the Dominican Republic, his lack of enthusiasm for an Inter-American Force, and his refusal to intervene in the universities to 'clean out the communists', Onganía led a coup to overthrow him. More important, it appears that the military were afraid of a Peronist victory in the elections due in 1967.

A week before the coup, the United States had decided to suspend delivery of twenty-five of the fifty Skyhawks, following a protest in the Senate Preparedness Investigating Subcommittee that the US Naval Air Reserve Wing had been receiving 'substantially inferior' types. After the coup, the USA also reversed its decision to deliver M-41 tanks.

The Argentinian response was to launch the Europe Plan in 1967. This was intended to expand the domestic defence industry with European help, and it is evidence of the new military unity that the first two major projects are the assembly of the French AMX-13 tanks and the assembly of two West German submarines.

A second feature of the demand for weapons in Latin America is inter-state rivalry. From an examination of the correspondence between arms procurement in the five major Latin American recipient countries – Argentina, Brazil, Chile, Peru and Venezuela – it might be inferred that the level of armaments considered commensurate with the status of the military establishment in any one country is judged with reference to the level of armaments possessed by the military establishment of another country.

Argentina and Brazil, as the largest recipients, tend to compete with one another. Chile generally follows the Argentinian lead. Peru, which has always displayed special concern with Chile's military posture – a concern which dates back to the war in the 1870s, when Chile annexed a large part of Peruvian territory –

justifies rather large purchases in terms of Chile's acquisitions. In the past, Venezuela has maintained a superiority in air-force equipment over all other Latin American countries, but has made no attempt to match naval procurement: this may well reflect different political roles for the services in Venezuela. In 1953, for example, Brazil purchased seventy Meteors from Britain. Argentina ordered F-86 Sabres from Canada in 1955, although the order was cancelled after the 1955 coup. Chile acquired B-26 bombers from the United States and five Vampires from Britain. Peru over-reacted by acquiring not only B-26 bombers and F-86 Sabres, but also Hawker Hunters and Canberras. Between 1955 and 1957, Venezuela acquired fifteen British Venoms, twenty-five F-86 Sabres from the United States and ten Canberras from Britain. In 1958, Argentina and Brazil ordered aircraft carriers within weeks of each other, although the Brazilian aircraft carrier was not delivered until 1961. A similar pattern is discernible in the recent round of combat aircraft purchases and naval re-equipment.

In the past, this rivalry has been supported by the United States and, in particular, the United States has been careful to maintain a balance between Peru and Chile. Over the entire period, US military aid to Peru has been only $15 million higher than military aid to Chile. In 1951, the United States sold two cruisers each to Argentina, Brazil and Chile and in 1959 embarked on a naval aid programme under which it supplied four refurbished 'Fletcher' class destroyers to Brazil, three to Argentina, and two each to Peru and Chile. The USA also supplied two 'Balao' class submarines each to Argentina, Brazil and Chile and one to Venezuela.

THE ROLE OF THE UNITED STATES

Because of the US hegemony over Latin America – the dependence of Latin American countries on US investment, the ability of the USA to intervene militarily, the various collective security arrangements and assistance programmes which bring Latin

American countries more closely into the US orbit – the choice of weapons has in the past been heavily influenced by US decisions.

Indeed, Latin America is often described as the United States' 'backdoor', and ever since the enunciation of the Monroe Doctrine in 1823, US policy towards the area has been based on the dual aim of stability and the prevention of extra-regional incursions. Since the Second World War, the prevention of extra-regional incursions has been aimed primarily at socialist countries. Cuba is the only country which received Soviet military aid. The purchase of Czechoslovak small arms by Guatemala in 1954 provided the justification for indirect military intervention there. However, the USA has also opposed the extension of influence by West European countries through the sale of arms and the missions that accompany them.

Throughout the period, US military assistance has met with strong Congressional opposition. In particular, Congress has charged the Administration with shoring up military regimes. Successively lower ceilings have been placed on the size of the military-aid programme, and a number of restrictions on the content and direction of military assistance have also been imposed. For example, an amendment to the Military Sales Act of 1970 limits arms deliveries to regimes which 'deny social progress'.

The main importance of US military aid lies in the opportunities it creates for fostering close ties between the United States and the military establishments. However, to appease Congress, the programme has generally been justified on strategic grounds. Until 1960, the main strategic justification for military assistance was the collective defence of the Western hemisphere against external attack. An Inter-American Defense Board was established for co-operative planning, and Mutual Defense Assistance Agreements were signed with most of the Latin American countries.

It is clear that the US military-aid programme during the fifties was not intended to develop military forces capable of resisting an external enemy. Little was achieved by the Inter-American Defense Board. Since details of Latin American forces were known only to the United States, it was in any case incapable of preparing any comprehensive military plans. Military assistance was provided, in part, as payment for the assurances given in the bilateral treaties. Provisions such as the 'control of trade with nations which threaten the security of the Western hemisphere' ensured the United States of continuing support in foreign policy. Even under the naval-aid programme, it is unlikely that the United States really supposed that the refurbished Second World War destroyers and submarines could provide adequate defence against a sophisticated enemy.

Aid was provided in a haphazard manner. Each of the services had its own military mission in the different Latin American countries, but there was no co-ordination between them. Indeed, there was a tendency for US services to transfer their own rivalries and prejudices towards each other to their Latin American counterparts, thus exacerbating inter-service factionalism. There were also several programmes outside the scope of the military-assistance programme. The 'vessel-loan' legislation was one; the army and air force training programmes were others. At their training schools in the Canal Zone the US army and air force trained 4,619 students between 1950 and 1958, compared with 5,560 trained under MAP at the same schools.

The policy changed in 1960. The summary presentation of the proposed Mutual Defense and Assistance Program for the financial year 1964 stated:

Military assistance programs for Latin America were orientated to hemispheric conditions prior to 1960. As it became clear that there was no threat of significant external aggression, emphasis shifted to strengthening internal security capabilities for use against Castro-Communist activities or other internal disruption or banditry and to actions designed to contribute to economic and social development. Limited assistance is also given for such activities as harbor defense, coastal patrol, and surveillance.

By the financial year 1967, 76 per cent of the military-aid programme was devoted to internal security.

While the US Administration is undoubtedly seriously concerned with the possibility of another Cuban-type revolution and is committed to counter such a possibility in Latin America with considerable efficiency, the importance of counter-insurgency in the military-aid programme can be exaggerated. To policy-makers finding it increasingly difficult to justify a programme based on the external threat to the Western hemisphere, the Cuban revolution and Khrushchev's oft-quoted speech of January 1961 calling for wars of liberation presented the opportunity to

Table 21 Latin America (excluding Cuba): supplies of items suitable for counter-insurgency

| | US supplies | | | Non-US supplies | | |
	Heli-copters	Trainers	Patrol boats[a]	Helicopters	Trainers	Patrol boats[a]
1950–59	61	222	30	6	–	12
1960–69	301	357	41	48	99	15
1970–72	66	35	8	3	51	5
1950–72	**428**	**614**	**79**	**57**	**150**	**32**

[a] Including gun-boats and motor torpedo boats.
Source: SIPRI worksheets.

give the military-aid programme a 'new look'. It must have been with relief that the State Department was able, in 1964, to describe hemispheric defence as an 'outmoded concept'. In fact, the United States was still able to supply conventional sophisticated equip-ment under the credit-sales programme and under the vessel-loan legislation. In 1965, the USA agreed to supply Skyhawks and M-41 tanks to Argentina, M-41 tanks and destroyers to Brazil and F-86 aircraft to Peru. Countries such as Chile, Argen-tina and Brazil continued to receive a major share of the military assistance programme although they faced no internal 'threat'.

Indeed, the counter-insurgency programme can be described merely as a streamlined method of increasing the US influence among Latin American armed forces, through the emphasis on such things as training and civic action. As Professor Lieuwen stated in his book *Arms and Politics*:

The great importance attached to military assistance in securing Latin America's political co-operation flows in large measures from the political role of Latin America's armed forces and their continuing desire for more arms . . . Because of the roles military personalities play in government and politics, the United States, through its military programmes, makes a pointed effort to influence them. The mission programme, for example, which . . . serves no important military purpose, is nevertheless most useful in providing opportunities for cementing political as well as professional relationships between the sending and the recipient governments. Also the practice of training Latin American officers in the United States helps to secure their political sympathies.

Except for a brief period under the Kennedy Administration, the US government has made little attempt to discourage the political role of the military. And even during the Kennedy era politicians such as McNamara stressed 'the essential role of the Latin American military as a stabilizing force', while US Senators described Latin American officers as 'our staunchest supporters' and 'a strong anti-communist core'.

Training. Training has always been an important part of the military-assistance programme to Latin America. The proportion of military assistance devoted to training purposes has been roughly double the worldwide proportion. During the sixties, the emphasis has increased. The share of military assistance devoted to training averaged 8 per cent in the period 1950–64. By 1967, this proportion had risen to 16 per cent.

This increased emphasis was accompanied by an increased emphasis on the non-military aspects of training programmes. During the fifties it was argued that training was necessary to ensure the proper use of weapons. During the sixties, however, this aspect has rarely been mentioned, and instead training has been justified on the grounds that contact with US officers will develop the notion of a professional, that is, non-political, army, that Latin American officers trained in the United States are exposed to democratic principles and will return to tell their relatives and friends of the American mode of life, and that training programmes can encourage the modernizing, educative role of the Latin American forces.

In recent years, priority has been given to training in counter-insurgency. The bulk of Latin Americans are trained at the Army School in the Caribbean, renamed the School of the Americas, and at the USAF School in the Caribbean, both in the Canal Zone. Also stationed in the Canal Zone is the 'Special Action Force for Latin America 8th Special Force', which has seventeen mobile training teams for teaching counter-insurgency skills ready for dispatch all over Latin America. (These teams, known as MTTs, were responsible for training the Bolivian Rangers, which captured Che Guevara, and also for the successful counter-insurgency effort in Colombia.) Latin Americans are also trained at the Special Warfare School in Fort Bragg. Between 1960 and 1962, 112 Latin Americans were trained there.

Training in counter-insurgency is not only confined to military skills. At the School of the Americas, the Department of Internal Security is reported to provide 'instruction in every aspect of counter-insurgency: military, para-military, political, sociological, and psychological'. The same is also true of the course at Fort Bragg.

In 1962, despite the objection of Mexico and Brazil, the United States sponsored the establishment of the Inter-American Defense College at Fort MacNair in Washington. The College provides a six-month advanced programme for twenty-five to thirty-five senior general staff officers. According to the Center for International Studies at MIT:

The purpose of this training goes beyond teaching technical or tactical skills. It is intended to be a means by which Latin American officers become acquainted with their US counterparts, to improve relations between them, and to instill in them professional skills and attitudes in developing effective and sound relations.

These programmes have been least successful in separating professional and political interests. Many of the officers trained in the United States – among them General Onganía of Argentina – have participated in military coups. The fact that political subjects are taught in the training programmes suggests that this aspect has never been very important. More important are the ties developed between the US and Latin American military establishments and the commitment to defeat communism that such contracts may bring about.

Civic action. While the US government may recognize the progressive character of the military establishments, their view is not always shared by other sections of the local population. To ensure wider acceptance of this view is one of the main purposes of military civic action, that is, the use of military forces for projects which contribute to economic and social development. In his book *The Essence of Security*, R. S. McNamara pointed out that in Latin America these programmes have a powerful effect in altering 'the negative image of the military man as the oppressive preserver of the stagnant status quo'.

Civic-action programmes reached a peak in 1963 and thereafter declined. They were not particularly popular with either the military or civilians. And there is no real evidence to show that they improve the military image. With less than ten military regimes and many more countries threatened with such regimes, it is better to ensure that the military are friendly than that they are reformist.

The best way to ensure friendliness was to maintain the US monopoly over arms supplies and military missions. Although since 1940 the USA has maintained a monopoly over military missions in Latin America, it has been less successful in maintaining a monopoly over equipment supplies. This is particularly true of deliveries of sophisticated weapons. Although until 1969, when Argentina, Brazil and Chile ordered European submarines, all the submarines possessed by Latin American countries came from the USA, all the three aircraft carriers purchased by Argentina and Brazil have come from Europe, while the only missile possessed by Latin American countries is the British Seacat. The proportion of combat aircraft purchased outside the United States rose strikingly during the sixties.

There were probably two reasons why Latin American countries bought sophisticated equipment from Europe during the fifties. First, it represented, as it still does, a sign of independence from the United States. Secondly, it is probable that, with constant Congressional supervision, there were simply insufficient funds to meet all Latin American demands.

The emphasis on internal security during the sixties made it more difficult to defend sales of sophisticated weapons. Congress was no longer willing to authorize large grants for the delivery of such weapons and instead the United States appealed to Latin American nations not to buy them at all. At Punta del Este in April 1967, the presidents of the Western hemisphere were persuaded to express their intention 'to limit military expenditures in proportion to the actual demands of national security, in accordance with each country's constitutional provisions'. And, also in 1967, two amendments to the Foreign Assistance Act – the Symington and Conte-Long amendments – required that economic assistance be curtailed to any country buying sophisticated weapons it does not need and cannot afford. These amendments were incorporated into the Military Sales Bill of 1968, and expanded to cover military credit sales.

However, the main concern was with the ability of countries to buy from other sources, as is demonstrated by the recent history of Latin American arms purchases. In 1965, the USA agreed to supply fifty A-4 Skyhawks to Argentina, after Argentina had threatened to purchase equivalent French or British planes. It was argued that if the United States supplied key weapons to Latin American nations, it could maintain greater control over their use and over proliferation. But only twenty-five A-4s were delivered because of the shortages in Viet-Nam.

Following the Argentine lead, Peru, over-reacting, began to make inquiries about supersonic fighters, requesting the F-5 from the United States and the Lightning from Britain. At the time, some sources suggested that Peru was negotiating for the Lightning in order to persuade the United States to release the F-5 before 1969. Later it was revealed that Washington had put pressure on Britain not to supply the Lightning. The United States refused to supply the F-5 before 1969 but offered Peru twelve F-86 Sabres. The offer was refused. In 1967, the United States blocked the sale of six Canberras to Peru, arguing that the sale would cause too much financial strain and would be inconsistent with the Alliance for Progress. The same arguments were used to dissuade Peru from buying the Mirage. There was also the added argument that the purchase of the supersonic Mirage would mean the introduction of a new type of weapon into Latin America and would lead to a new arms race.

In October 1967, French sources reported that a deal to supply twelve Mirage 5s to Peru had been signed in August. Two weeks later the United States offered the F-5 to five Latin American nations – Argentina, Brazil, Chile, Peru and Venezuela. The State Department spokesman, Closkey, said: 'We expect the purchase of F-5s to be spread over several years and will not sufficiently affect the economic development expectations of the interested countries.' The following year, after Peru had announced its intention to buy the Mirage, Secretary Clifford defended the offer of F-5s on the grounds that it was a less sophisticated plane than the Mirage.

Yet the Mirage 5 Peru purchased is a simplified version of the Mirage III, developed in the same way as the F-5, especially for the developing countries' market. Although probably more expensive, there is no reason to suppose that it is significantly more sophisticated or inferior for internal security purposes.

The purchase of Mirages and seventy-eight AMX-13 tanks was announced by Peru in April 1968, and in early May it was reported that Britain was selling Peru six Canberras which had been built entirely with British finance. On 16 May foreign-aid officials warned Peru that they would 'be unable to come to any decisions' on 'new loans' for projects and programme work if Peru's budget for 1968 included 'unnecessary military expenditure', that is if Peru persisted in buying the Mirage. A report in the *International Herald Tribune* on 2 November 1967 stated that US diplomats had quietly warned Brazil that the purchase of the Mirage might jeopardize the US aid programme to Brazil. The following day the State Department denied that any sort of threat had been issued but pointed out that Congress was responsible for decisions on aid and was opposed to excessive military purchases.

It is clear from the fact that while the United States is prepared to offer the F-5, roughly the equivalent of the Mirage 5, and the A-4, only marginally inferior to the Mirage III, and yet apply pressure to prevent the purchase of Mirages that the main concern is with maintaining the US monopoly. Even the economic argument is not convincing: the French terms are probably as favourable as those offered by the United States. It is also difficult to find a convincing justification for the veto on the Canberras to Peru. Since the planes had been in service with the RAF for several years, they cannot have been very expensive. Nor did they represent the introduction of a new type of weapon into the area as Peru had already purchased eight Canberras in 1956, and Venezuela had purchased ten in 1957.

Subsequently there has been a more determined effort in Latin America to increase military independence from the United States. Both Argentina and Brazil have launched programmes to develop their domestic defence industries: Argentina is developing its vehicle and ordnance production, with a view to export, and Brazil is producing the Macchi jet trainer under licence.

The search for European combat aircraft has also intensified. The day after, the USA announced the sale of sixteen Skyhawks to Argentina and its willingness to supply fifty Skyhawks or F-5s to Brazil, Chile and Colombia, Brazil announced on 18 May 1970 the purchase of sixteen Mirage IIIs. Argentina ordered fourteen Mirage IIIs, later on in the year. And in December, Colombia announced the purchase of eighteen Mirage 5s, and an arrangement for forty-three pilots to train in France. In the meantime, Argentina had ordered twelve refurbished Canberras from Britain and Chile had ordered a further nine Hawker Hunters, in addition to the twenty-one ordered in 1967.

During 1972, Venezuela concluded a large tank deal with France and ordered fifteen Mirage IIIs and 5s but it also purchased twenty F-5s. These were bought from Canada because of the cheaper price but their armament, 100 Sidewinder missiles, came from the USA. Both Ecuador and Chile are in the market for fighter aircraft. In Ecuador, the Anglo-French Jaguar is reported to be preferred. There were numerous reports during the autumn of 1972 that Chile was about to conclude an agreement for Soviet weapons, including the MiG-21, on very generous credit terms. In view of the ambivalent political situation in Chile and the very strong position the USA has always taken concerning the presence of Soviet weapons in Latin America, such a deal would appear unlikely.

Naval programmes were also launched. Argentina refused a US offer to loan two submarines; instead two submarines were ordered from the Federal Republic of Germany to be assembled in Argentina. Argentina also purchased an aircraft carrier from the Netherlands and ordered two missile-firing frigates from Britain. Brazil and Chile followed Argentina's lead and each ordered 'Oberon' class submarines from Britain. Chile also ordered two 'Leander' class frigates, while Peru purchased two second-hand 'Daring' class destroyers from the British Ministry of Defence. In September 1970, Brazil ordered six Vosper Thorneycroft frigates, at a cost of $280 million, armed with Seacat, Exocet and Ikara missiles. Two of these frigates are to be built in Brazil. Other purchases from Europe include six West German coastal minesweepers, for Brazil, Exocet missiles for Peru and Chile, AMX-13 tanks, Panhard armoured cars and West German patrol boats for Ecuador, and Vosper patrol boats and Otomat missiles for Venezuela.

Already by March 1970, General Warren, responsible for the aid and sales programmes, was admitting that 'the USA is losing the military equipment market of Latin America'. At the same time, there has been a drastic reduction in grant aid programmes due to increasing Congressional restrictions. In the financial year 1969, programmes to Argentina, Brazil and Peru were all curtailed. The number of US military personnel posted to military missions in Latin America fell from 791 in July 1969 to 498 in November 1970.

It seems that US policy towards Latin America is approaching a crisis, and the radical nature of the regimes in Peru, Bolivia and Chile is causing considerable concern. As one US official stated:

'We may no longer have anyone to assist if the military in Latin America become part of the official leftist establishment and the guerillas turn respectable.' At the same time, the ability to influence the conservative regimes is reduced by the restrictions on military aid and by their increasing arms purchases from Europe. Congress is no longer so willing to authorize military equipment for counter-insurgency. After the war between El Salvador and Honduras, Senator W. Fulbright called for a complete halt in military aid to Latin America. When Assistant Secretary of State Charles A. Meyer told the Senate Foreign Relations Committee that military aid played a 'fundamental role in strengthening counter-insurgency forces where inadequate and inequitable economic and social structures' made governments vulnerable to subversion, Senator Church asked: 'Why shouldn't they be subverted?'

12 Domestic Defence Production in Third World Countries

In recent years, several of the more advanced Third World countries have attempted to produce their own major weapons, either through collaboration with rich countries or as an indigenous venture. The main reason for doing so is to reduce dependence on foreign suppliers, to avoid the political strings attached to arms imports and to ensure the availability of the necessary spares and supplies in times of crisis.

Twenty-seven Third World countries are known to produce military equipment required by their armed forces. Of these, twenty-four are producing small arms and eighteen are producing naval vessels, generally of a very simple design, and mostly patrol boats and support ships such as tugs, oilers and landing craft. In these fields, production is relatively easy and can be regarded as part of the normal industrialization process at its early stages. But at the same time it is in these fields that potential suppliers are most numerous and where, therefore, the dangers of dependence on outside suppliers are least.

From a military point of view, and for the sake of independence from outside suppliers, the indigenous production of aircraft and missiles is more significant. It is also more rare. Only eleven Third World countries have established aircraft industries. Of these, nine have produced indigenously designed military aircraft, prototype failures not included. Only Israel has a locally designed missile in current production.

Armoured fighting vehicles have been produced in six Third World countries. Only Brazil and South Africa claim success with indigenous designs.

Table 22 Survey of production of major weapons and components in Third World countries, 1950–72*a*

Country	Military aircraft			Guided missiles			Armoured fighting vehicles		Warships		Military electronics		Aero-engines	
	A	B	C	A	B	C	A	B	A	B	A	B	A	B
Argentina	×	×	×*b*	×*c*			×		×	×				×
Brazil	×	×	×*b*	×	×			×	×	×	×	×		×
Burma										×				
Chile		×								×				
China, People's Rep. of*d*	×	×		×	×		×	×	×	×	×	×	×	×
Colombia										×				
Dominican Republic										×				
Egypt	×	×	×*e*		×									×
Gabon										×				
Greece	×*f*													
India	×	×		×			×	×	×	×	×	×	×	×
Indonesia	×									×				
Iran	×*g*													
Israel	×	×			×	×		×		×		×	×	×
Korea, North										×				
Korea, South	×									×				
Libya			×*e*											
Mexico		×								×				
Pakistan	×			×			×*h*							
Philippines*i*	×			×			×		×		×			
Rhodesia										×				
South Africa	×				×	×	×	[×]		×*k*		×	×	×
Syria										×				
Taiwan	×	×												
Thailand	×								×	×				
Turkey	×*j*	×							×					
Viet-Nam, South	×													

A = Licensed production
B = Indigenous production
C = Co-development with a foreign company
[] = Unconfirmed

ORDNANCE

In this connection, it is interesting to note that very few countries have attempted to acquire self-sufficiency in the production of small arms. Only India and Israel can be said to be self-sufficient, and although Egypt claimed self-sufficiency in 1956, when it was producing the Swedish m/42 Ljungman rifle and the M/45 sub-machine-gun under licence, since that date Egypt has imported large quantities of Soviet and Czechoslovak rifles. Pakistan and North Korea also claim self-sufficiency, although Pakistan continues to import such weapons.

While many countries produce sub-machine-guns and machine-guns, few countries have established facilities for producing medium-range weapons such as artillery, mortars or grenades, or the necessary ammunition. The latter include only Argentina, Brazil, India, Israel and South Africa. Again of special interest is the fact that most countries produce this type of weapon under licence from foreign countries. Several countries have introduced modifications to foreign weapons, but only seven produce their own indigenously designed types. Argentina has produced a series of sub-machine-guns since 1943. The Dominican Republic

Notes to Table 22

a Including production planned in 1972, whenever these plans are estimated to be remotely possible.

b Negotiations under way between Argentina and Brazil in 1972.

e Argentina plans production of surface-to-surface and surface-to-air missiles.

d Production under Soviet licences up to 1960. Thereafter indigenous development based on Soviet models.

e Negotiations under way between Egypt and Libya in 1972, as well as between Egypt and eighteen Arab states for the establishment of joint defence industries.

f First agreement with Dassault–Lockheed–Olympic Airways (France–USA–Greece) consortium in January 1972, initially for repair, maintenance and overhaul facilities.

g First agreement with Lockheed (USA) in 1970 and with Agusta (Italy) in 1971, initially for repair, maintenance and overhaul facilities.

h The five-year plan for defence production launched in 1969 includes production of tanks.

i Philippine proposal in April 1972 for a five-year plan with US aid.

j Negotiations under way in 1972 with France/Federal Republic of Germany, possibly for production of the Alpha jet trainer. Discussions also held with the United States for eventual assembly of the F-104 and F-5 fighters.

k Advanced plans for naval production by 1972.

has produced its own Cal. 30 rifle and the Cristobal Model 2 carbine. India has produced the Ishapore rifle, among other types. The Israeli-designed sub-machine-gun Uzi is recognized as the best of its type by many experts and Israel is now developing a new machine-gun, known as 'Dror'. Mexico has designed several light machine-guns, and Turkey has been well known as a manufacturer of rifles since 1890.

ARMOURED FIGHTING VEHICLES

The most important projects at present in this field concern the production of armoured fighting vehicles under licence. Since 1965 India has produced a model of the Vickers medium tank, called the 'Vijayanta'. Israel has designed two so-called hybrid tanks based on American Shermans: the 'Isherman' tank consists of a Sherman chassis, French turret and British or French 105-mm. guns, while the 'Super Sherman' is made out of a Sherman chassis, Sherman M-50 and M-4 turret and French guns. Both have proved successful in desert warfare. Argentina assembles the French AMX-13 tank under a licence agreement of 1968, and South Africa has for many years assembled both the AMX-13 and Panhard armoured cars under licence. Brazil has designed an armoured reconnaissance vehicle. South Africa claims to have designed a light tank. Military trucks are not included here, because they are produced in several of the countries which possess automobile industries.

AIRCRAFT

The types of aircraft produced in Third World countries are mostly light planes, trainers and transports. Only four aircraft – produced in Brazil, India, Israel and South Africa – have jet engines, and these are all imported. The engines and propellers required for piston-engined planes are also generally imported. Indeed, only two countries – Argentina and India – have produced indigenously designed aero-engines for military aircraft. Egypt attempted to produce a turbojet engine to power a supersonic fighter, but the project has been abandoned. Five countries produce engines under licence, in connection with licensed aircraft projects. Rolls Royce engines are produced in Argentina, Brazil, India and South Africa. The French Artouste is produced in India, and Turbomeca engines are under production in Israel.

Only three Third World countries have designed and developed jet fighters. The Argentinian I.A. 58 counter-insurgency aircraft entered production in 1972 for a first batch of fifty planes for the air force. The plane is expected to have a significant export potential for other Latin American countries: in fact, Peru has already ordered twenty-five aircraft. Although this first version is powered by a French turboprop engine, the development of a jet-powered version, also with a French powerplant, is proceeding, as is the development of a high-speed liaison version.

The Indian HF-24 was originally designed as a supersonic fighter. The project was started in 1956, but by 1972 only about sixty-five aircraft had been produced, without yet reaching the planned Mach 2 speed capability. The main difficulty has been in obtaining a suitable engine. Initially India was to purchase the NATO-backed Bristol-Siddeley BO3 12 turbojet, but after the development of this engine was cancelled, Soviet engines were tried instead. The Klimov VK-7 turbojet proved impossible to fit to the existing airframe of the HF-24 plane, and in 1961 the Soviet RD 9-F axial-flow engine was bought. A licence production agreement for this engine was signed the following year, despite the fact that it too needed extensive modification before it could fit the airframe, and that at most it could only provide a speed of Mach 1·4. Eventually the modified Soviet engines were found to be 30 per cent below specification. But the project was not cancelled until February 1964, when the Soviet Union finally stated that these engines could not possibly be modified to the Indian requirements.

The Indians then tried co-operation with Egypt, trying to fit the Helwan E-300 engine to the HF-24 airframe. Interestingly, at this time the heads of these projects in both Egypt and India were

German scientists. The cancellation of the Egyptian programme put an end to this venture. A Public Accounts Committee reported to the Indian Parliament in 1966 that total expenditure on these abortive programmes for the Mach 2 engine was more than $3 million. The present aircraft are powered by two British Orpheus 703 turbojets, producing a speed of Mach 1·02. But the future plans involve re-engining the aircraft with the Rolls Royce/ Turbomeca Adour, which at last will provide the Mach 2 speed. By 1972 the indigenous content of the H F-24 was stated to be 70 per cent. The engine, the entire undercarriage, the breaking system and the communications and electronic equipment are still being imported.

Egypt also developed a jet fighter, based on a Spanish project, the HA-300, which came into being shortly after the Second World War under the leadership of the German constructor Willy Messerschmidt. When the Spanish government decided to cancel the project in the late fifties, an agreement was reached for the transfer of the entire programme to the aircraft works at Helwan, Egypt. But numerous difficulties were encountered, and the project was abandoned in 1969.

Most countries which have established aircraft industries produce aircraft under licence. The Italian Aermacchi M.B.326 armed trainer is in current licence production in Brazil and South Africa. South Africa has also obtained the licence for the French Mirage III and F-1. India produces the Soviet MiG-21 in two versions, and the French Alouette III helicopter, and considers re-opening the production of the British light fighter, the Gnat. The USA has not sold any production licence of more sophisti- cated aircraft: Taiwan is producing the Pazmany PL 1 mono- plane and the Bell 205 helicopter.

Licensed production can mean anything from mere assembly to the local manufacture of nearly all parts and components. Only Israel has reached the latter stage. Indeed Israel has made several modifications to the Fouga Magister, which it produces under licence, not only to the aircraft itself but also to the jigs and tools needed to manufacture it. In other Third World countries, nearly all the components are imported, including the engines and electronic equipment. One reason, among many, for this is the unwillingness of licensing countries to part with manufacturing know-how. India, in particular, has had such difficulties with respect to the Soviet Union – the difficulty in obtaining design plans prevented the Indians from making desired modifications to the MiG-21. The MiG programme negotiations started in 1962, but it got under way only after 1964 when the Soviet Union agreed to provide technical aid for the construction of the three factories needed to produce airframe, engine and electronics. Production started in 1966, and eventually reached the stage of assembly of locally produced parts in 1971. In 1972 the indigenous content of the Indian-built MiG-21 was only about 60 per cent. About 130 out of a production run of 154 planes have been produced, and in 1970 the Soviet Union finally agreed to sell the production licence for the improved STOL version, the MiG-21(M). The new programme reportedly involves 150 aircraft up to 1974. The favoured position of Israel results partly from the fact that foreign firms expect to get valuable returns from the modifications adopted by Israel and partly also from the fact that foreign firms are more willing to co-operate with another industrialized country.

ROCKETS AND MISSILES

Unguided rockets are relatively simple to produce and could be manufactured by a number of countries if they were considered more useful militarily. However, only Brazil, which manufactures a range of bombardment rockets, has chosen to do so, although several countries have launched rather more sophisticated research rockets, presumably intended in part as preparation for the production of missiles.

Missiles, however, are much more difficult to produce, the main problem being the guidance system. Egypt attempted to develop three types of surface-to-surface missiles – Al Zafir, Al Kahir and Al Ared – and Nasser witnessed the test firing of the first two types on 21 July 1962. The third type, Al Ared, was officially fired on 23 July 1963. These were single-stage rockets, with ranges of 380 km., 600 km. and 700 km. respectively, and at least one of them is said to have employed a guidance system similar to the French Véronique research rocket. All three were displayed in the Cairo military parade in 1965, but there is no evidence that the missiles are or have been operational. The Egyptian missile programme was directed by German scientists, just as its jet-fighter and jet-engine projects were, and all of them came to a halt after 1965. So far there is nothing more than rumours about Egyptian wishes to restart these programmes, possibly in co-operation with Libya.

The only indigenously designed missile which has entered production in a Third World country is the Israeli Gabriel ship-to-ship missile, developed with the assistance of several French firms. A wire-guided anti-tank missile is also under development in Brazil. Elsewhere, notably in India and Pakistan, missiles are produced under licence from foreign manufacturers.

NAVAL VESSELS

The construction of naval vessels is largely concentrated in Latin America and Asia. It is somewhat surprising that so little effort has been made in South Africa to construct naval vessels, although recently South Africa announced plans to produce submarines. It is, perhaps, less surprising that naval building has been so limited in Israel and Egypt – indeed, it is non-existent in Egypt – although this may reflect the emphasis on land wars or the dominance of major powers in the Mediterranean. Only two Third World countries – Argentina and India – have undertaken the construction of ships in the destroyer-frigate class since 1950. In addition Argentina plans to assemble West German submarines, and Brazil will assemble two fast frigates under British licence. All these are based on foreign designs and imported engines, armament and electronic equipment. Brazilian shipyards are now building six coastal patrol vessels, two river patrol vessels and a naval tanker. Chilean shipyards are also geared to naval production and turned out their first 400-ton submarine chaser at the end of 1971. Further, North Korea is building two fast submarine chasers, and South Korea is building two patrol vessels. Rhodesia is considering military hovercraft. Thailand is building eighteen patrol boats with US supplied engines and machine-guns, with US aid.

THE PROBLEMS

The shortage of financial resources, the absence of appropriate materials, the limited nature of defence-related industries such as electronics, and the shortage of skilled personnel are all features of a developing country which make the establishment of a truly indigenous defence industry extremely difficult. While self-sufficiency can be achieved over a wide range of small arms and small naval vessels, the dependence on foreign assistance in the manufacture of more sophisticated weapons is likely to remain very great. Only Israel is in a position to manufacture domestically most of the parts for a particular weapon and even there the weapons and components have been largely based on foreign designs. It was not possible to survey the types of material required for defence production and their availability in developing countries, although it is clear that most countries will have to import, for instance, the special-quality steel and aluminium required for aircraft production.

The role of foreign scientists in the production of aircraft missiles and related equipment has been major. The Indonesian aircraft industry is the only one to have been established without the import of foreign scientists. Of special interest is the role of former German engineers who have been active in Argentina, Brazil, India and Egypt. Dr Kurt Tank, Focke-Wulf's war-time chief designer, appeared in Argentina some time after the Second World War, and in 1950 he produced a design for the swept-wing jet fighter 1-A-33 Pulqui II. He was supported by a team of German engineers and at least one German test pilot. But Pulqui II never reached the production stage and, with the overthrow of Perón in 1955, Dr Tank left for India, where he headed the design team of the supersonic fighter HF-24 Marut. Brazil also employed a number of European designers, for example Max Holste (French), Heinrich Focke (German) and Paul Baumgartl (Austrian) – famous names of the pre-Second World War European armaments industry.

The history of foreign scientists in Egypt provides a striking illustration of the dangers inherent in this type of dependence. When the HA-300 jet-fighter project was transferred to Egypt in 1959, it was accompanied by German and Spanish workers and technical personnel, and headed by Willy Messerschmidt. The E-300 turbojet engine, which was intended to power the HA-300, was developed under the leadership of the Austrian aeronautical engineer Dr Ferdinand Brandner, who had earlier worked on the Kuzhetsov NK-12m turboprop and other Soviet turbine engines.

It became necessary to set up recruiting activities in Switzerland in order to obtain the qualified personnel from other Western countries. Approximately 100 Spanish engineers and designers were reported to have been in Egypt at the start of the project and they were followed by German, Austrian and US teams of designers and engineers. Foreign scientists, mainly German, were also employed on other Egyptian defence projects: for example, the missile programme was initiated in 1960 under the leadership of Professor Wolfgang Pilz, a wartime associate of Werner von Braun. By 1962, there was a total 250 West German rocket experts and technicians in Egypt. But, increasingly, the rocket and aircraft programmes were subject to Israeli sabotage operations against factories and laboratories and the lives of many of the foreign scientists were endangered, so that by 1965 most of the senior scientists had left Egypt. Only Brandner remained until 1968. When, with the crisis in Arab–German relations in 1965, the Federal government gave German scientists the choice of returning to the Federal Republic of Germany or having their citizenship revoked, several scientists chose to return to Germany. Others have since disappeared from Egypt, apparently as a result, directly or indirectly, of Israeli sabotage operations, and only a maximum of ten still remain in Egypt, working, it is assumed, on the missile programme. The virtual disintegration of the Egyptian defence programme is mainly attributable to the departure of foreign scientists and engineers.

Another aspect of foreign assistance for domestic defence production is foreign investment: for a number of countries, certain production facilities consist of the establishment of subsidiaries by foreign firms. For instance, the French company Turbomeca has set up an engine factory in Israel. A number of British electronics firms have set up factories in South Africa. Imperial Chemical Industries Ltd also has a subsidiary in South Africa which, among other things, produces explosives for the South African armed forces. Particularly notable in this respect is Brazil. Several foreign companies have made a significant contribution to Brazil's aircraft industry. Rolls Royce do Brazil Limitada has been in existence for many years. In February 1968 it was announced that Dornier of Germany intended to build a $25 million factory in Brazil for the manufacture of Do 27 and Do 28 transports, as well as the Dornier Skyservant.

But the establishment of factories by foreign firms does involve some risk. Despite the fact that the Brazilian government has actually encouraged foreign firms, at least one company has been taken over. With the agreement to manufacture Fokker aircraft in Brazil, Fokker took over the state-owned factory at Ilha do Governador and formed the company Fokker Industria Aeronautica S.A. do Brazil. But in the late fifties it is reported that the company was taken over by the Brazilian government with no compensation to Fokker. Plans to produce the Fokker F-27 under licence have since then been abandoned.

However, foreign investment also involves risks for the country in question. Were a foreign firm to pull out in time of crisis or war, little indigenous manufacturing capacity would remain.

Another problem associated with domestic defence production concerns production costs. Although the conclusions in this section are based on estimates for the cost of producing military aircraft in India, they probably hold true for the production of missiles and electronic equipment and, to a lesser extent, for armoured vehicles and large naval vessels, for a country at a similar stage of development. They show that indigenous production is considerably more expensive than importing.

An examination of the differing breakdowns for producing aircraft in India and Britain indicates some of the disadvantages for developing countries. First of all, in the West labour costs account for a relatively low share of total costs: for a typical aircraft, they vary from 10 to 15 per cent of total production costs. This, in itself, suggests that such production may be inappropriate in developing countries, since the supply of cheap labour is one of the main advantages a poor country possesses over a rich country. In India, labour costs vary from 1 to 5 per cent of total production costs. Secondly, material costs are likely to be high. In India, the share of material costs in total production costs varies from 40 to 80 per cent, while in Western countries the share varies from 35 to 40 per cent. Material costs are not only high because of indigenization but also because the import of parts tends to be more expensive than the import of complete aircraft. This can be due to differing transport costs, to manufacturers' pricing practices, and to modifications made to suit the purchasing country.

The licensed production of the British HS 748 transport aircraft in India, for example, has involved considerable financial difficulties. In 1956 it was claimed that by producing this plane in India the cost would be $320,000, compared with the import price of $1 million. But the current production cost is quoted as $1·49 million. Only twenty-four planes have been delivered, and none is used in the tactical transport role for which it was originally intended. The future cost of the licensed production of the French SA 315B Lama high-altitude helicopter will also very likely reflect the fact that it was specially designed in France to meet Indian requirements.

All the aircraft turned out to be more expensive to produce at home than to buy from abroad. The increase in procurement costs as a result of domestic production ranges from 50 per cent for the HS 748 to 90 per cent for the Gnat. The very high increase in costs for the Gnat is the result of indigenization. As more material is purchased domestically, preferential prices have to be paid to domestic producers.

There are also other difficulties which add expense for a developing country. A number of items, such as testing facilities, which developing countries do not possess, must be constructed from scratch or with the use of foreign facilities. Both alternatives are expensive and time-consuming. For example, the entire fuselage section of the Egyptian HA-300 had to be shipped to England for testing of the pressurization and air-conditioning system. Similarly, the non-availability of a particular component can lead to a considerable slowing-down of the production rate, thus increasing overhead costs, if the component has to be acquired from a foreign country.

Finally, developing countries are unlikely to reap the full benefits of economies of scale. There is evidence that 'learning' tends to be slower in developing countries, but, more importantly, developing countries do not generally have such long production runs as rich countries. Not only are rich countries able to afford larger numbers of aircraft for their own use, but they also have greater export potential. Indeed, most licence agreements forbid exports by the licensee to certain specified countries, so that, for instance, Israel cannot export the Fouga Magister to French ex-colonies.

The above discussion and estimates do not include Research and Development costs. The total costs of the HF-24 and HJT-16 would be very much higher were these to be included, but unfortunately there is very little available information about comparative R & D costs. R & D expenditure represents an addition to the stock of technological know-how. For a country with very limited experience it is to be expected that R & D expenditures will have to be very great if aircraft comparable to those produced in rich countries are to be designed and developed domestically.

Finally, there are a number of planning problems to be considered: to establish a defence industry requires careful planning and organization. A major difficulty for several countries has been the fact that political and prestige considerations have affected both the choice of projects and the growth of the industry, as the possession of a sophisticated defence industry is often regarded as an attribute of power. This is of course true of both rich and poor countries. The ability to produce complete aircraft and in particular to produce jet fighters or missiles, provides a demonstration of modernization which the ability to overhaul and maintain weapons or to produce small arms cannot compete with. Probably for this reason, several countries such as India and Argentina have embarked on very ambitious projects, hastily planned and often doomed to failure. This also appears to be the case with the Egyptian aircraft and missile programmes. The success of the Israeli defence industry is partly attributable to the fact that, by force of circumstance, Israel's first priority has been military self-sufficiency as opposed to the production of prestige items.

Political considerations can affect the choice of weapons in another way. A country embarking on the production of equipment under licence must choose the weapon in the same way as it would a direct import. For political reasons, certain suppliers may be ruled out or others may be unwilling to meet demands.

The case of the development of Israel's arms industry is outstanding in this context, because it has managed to avoid most of the problems described above. The explanation for this is mainly that Israel is not an underdeveloped, semi-industrialized country. It possesses many of the skills and techniques that other countries lack. The criteria for starting projects have been their military usefulness and their export potential. It is significant that the Israeli aircraft industry, for example, has had only one prototype failure, compared with at least ten in Argentina. The priorities for Israel have been to develop a capability to maintain and overhaul all weapons, to produce all spares and ammunition, and to modify foreign types of weapons to suit its military requirements. There is little evidence of prestige considerations, which proved so expensive in some cases in India. The Israeli plans for exporting 30–40 per cent of its military output reflect the intention to pay for the defence industry with earnings from foreign sales. Co-operation with foreign firms has been vital to the development of the arms industry, although it appears to have been contracted on a commercial basis rather than as military aid. The foreign firms have often benefited from Israeli designs and modifications. For instançe the French export success, the Mirage 5, was essentially the result of Israeli modifications to the Mirage III.

The ordnance industry has benefited from co-operation with the Fabrique Nationale of Belgium. In 1961 Belgium bought the manufacturing licence of the Israeli-designed Uzi sub-machine-gun, and in return Israel was allowed to manufacture the 7·62 FN rifle. French companies have played an essential role for the aircraft industry and the missile programmes, as well as US companies.

The first project in the field of aircraft production undertaken by the state-owned Israel Aircraft Industries (IAI) was the licenced production of the French Fouga Magister jet trainer, which started in 1960. The Magister was used to gain experience for future projects, and some of the Israeli tooling was reported to be more advanced and sophisticated than that of the French. Within a short period IAI was reported to be producing more than 80 per cent of the primary components, and production continued until 1968. Some of these planes were sold to Uganda.

In mid-1967 the first indigenous aircraft project was announced: the STOL transport Arava, especially designed for export to developing countries. In 1972 there were reports of an unexpected cost increase for the civil version of Arava, illustrating the financial problem involved in indigenous production even for a country such as Israel. But the military version has received flight certification, and current plans state the rate of production to be one per month. Thirty options on the Arava are held by a number of developing countries, and the Israelis count upon the US market for the civil version.

In the same year as the plans for Arava appeared, IAI succeeded in buying the full design and production rights for the US Jet Commander. This solution was applied after difficulties with the indigenous design of an executive jet, a project that was abandoned because of the unacceptable costs. In addition IAI inherited a marketing system in the US that will be able to handle both the Jet Commander aircraft, re-named Commandore Jet, and the Arava. This project is aimed only at export.

The engine and electronics industries are also advancing, with French and US co-operation. French firms have assisted Israel in the development of rocketry. The MD 660 surface-to-surface missile, capable of carrying a nuclear or high-explosive warhead, was developed in France, while financed by Israel. The Gabriel ship-to-ship missile was developed in Israel but with the co-operation of several French firms.

The achievements of the Israeli industry should not necessarily be taken as an example of the practicability of defence production in Third World countries in general. To follow the Israeli example, a country will probably need the same degree of industrialization and educated manpower, financial resources and the opportunity of co-operating with foreign firms, plus the intention to export. It should also be kept in mind that Israel still depends heavily on imports of foreign weapons, like the Phantom and Skyhawk planes, and this in itself suggests that the road to self-sufficiency for most developing countries is a very long one.

Part Four

Control of the Arms Trade

13 Proposals Concerning the Arms Trade

The regulation of the arms trade first became a subject for international negotiation in connection with the African slave trade at the end of the last century; indeed, the Brussels Act of 1890 was the only international measure regulating the arms trade which ever came into force. There was a fairly intense period of international negotiation at the end of the First World War within the framework of the League of Nations; the high-water mark of interest was the Geneva Conference of 1925, which dealt exclusively with the arms trade. This was the period when a great many people considered that the build-up of armaments was one of the major causes of the war, and they were strongly suspicious of the role of the arms trade in general, and private arms dealers in particular, in this build-up.

The 1925 Geneva Convention on regulation of the arms trade never came into force, and, although the arms trade continued to be a topic dealt with in international discussions until the mid-thirties, there was never much prospect of an agreement, particularly after the failure of the Disarmament Conference in 1933.

One result of the efforts of the League of Nations was the publication of the statistical yearbooks on armaments and on the arms trade, which continued to be published up to 1938. Also during this period, a number of governments – perhaps partly influenced by the proposals for government licences for arms exports put before the League of Nations – acted to bring the private arms trade in their countries under some sort of governmental control.

Since the 1930s, the regulation of the arms trade has never again been a major subject of international discussion. After the Second World War, the main aim of the arms-trade proposals of the thirties was achieved, in so far as the arms trade was now largely in the hands of governments, and the role of private arms

Table 23 Past proposals and other measures for the regulation of the arms trade[a]

Proposal	Proposed by	Date	Main content
Pre-Second World War			
1. Brussels Act	13 European states, USA, 3 non-European	1890	Regulation of arms traffic to North Africa
2. Covenant of the League of Nations	League members	1919	Supervision of trade in arms
3. Saint-Germain Convention	Allied powers	1919	Regulation of arms trade with European states defeated in First World War and with certain parts of the Middle East and Africa
4. Treaty of Washington	USA	1922	Isolated attempt to regulate naval armaments
5. Geneva Convention	League of Nations Conference	1925	Arms traffic to be entirely government-controlled; publication of arms trade; prohibited areas
6. Special Commission Draft	League	1926	Publicity of state manufacture of arms
7. League Plan	League	1929	(Only discussed in connection with disarmament) Sanctions on aggressor; assistance to innocent
League proposals in connection with a general disarmament treaty			
The Disarmament Conference, 1932			
1. Spanish plan	Spain, at opening of conference	1932	International and national supervision of private and state manufacture of arms

[a] See notes at end of table

Table 23 – contd

Proposal	Proposed by	Date	Main content
2. Special Committee[b] agreement, following opening of conference, based on Spanish plan		1932	Supplementary agreement of general disarmament for control of arms trade and manufacture
3. French plan	France (supported by Poland, Spain, Holland, Scandinavia), to League	Feb. 1933	Abolish private manufacture and check state manufacture of arms
4. Turkish proposal	In Special Committee discussions	1933	Internationalization of arms manufacture a condition for abolishing private manufacture
5. Persian proposal			
6. French plan	France, to Disarmament Conference	May 1933	Under a disarmament agreement, the Permanent Disarmament Commission of the League was to supervise and record arms transfers and production

Other than disarmament

1. Roosevelt recommendation	USA, to Geneva Conference	1934	International supervisory body for arms trade
2. US arms trade convention	USA, to League	1934	Permanent Disarmament Commission to publish arms trade and manufacture; supervision and inspection rights

[b] See notes at end of table

Table 23 – *contd*

Proposal	Proposed by	Date	Main content
Post-Second World War			
International: UN/CCD (Conference of the Committee on Disarmament)			
1. Resolution 42 (1)	UN General Assembly	1946	Call on Security Council to determine information on armed forces and armaments
2. Draft resolution	France and Norway, to UN General Assembly	Nov. 1949	Full publicity of armed forces
3. Draft resolution	By USSR, to Security Council	Feb. 1949	Information on conventional armaments and nuclear weapons
4. Maltese Draft Resolution	Malta, to First Committee of UN General Assembly	Nov. 1965	Publicity of arms transfers
5. Four-Power Draft Resolution	Denmark, Norway, Iceland and Malta, to First Committee of UN General Assembly	Nov. 1968	Request for inquiry among member states on publicity of arms transfers
Counterproposal	Congo (K)	1968	Freeze on offensive weapons
Counterproposal	Tunisia	1968	Ceiling on military expenditure in underdeveloped countries
6. US initiative	US delegate to CCD	Spring 1970	Regional arms limitation
7. Swedish initiative	Swedish delegate to CCD	Spring 1970	Arms trade; recommendation to investigate the problem

Table 23 – contd

Proposal	Proposed by	Date	Main content
International forum other than UN			
WEU Document 500	Western European Union	1969	Limit heavy equipment; registration of arms trade
Official statements			
1. Khrushchev press conference, London	USSR	27.4.1956	Embargo on Middle East
2. Draft Declaration	USSR	11.2.1957	Embargo on Middle East
3. Khrushchev interview with *The Times*	USSR	31.1.1958	Embargo on Middle East
4. Soviet memorandum to USA, France, UK	USSR	5.5.1958	Embargo on Middle East
5. Address by Irish Foreign Minister Aiken, to General Assembly	Ireland	23.9.1959	Regional embargoes; regional agreements not to acquire certain arms
6. Statement by Dean Rusk	USA	2.1.1964	Destruction of obsolete weapons
7. Johnson message to Eighteen-nation Disarmament Committee	USA	27.1.1966	Regional agreements not to acquire certain arms
8. Foster statement to ENDC	USA	19.4.1966	Regional agreements not to acquire certain arms
9. Johnson address to Foreign Policy Conference for Educators	USA	19.6.1967	Registration of all arms imports to Middle East
10. Dean Rusk news conference	USA	19.7.1967	Ceiling on Middle East arms race; registration of arms transfers

Table 23 – contd

Proposal	Proposed by	Date	Main content
11. Johnson message to ENDC	USA	16.7.1968	Regional initiatives for restraints on arms imports; registration by suppliers
12. Soviet government memorandum	USSR	July 1968	Regional reductions of armaments
Latin America			
1. Colombia–Peru treaties		1831 and 1840	Ceiling on military personnel
2. Argentina–Chile agreements		1902 and 1903	Naval disarmament
3. Central American Republics Convention		1923	Ceiling on armed forces; arms export prohibition
4. Costa Rican initiative		5.3.1958	Proposal to the OAS: no import of arms from non-US suppliers; ceiling on armed forces
5. Chilean initiative		Nov. 1959	No definite proposals
6. OAS		Dec. 1962	Reduction of armaments
7. OAS Punta del Este		April 1967	Limit military expenditure
US research related especially to arms trade			
1. MIT Study		1964	Control of arms traffic and production; restriction by all suppliers on arms to the Middle East; arms-trade registration of shipments to all non-governmental purchasers in Africa; provision of military aid directly to OAU and to African police force

Table 23 – contd

Proposal	Proposed by	Date	Main content
2. ICY Report (Report of the Committee on Arms Control and Disarmament of the National Citizens' Commission on International Cooperation)		28.11.1965	Regulation of arms traffic; publication of yearbook on international arms transfers and UN registration system
3. ACDA: Fifth ACDA Report. ACDA Special Study: 'The Reporting on International Arms Transfers'		19.1.1966	End-use restrictions on arms exported
		30.6.1968	Registration of arms trade
4. The Fulbright Study (Senate Study on Arms Sales and Foreign Policy)		25.1.1967	US initiative in organizing regional conventional weapon-free zones

Notes:

a In addition to the more significant proposals for arms-trade regulation discussed in the text, this chronological list includes various other suggestions for measures made within the context of general disarmament discussions. The discussions have tended throughout the period to centre on the same topics, which means that the proposals are often repetitive. This list, then, is a sample of the most meaningful suggestions for measures for supervision of the international trade in arms.

b This was the first time the USSR participated in a discussion on the arms-trade issue.

dealers was reduced to a very minor one indeed. The debate has been taken up in the United Nations, but only incidentally and only by some of the smaller countries. Malta and Denmark prepared draft resolutions in 1965 and in 1967/8, both dealing with publicity for the arms trade, but both were rejected by the United Nations.

There was some rise in general interest in the subject of the arms trade in the second half of the sixties, and some research was started, particularly in the United States. There was a critical examination in the US Congress of the role of the US government as an arms trader, and in Europe there was some questioning of the arms trade after the Nigerian–Biafran Civil War, the Arab–Israeli war of 1967 and the embargo on arms to South Africa. However, no further substantive proposals for international action have been put forward.

The failure of such proposals as there have been is no more surprising than the failure of the various post-war proposals for general disarmament, given the political climate of the past twenty years. The proposals have not sufficiently taken into account the very strong political and economic pressures behind the arms trade, pressures which have proved to be stronger than the pressures for regulation. The United States has been lukewarm about any proposals: the Soviet Union has been opposed to any special measures to deal with the arms trade, outside general disarmament negotiations; and Third World countries have been strongly opposed to any kind of interference with their supplies. The proposals have so far not come properly to grips with the problem of discrimination between producing and non-producing countries. To sum up, the proposals for regulation or supervision of the arms trade were never based on a careful analysis of causes and consequences.

ASSESSMENT OF THE PROPOSALS

Most proposals about the arms trade have been made because of concern with the build-up of armaments, outside the direct NATO–Warsaw Pact confrontation, in developing countries. Given that most of these countries are non-producers, at least of sophisticated weapons, the arms trade is the route by which these armaments build-ups take place; so the arms trade naturally springs to mind as a possible instrument for slowing down the process. A second source of concern – though it has not been made explicit in most of the post-war proposals – is that the supply of weapons is one of the routes by which the competition between the major powers spreads round the world.

The object of the proposals, then, in this field is to slow, stop or indeed possibly reverse the build-up of weapons stocks in developing areas, and to find ways for reducing the degree to which the major East–West arms race infects Third World countries.

There is probably general agreement that these objectives are desirable – just as there is general agreement that multilateral arms limitation or disarmament is desirable. There is a strong case for saying that the greater the supply of weapons round the world, the greater is the chance that military solutions will be sought for the many disputes in the world today. Further, the economic resources used up are considerable – not least the wastage of skill in the operation and maintenance of weapons.

However, in approaching the problem of arms build-ups in developing countries, there is the question whether in fact the control of trade, alone, is the most appropriate instrument. Certainly there is a strong case for altering the present situation. The consequence of doing nothing may be very serious – and this should be continually said – but one criterion of a good proposal is that it should have some chance of success. Past proposals, which have failed to take into account the political situation in non-producing nations and the relationship between the arms build-ups in these countries and those in the producing countries, have had little value except to draw attention to the problem.

In the following sections, various obstacles to regulating trade in arms alone are analysed. This is followed by a discussion of certain limited proposals concerning publicity, and proposals concerning production as well as trade in Third World regions; then the various criteria on which the policies of supplying countries are, or could be, based are examined.

Obstacles to the regulation of trade alone

There are two major obstacles in the way of the success of arms-trade proposals. First, developing countries complain that in the nature of things they are discriminatory, as indeed they are. The proposals are in linear descent from the Brussels Act of 1890 and from the proposed Convention of Saint-Germain of 1919, both of which devoted most of their attention to attempts to regulate the supply of arms to prohibited areas. One implication of these proposals was that in some areas of the world peoples of European stock should maintain a monopoly over the possession of weapons.

In the view of the developing countries, this is an untenable position. They claim that they have the same right to possess arms as any developed country, and they consider it inseparable from the sovereign right to protect their security both from internal and external threats. These countries also point out that the vast bulk of the world stock of weapons is in the hands of the developed countries, and they do not see any particular reason to support arms-trade proposals in their areas while developed countries are permitted to pile up their much larger stocks of weapons. It is probable that developing countries might have been more positive towards proposals for the regulation of the arms trade if they had been accompanied by measures for regulating the arms race in developed countries as well.

On the other side, most non-producing countries have been involved in various actual or potential conflicts – mostly territorial claims – with other countries in the region, and under these circumstances they have considered it necessary to retain full freedom to procure weapons. Many developing countries also consider arms purchases vital for their various internal needs, or as backing for their foreign policy. They are disturbed that restrictions might be imposed at the discretion of developed countries, and object that proposals which would deprive them of weapons for these purposes are discriminatory.

An example of a situation in which non-producing countries may feel the danger of discriminatory treatment particularly keenly is the case in which certain Third World countries are protected by a producing nation through an alliance or other military agreement. Countries which are not so protected feel that arms-trade restrictions would provide an advantage to an adversary who had this protection. The non-aligned countries have argued that to reduce the risks involved in this sort of situation, proposals for the regulation of the arms trade should be accompanied by agreements terminating defence treaties between producing and non-producing countries.

The producing country may also be another country in the same region which meets some of its requirements from indigenous production. The fact that most of the producing countries in the Third World have been engaged in conflicts with other non-producing countries in the area is one of the reasons for the pronounced opposition of the latter to any proposal confined only to regulating arms supplies. This is one of the main barriers to arms-trade regulations in almost all regions. In the Far East and South Asia, India and, to a lesser extent, Indonesia produce weapons. In the Middle East, Israel has a relatively advanced defence industry. In Africa, the defence production by South Africa is of major importance. In Latin America, Argentina and Brazil produce weapons. In most of these cases there exist neighbouring non-producing countries which feel a threat from this indigenous production of arms.

It follows that any proposal to regulate arms supplies, if it is to have any chance of acceptance by developing countries, must take several factors into account. First, it must deal with production (or possession) as well as trade, not only in the non-producing countries but in the producing countries as well; in this way it would explicitly recognize the existence of arms races in the rich countries as well as the poor. Secondly, it must take into consideration the demand for weapons which exists in developing countries, either as a result of their internal political situation or their relations with other countries in the region. Thirdly, it must deal with the problems connected with the existence of military alliances or defence agreements between developed and developing countries; for instance, there should be some guarantee against military intervention by outside powers.

Supply-side constraints. Even though agreements to regulate the arms trade alone have proved contrary to the interests of the importing nations, the supplying countries could, by virtue of their monopoly position, agree to regulate trade without taking into account the views of the importing nations. That they have not done so in itself suggests that there are strong constraints on the supply side as well, and this is the second major sort of obstacle to any effective agreement on arms trade.

There are two main reasons for objection on the part of suppliers. First, the supply of weapons is used by the big powers – in particular the United States and the Soviet Union – as an instrument of policy. It has been one way in which the conflict between them has been spread through the world. If one were to subtract from the arms trade those weapons which have been supplied by the two great powers, not only would world arms races be reduced, but also there would be much less risk of the spread of the East–West confrontation. Secondly, the military commitments of the big powers to Third World countries are to a great extent subsidiary consequences of the major arms race. It may well be assumed that as long as this race continues unabated it will also be an obstacle to regulating arms trade with Third World countries.

There are circumstances in which these constraints might be reduced: if relations between the United States and the Soviet Union improve, then various local conflicts which have been wholly or partly incorporated into the world power struggle will become easier to solve; the local demand for weapons would then fall, and the big powers themselves might find it easier to come to some agreement regulating supplies. Also, if the big powers were to come to any agreement on the arms race between themselves, the climate would be more favourable for them to agree about arms supplies to Third World countries.

The strong pressure to continue arms supplies to the Third World is not restricted to the United States and the Soviet Union. In Britain and France a domestic armaments base is considered necessary for an independent stance in world affairs, and these countries could not retain the existing structure of their armament industries without exports.

POSSIBLE PROPOSALS

There are therefore strong forces in being for the continuance and indeed expansion of arms supplies to developing countries. On the supply side, in addition to the great powers' use of arms supplies in their policies, there are economic pressures at work – particularly in Britain and France. On the demand side, there are strong objections to anything that savours of discrimination. So both major supplying countries and recipient countries tend to be opposed to any arms-trade proposal – which leaves relatively few countries in favour.

In general, therefore, the most fruitful approach to the problems of arms build-ups in Third World countries is not so much through proposals concerning the arms trade alone, but rather through arms regulation or non-armament agreements: that is to say, through agreements which concern the possession of weapons rather than the methods of acquiring them, though some control over the methods of acquiring them would probably be part of any agreement.

Registration and publication. The only arms-trade proposal discussed in the United Nations has been the registration of international arms transfers. The idea that increased publicity would limit the arms traffic prompted the *Statistical Year-Book of the League of Nations*, which was published annually from 1924 to 1938. But the reception to post-war proposals for registration indicates the difficulties involved in imitating the inter-war practice, let alone improving upon it, although many critics of the proposal made it clear that they would react more favourably to proposals for registration if they covered production as well as trade and if they were world-wide.

There are generally two sorts of arguments put forward to support the contention that increased publicity limits the procurement or sale of weapons. First, it is argued that countries in conflict as a rule tend to overrate their enemy's military capability and arm accordingly. If all transactions were open and above board, such countries might feel secure with a smaller military capability. Furthermore, in their public statements, defence establishments themselves tend, in general, to exaggerate the enemy's strength, and an authoritative international publication would be some corrective to this.

The second argument about publicity also depends on the peace-loving inclinations of the general public. It is argued that if the entrammelment of supplying countries, via the arms trade, in Third World countries were publicized, then public pressures would be exerted to reduce the export of weapons. In practice, this has been the case in a number of supplying countries where facts about the export of weapons have been made known. In the United States, it was revealed in 1967 that the Export–Import Bank was heavily involved in the financing of arms exports, with the aid of a Department of Defense guarantee. The revelation resulted in an intense public debate and Congress passed a law forbidding the Export–Import Bank to finance arms exports to developing countries and limiting the ability of the Defense Department to provide such loans. Similarly, the Nigerian civil war provided the occasion for public debates in a large number of supplying countries. And in several cases these resulted in arms embargoes on both Nigeria and Biafra. There are contrary examples, such as some public protest in France against the decision to impose an embargo on Israel after the June 1967 War. But it is probably fair to say that if governments were prepared to publish fuller details of their arms exports, public pressure would generally operate in a restrictive direction.

An international proposal to register the production and trade of weapons would be one way of legalizing such publicity. It might begin by being a proposal for a register of one category of weapons only – taking as a start a category about which there is at the moment most information, say, warships. The advantage of secrecy would not be lost to any significant extent by a proposal of this kind: warships, certainly once afloat, can hardly be concealed. If the idea were accepted for warships, it might then be accepted for other weapons, first for military planes or tanks, and then other sorts of weapons which are easier to conceal.

Third World countries may be willing to accept a register if it also covers production, but the producing nations might well not agree. One difficulty in particular is that at the moment much more information is published about Western countries' weapons output than about Warsaw Pact weapons output. There has already been opposition on the Warsaw Pact side to a proposal which appears to them to be a unilateral concession, their objection being that this is not a disarmament or an arms regulation proposal, but merely a ruse by the West to gain information.

The main reason given by the recipient countries for not publishing details of supplies is that they feel this would threaten their security, and be another example of discrimination. The connection between secrecy and security is a dubious one: and this objection would be overcome to the extent that supplying countries were prepared to publish details of their arms production as well.

Regional proposals

A second approach to arms limitation in the Third World which has attracted wide attention has been regional arms-limitation agreements. A full examination of these proposals falls outside the scope of this study. However, they have important implications for the arms trade.

It is in those regions where conflicts have not become polarized, where local conflicts do not reflect East–West competition, that the possibility for arms-limitation agreements are greatest. In the Far and Middle East, a prerequisite for such agreements would be some form of conflict settlement and the reduction of outside military commitments in the regions. In Latin America, with the exception of Cuba, competition is confined to the Western powers. Armed inter-state conflicts are almost non-existent and weapons are acquired for counter-guerilla activities and to serve the purposes of a politically conscious military establishment. In Africa, the role of the two great powers has been very limited in the military sphere: armed conflicts have been few and weapon purchases have been low. Black African nations generally recognize that their conventional military inferiority in relation to South Africa is unlikely to be overcome soon.

The market for weapons is a seller's market. But one can conceive of various ways to increase the bargaining position of the buyers. The obvious way would be for Third World countries to purchase their weapons on an international or regional basis. Theoretically, they might develop a buyers' association through which all military equipment and services were channelled.

There are, of course, immense obstacles to such an institution. Countries in conflict would hardly agree to buy weapons from the same source. Then there is the problem of developing criteria for each purchaser's military needs. If the association were to avoid judgements about who is entitled to weapons and how much, then the criteria would have to be based on ability to pay. It is unlikely that poorer countries and guerilla movements, particularly if they were not recognized by the association, would accept such a system and reject offers of military aid from individual supplying countries outside the framework of the association, unless supplying countries also were ready to accept the association and operate according to its rules. Finally, it would not entirely remove the relationship between supplier and recipient nations. If recipient nations are to specify their weapon types, then the supplying countries will still be able to promote individual sales of weapons, make credit arrangements and provide technicians.

However, there are grounds for supposing that, on a smaller scale, some such ideas might be tried out in certain regions. The African Liberation Committee (ALC) of the Organization of African Unity provides an example of such an association in embryo form.

Something on the lines of the ALC might be developed as a buyers' association in Africa. This would increase the military independence of African nations and strengthen their bargaining position *vis-à-vis* outside powers. It would not be difficult to envisage some form of joint African aid to those governments that might feel directly threatened by white regimes in Southern Africa. There is already some interchange of training and military services among African countries as well as with other Third World countries, for instance, Israel and India. There is reluctance among several countries to accept military aid from the two great powers and a tendency to acquire military equipment and services from a number of different sources. Both these aspects of military policy reduce the possibilities for polarization and could be institutionalized.

Africa is not the only region where this type of policy might be followed. There have already been attempts to co-operate on military purchases among Arab countries. This has largely been related to funding, but there have also been joint Arab purchasing missions. The problem in the Middle East is that polarization already exists and no recipients' agreement on arms limitation will be reached without some settlement of the conflict, which requires the co-operation of the great powers. There are likely to be similar barriers to this type of policy in the Far East and South Asia.

Latin American countries have recently been purchasing sophisticated weapons from Europe, which has, to some extent, reduced their military dependence on the United States. However, such is the dependence of most Latin American regimes in other fields that a buyers' association, whether independent of the OAS or not, could not appreciably alter the situation. Also, under present circumstances, East–West competition is unlikely to make itself felt in the region.

Arms-limitation agreements in Africa. Africa has always been regarded as a potential area for arms regulation and disarmament. Defence spending is low and the weapons at present possessed by African nations are relatively unsophisticated. Only thirteen countries, out of thirty-five, possess combat aircraft with jet engines. Only Ethiopia, Uganda, Nigeria and the Sudan have supersonic fighters. Only nine countries possess tanks. Only Ghana and Nigeria have navies with equipment heavier than patrol craft. And Zambia is the only Black African country to possess missiles.

The main barrier to an arms-limitation agreement in Africa is the conflict with the white Southern African regimes: an effective arms embargo on South Africa, Portugal and Rhodesia would be necessary if such an agreement is to be reached. However, it can be argued that, with or without an embargo, these regimes will still be very much stronger in conventional military terms than the forces opposed to them. Developing countries are likely to be at a disadvantage in a conventional war, using sophisticated weapons, with industrial countries, and, even if South Africa and Portugal were denied weapons from outside sources, they would still have some domestically produced weapons at their disposal.

If a military solution to the conflict is attempted, it is unlikely to be a war fought with major sophisticated weapons. It is more likely to take the form of a guerilla war waged within countries with white regimes. It is therefore not unreasonable to propose a limitation on certain categories of sophisticated weapons in the region. There still remains, however, the problem of meeting air attacks on those countries playing host to the guerillas, so that an arms-limitation agreement would have to make some provision for the air defence of these countries. A possible solution to this problem would be an international arrangement to construct such an air-defence system. Its implications are analogous to those of providing peace-keeping forces.

It is not the first time that multilateral military assistance has been suggested. In 1964, Congo (Kinshasa) and the United States jointly proposed a multilateral training programme for the Congolese armed forces, to be carried out under UN auspices, in connection with the UN withdrawal. A number of countries agreed to participate in the programme, including Norway, Belgium, Canada, Britain and Italy, but their plan was eventually abandoned. The main objection to it in the UN was its Western bias. But this could easily be overcome in any future proposal of this kind.

Arms-limitation agreements in Latin America. There is a precedent for regional arms-limitation agreement in the Latin American nuclear-free zone. It was suggested by the USA at Punta del Este in April 1967 that there should be an agreement to exclude other categories of weapons as well. The weapons suggested were supersonic aircraft, naval vessels heavier than destroyers, tanks over thirty tons and missiles. But today all these categories of weapons, except for heavy tanks, are possessed by one or more of the Latin American countries. Therefore, such an agreement would have to be a disarmament agreement, as opposed to a non-armament agreement.

It is not inconceivable that Latin American countries would be prepared to accept an agreement which placed a ceiling on defence spending or limited future arms purchases. But the significance of such an agreement would not be very great. Latin American regimes have been most inclined to oppose US policies concerning the purchases of sophisticated weapons. These weapons have a function in preserving the political role of the military establishment and in perpetuating rivalries between various branches of the military establishment. Nevertheless, defence spending has been low, and in other fields of military procurement Latin American countries appear to have accepted US recommendations.

Latin American countries are perhaps more likely to accept a ceiling on defence spending than an agreement to limit future purchases of weapons. The former would merely formalize the present situation. The latter might have some effects on the role of the military establishment. The resources released by such a ceiling would not be very substantial and, given the structure of most Latin American countries, might not contribute much to the economic and social development of the countries as a whole. The risk of war posed by the present situation is small. The main Latin American conflicts are internal conflicts and these would not be affected by a disarmament or non-armament agreement. Nevertheless, there is a strong case for arguing that any agreement to regulate arms procurement is an advance, since it provides a precedent for similar agreements in other parts of the world.

Supplying policies

Every supplying country makes decisions about arms exports on the basis of some implicit or explicit criteria. It is worth examining different categories of criteria and considering the consequences of their adoption.

The first group of criteria are the restrictive ones. Countries such as Sweden and Switzerland, and to a certain extent the Federal Republic of Germany and Japan, apply the principle that no arms should be supplied to countries engaged in armed conflicts and, in some cases, to countries likely to be so engaged. Since the acquisition of arms is likely to reflect a conflict situation, however latent, a variant of this policy would be one in which no arms were exported at all. A country might decide that its role in international affairs was such that it should avoid the arms trade altogether. For example, during the recent arms-trade debates in Switzerland it was suggested that there is a basic incompatibility between the Swiss form of neutrality (including the fact that many international organizations, in particular the Red Cross, are based in Switzerland) and Swiss arms exports.

There are two problems with this sort of approach. First, it implicitly lends support to the stronger parties in a conflict. Secondly, if the spread of East–West competition to Third World countries is to be limited, then those smaller countries which adopt such principles might represent more appropriate sources for weapons than, say, the Soviet Union and the United States.

There would be a genuine difficulty if, for example, all the major arms suppliers except the United States and the Soviet Union adopted the principle of refusing to supply countries engaged, or likely to be engaged, in conflict, for this would force countries even further into the hands of the two great powers. Countries are obviously chary of buying from suppliers who might cut off supplies of ammunition or spares if a conflict began.

A possible compromise arms-trade policy for individual countries is one in which a general principle is laid down that arms should not be supplied to countries in conflict, but where the executive should be entitled to go against this general rule in particular circumstances, if it is prepared to announce the fact and justify its action. A policy of this kind would leave open the possibility of arms supplies to parties to a conflict on the basis of some overriding principle. This is to some extent similar to the third and fourth types of policy described below except that, as a general rule, the principle of not supplying countries in conflicts is still observed.

The second type of policy, the antithesis of the restrictive policy, is to supply arms to all who request them on a commercial basis. In this case, the criterion for arms exports is ability to pay. This policy does not reflect any particular political sympathies and, since there is no form of subsidy, the entrammelment of the supplying country in the recipient country's affairs is limited. The disadvantages of this approach are that it is likely to lead to an overall increase in the flow of weapons and that it lends implicit support to the wealthier recipient nations.

A third type of policy is to base decisions concerning arms exports on the political sympathies of the supplying countries with the recipient countries. These are clearly the criteria adopted by the Soviet Union and the United States, and it is these criteria which can lead to the competitive arming of client states.

A fourth type of policy is one which determines support for particular recipient countries on the basis of internationally agreed principles. The UN Security Council resolution embargoing all arms to South Africa and certain categories of arms to Portugal reflects the principle that no arms should be supplied to racist regimes or to support colonial wars. In a sense, this fourth type of policy was also applied by the League of Nations in the inter-war years: the particular principle applied then was of opposition to the aggressor. After Italy invaded Ethiopia, the League of Nations instructed members in 1935 to impose an arms embargo on Italy, and went a stage further in urging countries such as Switzerland, which had also imposed an arms embargo on Ethiopia, to remove it.

The application of such principles has the advantage of treating conflicts as manifestations of a broad set of international problems and disturbances, and not as isolated bouts of violence. It also avoids the competitive arming of parties to conflicts.

But there are great difficulties about extending this approach and making it more effective. The interests of particular supplying countries might well result in differences of interpretation of the principles. Already these interests have inhibited the effectiveness of the South African and Portuguese embargoes. Further, many of the states in the Third World are aligned either with the United States or with the Soviet Union, and consequently in any conflict the power with which they are aligned tends to judge that the other party is in the wrong. These divisions mean that there would probably not be many conflicts where the United Nations – either the Security Council or the General Assembly – would reach the degree of unanimity which the League of Nations reached about Italy and Ethiopia.

Possibilities for supply-side arms-trade restraint.   Since the two great powers supply the bulk of the Third World's weapons, the main chance of this flow being reduced, in the absence of any international agreement, lies in their policies. There are few signs at the moment of any slowing-down in the flow: but there are circumstances in which it could be envisaged.

The most likely possibility is that the competitive supplying countries may wish to restrain the conflict between their recipients before they themselves become involved. Where interests coincide, there is the possibility of agreement: the interests of outside powers in restraining the Arab–Israeli War may be one such example. Since the breakdown of arms limitation under the Tri-partite Declaration of 1950, there have been a number of tentative suggestions for an arms embargo on the Middle East, particularly from the Soviet Union. In earlier years one of the obstacles was the Western unwillingness to give up their military commitments to the Baghdad Pact (now CENTO); another has been the failure to reach a peace settlement. In particular, since 1967, the Soviet Union has insisted that Israeli withdrawal from Arab territories occupied in the June War should be a precondition for an agreement to limit arms supplies. If there were to be a peace settlement in the Middle East, then some agreement between the four powers on arms supplies would probably have to be a part of it. Whether such an agreement could win the support of the recipient countries is an open question: basically it would have to be a suppliers' agreement.

Another supply-side possibility is the scrapping of surplus stocks. When a US proposal for scrapping bombers was made in 1964, one of the arguments for it was that it would keep those weapons out of the hands of other countries. 'Dumping' – the passing-on of surplus weapons by the armed services in order to acquire new types – is, for a variety of reasons, not such an abuse in the United States today as it was in the fifties. Nevertheless, the United States government still has an interest in supplying surplus weapons to certain recipients, such as Taiwan, since this has been a way of evading Congressional restrictions on military aid. It is not known how the Soviet Union views such supplies. But agreements on scrapping do not have to take the form of agreements between the United States and the Soviet Union; it is possible that NATO countries, on their own, might agree, for instance, to scrap the obsolete tanks now lying idle in Western Europe. Not only would such an agreement reduce the ability of recipient countries to acquire weapons at low cost, but it would also reduce the total stocks available for supply.

There are more general possibilities. It is conceivable that there could be a really marked reduction of tension between the United States and the Soviet Union – possibly accompanied by a genuine arms-limitation agreement on their own strategic weapons; or there could, in both countries, be some move towards isolationism. In any of these circumstances, the amount of military aid given might be increasingly questioned: and there might be strong pressure to reduce the total. There have already been such pressures in the US Congress, largely evaded by the executive by the device of including military aid in other parts of the budget than the military-aid bill. There is no way of knowing whether there has been anything equivalent in the Soviet Union: presumably there are some groups who feel that the resources devoted to military aid could be better used. Any reduction in the military aid component of arms supplies would have the further advantage that it would reduce the political indebtedness of recipient countries to supplying countries, and would also reduce the two great powers' share of the market; one reason poorer countries choose to acquire weapons from the United States and the Soviet Union is that they get them cheaply.

The effectiveness of any agreement between the United States and the Soviet Union – tacit or explicit – to restrain arms supplies to Third World countries would be considerably increased, of course, if other major suppliers were party to it. If any agreement were confined to the United States and the Soviet Union, weapons exports from other countries such as France and Britain would probably rise – though not by any means by the full amount of the US and Soviet reductions, however, since these other countries subsidize their exports so much less. Any wider suppliers' agreement would have considerable consequences for the international position of many medium-sized supplying countries. They tend to consider a domestic armaments base as necessary for an independent stance in world affairs: and many would find it difficult to retain the present structure of their armaments industries without exports. Any agreement of this kind would naturally discriminate against Third World countries.

CONCLUSIONS

The build-up of stocks of weapons in Third World countries is one of the new and disturbing features of the post-war world. It is doubtful, however, whether proposals concerning the regulation of the arms trade alone are the most appropriate instrument for limiting them – mainly because such proposals inevitably discriminate against non-producing countries.

Any registration proposal, therefore, would certainly have to cover production as well as trade if it were to have any chance of acceptance by Third World countries. The most fruitful approach to actual regulation or limitation of weapons would seem to be through regional recipient-country agreements which would also cover production as well as trade. In the regions where the competing military commitments of the great powers are important, there is no prospect of any such agreement being reached until there is more progress in settlement between the United States and the Soviet Union. It is in the regions where the links with the major arms race are weakest that the possibility of agreement is greatest – for instance, Latin America and Sub-Saharan Africa.

One of the important characteristics of the arms trade is that, along with other factors, it links arms races in the Third World to the major East–West confrontation; one object of any proposal should be to weaken this link and reduce the military dependence of non-producing countries.

On the supply side, there is the possibility that some countries might adopt more restrictive policies, though this does not seem very likely at the moment. The key question concerns the policies of the United States and the Soviet Union. If for any reason (and such reasons can be imagined) their interest in the competitive arming of Third World countries diminished, this would be the most important single development moderating the build-up of weapon stocks in the Third World, though, of course, it would increase world military inequality.

Bibliography

The purpose of this bibliography, which is based on the list contained in the complete version of the SIPRI publication *The Arms Trade with the Third World*, is to provide an account of the types of literature used in the SIPRI study. It does not claim to be comprehensive, in that it does not cover international newspapers, journals, parliamentary debates or public accounts, which were used extensively.

This bibliography is also intended to provide the reader with a list of material for further study. In order to make it more useful for the reader in this respect, an attempt has been made to classify the books and government publications into six broad categories, dealing with the arms trade and related subjects.

ARMS TRADE AND MILITARY ASSISTANCE

Albrecht, Ulrich: *Der Handel mit Waffen*, Munich, 1971.

Bell, M. J. V.: *Military Assistance to Independent African States*, Adelphi Paper No. 15, London, 1964.

Browne and Shaw Research Corporation: *The Diffusion of Combat Aircraft, Missiles and their Supporting Technologies*, Waltham, Mass., 1966.

Haftendorn, Helga: *Militärhilfe und Rüstungsexporte der BRD*, Düsseldorf, 1971.

Hovey, Harold A.: *United States Military Assistance. A Study of Policies and Practices*, New York, 1965.

Joshua, Wynfred, and Gibert, Stephen P.: *Arms for the Third World, Soviet Military Aid Diplomacy*, Baltimore, 1969.

Lefever, Ernest W.: *US Military Training Programs for Developing Countries*, Brookings Institution, Washington.

Ra'anan, Uri: *The USSR Arms the Third World: Case Studies in Soviet Foreign Policy*, Cambridge, Mass., 1969.

Stockholm International Peace Research Institute: *Arms Trade Registers: The Third World*, Stockholm, 1974.

326 The Arms Trade with the Third World

Sutton, J. L., and Kemp, G.: *Arms to Developing Countries 1945–1965*, Adelphi Paper No. 28, London, 1966.

Thayer, G.: *The War Business: The International Trade in Armaments*, London, 1969.

Wolf, Charles, Jr: *Military Assistance Programs*, Rand P-3240, Santa Monica, 1965.

Center for International Studies, Massachusetts Institute of Technology

Leiss, A. C., Kemp, G., Hoagland, J. H., Refson, J. S., and Fischer, H. E.: *Arms Transfers to Less Developed Countries*, C/70–1, Cambridge, Mass., 1970.

Leiss, A. C.: *Changing Patterns of Arms Transfers, Implications for Arms Transfer Policies*, C/70–2, Cambridge, Mass., 1970.

Kemp, G.: *Classification of Weapons Systems and Force Designs in Less Developed Country Environments. Implications for Arms Transfer Policies*, C/70–3, Cambridge, Mass., 1970.

Refson, J. S.: *U.S. Military Training and Advice, Implications for Arms Transfer Policies*, C/70–4, Cambridge, Mass., 1970.

Kemp, G.: *Some Relationships Between US Military Training in Latin America and Weapons Acquisition Patterns: 1959–1969*, C/70–5, Cambridge, Mass., 1970.

Hoagland, J. H.: *World Combat Aircraft Inventories and Production: 1970–1975. Implications for Arms Transfer Policies*, C/70–6, Cambridge, Mass., 1970.

Swedish Government publications:

Statens Offentliga Utredningar: SOU 1970:63, Handelsdepartementet, *Svensk krigsmaterielexport*, Stockholm, 1970.

Swiss Government publications:

Bericht der Expertenkommission an den Bundesrat über die Schweizerische Kriegsmaterialausfuhr (Motion Renschler), November, 1969.

UK Government publications:

Sale of Military Equipment Abroad, Second Report from the Select Committee on Estimates, session 1958-9.

The Simonstown Agreements: Britain's defence and the sale of arms to South Africa, London, September, 1970.

US Government publications:

Senate Foreign Relations Committee
Amending the Foreign Military Sales Act, Report by Mr Fulbright from the Committee on Foreign Relations, US Senate, 91st Congress, 2nd Session, 12 May 1970.
Arms Sales and Foreign Policy, Staff Study Prepared for the Use of the Committee on Foreign Relations, US Senate, 90th Congress, 25 January 1967.
Arms Sales to Near East and South Asian Countries, Hearings before the Subcommittee on Near Eastern and South Asian Affairs, Committee on Foreign Relations, US Senate, 90th Congress, 1st Session, March, April, June 1967.
Foreign Military Sales Act Amendment: 1970, 1971, Hearings before the Committee on Foreign Relations, US Senate, 91st Congress, 2nd Session, 24 March and 11 May 1970.

House Foreign Affairs Committee
Aircraft Sales in Latin America, Hearings before the Subcommittee on Inter-American Affairs of the Committee on Foreign Affairs, House of Representatives, 91st Congress, 2nd Session, 29 and 30 April 1970.
Amending the Foreign Military Sales Act, Report of the Committee on Foreign Affairs, House of Representatives, 91st Congress, 2nd Session, 5 March 1970.
Export–Import Bank and Credit Sales of Defense Articles, Hearings before the Committee on Banking and Currency, House of Representatives, 90th Congress, 1st Session, 17 July 1967.
The Foreign Military Sales Act, Hearings before the Committee on Foreign Affairs, House of Representatives, 90th Congress, 2nd Session, 26, 27 June 1968.
The Foreign Military Sales Act, Report of the Committee on Foreign Affairs, House of Representatives, 90th Congress, 2nd Session, 3 July 1968.
To Amend the Foreign Military Sales Act, Hearings before the Committee on Foreign Affairs, House of Representatives, 91st Congress, 2nd Session, 5 and 17 February 1970.

Other

Composite Report of the President's Committee to study the United States Military Assistance Program (Draper Report), Washington, 1959.

REFERENCE WORKS ON ARMS AND ARMED FORCES

Aviation Advisory Services, Ltd: *International Airforces and Military Aircraft Directory*, Essex, England, periodical.

Booth, R.: *The Armed Forces of African States 1970*, Adelphi Paper No. 67, London, 1970.

Coward, H. R.: *Military Technology in Developing Countries*, CIS/MIT, Cambridge, Mass., 1964.

Green, W., and Fricker, J.: *The Air Forces of the World*, London, 1958.

Green, W.: *The Observer's World Aircraft Directory*, London, 1961.

Green, W.: *The World's Fighting Planes*, London, 1965.

Institute for Strategic Studies: *The Military Balance*, London, annual.

Jane's All the World's Aircraft, London, annual.

Jane's Fighting Ships, London, annual.

Jane's Weapon Systems, London, 1970.

Military and Police Forces in the Republic of South Africa, UN Publication, New York, 1967.

Moyer, F. A.: *Special Forces Foreign Weapons Handbook*, Boulder, Col., 1970.

SIPRI Yearbook of World Armaments and Disarmament 1968/69 and 1969/70, Stockholm, annual.

World Armaments and Disarmament, SIPRI Yearbook 1972, 1973 and 1974, Stockholm, annual.

Taylor, J. W. R.: *Combat Aircraft of the World*, London, 1969.

Wood, David: *The Armed Forces of African States*, Adelphi Paper No. 27, London, 1966.

Wood, David: *The Armed Forces in Central and South America*, Adelphi Paper No. 34, London, 1967.

THE POLITICAL AND SOCIAL ROLE OF THE ARMED FORCES

Van Doorn, Jacques, ed.: *Armed Forces and Society*, The Hague, 1968.

Van Doorn, Jacques, ed.: *Military Profession and Military Regimes*, The Hague, 1969.

Hanning, H.: *The Peaceful Uses of Military Forces*, New York, 1967.
Hurewitz, J. C.: *Middle East Politics: The Military Dimension*, London, 1969.
Johnson, John J., ed.: *The Role of the Military in Underdeveloped Countries*, Princeton, 1962.
Lieuwen, Edwin: *Arms and Politics in Latin America*, New York, 1961.

THE ECONOMICS OF ARMS PRODUCTION

Asher, Harold: *Cost–Quantity Relationships in the Aircraft Industry*, Rand R-291, Santa Monica, 1956.
Baldwin, W.: *The Structure of the Defense Market, 1955–64*, Durham, N.C., 1967.
Harlow, C. J. E.: *The European Armaments Base: A Survey*, Part 1: Economic Aspects of Defence Procurement; Part 2: National Procurement Policies, ISS, London, 1967.
Melman, Seymour, ed.: *The Defense Economy, Conversion of Industries and Occupations to Civilian Needs*, New York, 1970.
Society of British Aerospace Industries: *Into the Seventies, A Future Plan for Britain's Aerospace Industry*, London, 1969.
Union Syndicale des Industries Aéronautiques: *L'Industrie aéronautique et spatiale, 1967–68, Rapport du bureau*, Paris, 11 July 1968.
Worcester, Richard: *Roots of British Air Policy*, London, 1966.

UK Government publications:

Report of the Committee of Inquiry of Aviation under the Chairmanship of Lord Plowden 1964–65: Presented to Parliament by the Ministry of Aviation, London, December 1965.

INTER-WAR PERIOD

Chamberlain, Joseph P.: 'The Embargo Resolutions and Neutrality: Text of the Resolutions, the Treaty of St Germain and the Trade in Arms Convention', *International Conciliation* (Carnegie Endowment for International Peace), No. 251, June 1929.
Drexel, Constance: 'Armament Manufacture and Trade', *International Conciliation*, No. 295, December 1933.

Engelbrecht, Helmuth Carol, and Hanighen, Frank Cleary: *Merchants of Death. A Study of the International Armament Industry*, London, 1934.

Morgan, Laura P.: 'Armaments and Measures of Enforcement', in *World Organization, A Balance Sheet of the First Great Experiment*, American Council on Public Affairs, Washington, D.C., 1942.

Noel-Baker, P.: *Disarmament*, London, 1926.

Noel-Baker, P.: *The Private Manufacture of Armaments*, London, 1936.

Royal Institute of International Affairs, *Survey of International Affairs, 1920–1935*, London, annual.

Sloutzki, N. M.: *The World Armament Race, 1919–1939*, Geneva Research Center, Geneva Studies, Vol. 12, No. 1, July 1941.

White, Freda: *Traffic in Arms*, League of Nations Union, Fourth Edition, London, April 1934.

GENERAL BACKGROUND MATERIAL

Ambekar G. V., and Divekar, V. D., eds.: *Documents on China's Relations with South and South East Asia 1949–1962*, London, 1964.

Angola Committee: *Portugal and NATO*, Amsterdam, 1969.

Armbruster, Frank E.: *China Briefing*, Chicago, 1968.

Ballantine, Joseph W.: *Formosa, A Problem for United States Foreign Policy*, Brookings Institution, Washington, 1952.

Barber, William F., and Ronning, C. Neale: *Internal Security and Military Power. Counterinsurgency and Civic Action in Latin America*, Ohio, 1966.

Barnet, R. J.: *Intervention and Revolution*, New York, 1968.

Barnett, A. Doak: *Communist China and Asia, Challenge to American Policy*, New York, 1968.

Bloomfield, L. P., and Leiss, A. C.: *The Control of Local Conflict*, CIS/MIT, Cambridge, Mass., 1967.

Browne and Shaw International Studies Division, *The Control of Local Conflict: Case Studies*, prepared for US ACDA 'Far Eastern Case Studies', Massachusetts, 1969.

Brown, William Adams, Jr, and Opie, Redvers: *American Foreign Assistance*, Brookings Institution, Washington, 1953.

Buchan, A., ed.: *China and the Peace of Asia* (Studies in International Security, No. 9), London, 1965.

Burnett, B. G., and Johnson, K. F.: *Political Forces in Latin America*, Belmont, Calif., 1968.

Butwell, R.: *South East Asia Today and Tomorrow*, London, 1969.

Clubb, O. E., Jr: *The US and the Sino-Soviet Bloc in South East Asia*, Washington, 1962.

Cooley, J. K.: *East Wind Over Africa*, New York, 1965.

Copeland, Miles: *The Game of Nations*, London, 1969.

Dallin, David J.: *Soviet Foreign Policy after Stalin*, Philadelphia, 1961.

Dasgupta, J. B.: *Indo-Pakistan Relations 1947–1955*, Amsterdam, 1958.

Emerson, R.: *Africa and US Policy*, Englewood Cliffs, N.J., 1967.

Fall, Bernard B.: *The Two Viet-Nams*, London, 1963.

Fifield, Russel H.: *South East Asia in US Policy*, New York, 1963.

Gerassi, J.: *The Great Fear: The Reconquest of Latin America by Latin Americans*, London, 1967.

Halperin, M.: *China and the Bomb*, London, 1965.

Halperin, M., ed.: *Sino-Soviet Relations and Arms Control*, Massachusetts, 1967.

Hamrell, Sven, and Widstrand, Carl Gösta: *The Soviet Bloc, China and Africa*, Uppsala, 1964.

Himmelstrand, U.: *Världen, Nigeria och Biafra*, Stockholm, 1969.

Hinton, H.: *Communist China in World Politics*, Boston, 1966.

Horowitz, D.: *From Yalta to Vietnam, American Foreign Policy in the Cold War*, Harmondsworth, 1967.

Howard, Michael, and Hunter, Robert: *Israel and the Arab World: The Crisis of 1967*, Adelphi Paper No. 41, London, 1967.

Hsieh, Alice: *Communist China's Military Policies, Doctrine and Strategy*, Rand P-3960, Santa Monica, 1968.

Jordan, Amos A., Jr: *Foreign Aid and the Defense of Southeast Asia*, New York, 1962.

Kahin, G. M.: *The Asian–African Conference, Bandung 1955*, Cornell, 1956.

Kahin, G. M., ed.: *Governments and Politics of Southeast Asia*, Ithaca, N.Y., 1959.

Kahin, G. M., and Lewis, J. W.: *The United States in Vietnam*, New York, 1967.

Kavic, Lorne: *India's Quest for Security*, Berkeley, 1967.

Kemp, Geoffrey: *Arms and Security: The Egypt–Israel Case*, Adelphi Paper No. 52, London, 1968.

Kennedy, D. E.: *The Security of Southern Asia*, London, 1968.

Khan, Ayub: *Friends not Masters*, Lahore, 1967.

Kitchen, Helen, ed.: *A Handbook of African Affairs*, New York, 1964.

Lacouture, Jean: *Ho Chi-Minh*, Stockholm, 1969 (Penguin Books, 1969).

Lacouture, Jean: *Vietnam between Two Truces*, New York, 1966.

La Feber, Walter: *America, Russia, and the Cold War, 1945–1966*, New York, 1967.

Laqueur, Walter Z.: *The Soviet Union and the Middle East*, London, 1959.

Larkin, Bruce D.: *China and Africa, 1949–1970*, University of California Press, 1971.

Lefever, Ernest W., and Joshua W.: *United Nations Peacekeeping in the Congo 1960–64*, Brookings Institution, ACDA RS/63, Washington, 1966.

Loftus, Joseph E.: *Latin American Defense Expenditures, 1938–1965*, Rand RM-5310, Santa Monica, 1968.

Lusignan, Guy de: *French-Speaking Africa since Independence*, London, 1969.

McKay, Vernon: *Africa in World Politics*, New York, 1963.

McLane, Charles B.: *Soviet Strategies in Southeast Asia, An Exploration of Eastern Policy under Lenin and Stalin*, Princeton, 1966.

McNamara, Robert: *The Essence of Security – Reflections in Office*, London, 1968.

Menges, C.: *Military Aspects of International Relations in Developing Areas*, Rand P-3480, Santa Monica.

Mozingo, David: *Sino-Indonesian Relations 1955–1965*, Rand Memorandum, Santa Monica, 1965.

Myrdal, Gunnar: *Asian Drama*, New York, 1968 (Penguin Books, 1968).

Nielsen, W. A.: *The Great Powers and Africa*, London, 1969.

Nkrumah, K.: *Ghana*, London, 1959.

Nkrumah, K.: *Africa Must Unite*, London, 1963.

Nutting, Anthony: *No End of a Lesson – The Story of Suez*, London, 1967.

Odinga, Oginga: *Not Yet Uhuru*, London, 1967.

Polk, William R.: *The United States and the Arab World*, Cambridge, Mass., 1965.

Purcell, Victor: *The Chinese in South East Asia*, London, 1965.

Rivkin, Arnold: *Africa and the West*, New York, 1962.

Snow, Edgar: *Red Star over China*, New York, 1961 (Penguin Books, 1970).

Stanley, John, and Pearton, Maurice: *The International Trade in Arms,* Chatto and Windus, for the International Institute for Strategic Studies, 1972.

Tang Tsou, ed.: *China in Crisis,* Vols. I and II, Chicago, 1968.

Thompson, W. Scott: *Ghana's Foreign Policy 1957–1966,* Princeton, 1969.

Varga, E.: *Fundamental Problems of the Economics and Politics of Imperialism,* Moscow, 1953.

Whiting, A.: *China Crosses the Yalu,* New York, 1960.

Wolf, Charles, Jr: *Foreign Aid: Theory and Practice in Southern Asia,* Princeton, 1960.

US Government publications:

Senate Foreign Relations Committee
Background Information relating to Southeast Asia and Vietnam, Committee on Foreign Relations, US Senate, 89th Congress, 1st Session, 14 January 1965.

Foreign Assistance Act of 1968, Hearings before the Committee on Foreign Relations, 90th Congress, 2nd Session, 13, 14 March, 14, 17 May 1968.

Foreign Assistance Act of 1968, Report of the Committee on Foreign Relations, US Senate, 90th Congress, 2nd Session, 26 July 1968.

Foreign Assistance Act of 1969, Hearings before the Committee on Foreign Relations, US Senate, 91st Congress, 1st Session, 14, 15, 18 July and 6 August 1969.

Foreign Assistance Act of 1969, Report by Mr Mansfield (for Mr Fulbright) from the Committee on Foreign Relations, US Senate, 91st Congress, 1st Session, 10 December 1969.

Mutual Security Act of 1951, Hearings before the Senate Committee on Foreign Relations and the Committee on Armed Forces, US Senate, 82nd Congress, 1st Session, July and August 1951.

Supplemental Foreign Assistance Authorization, 1970, Hearings before the Committee on Foreign Relations, US Senate, 91st Congress, 2nd Session, 10, 11 December 1970.

United States Military Policies and Programs in Latin America, Hearings before the Subcommittee on Western Hemisphere Affairs of the Committee on Foreign Relations, US Senate, 91st Congress, 1st Session, 24 June and 8 July 1969.

United States Security Agreements and Commitments Abroad, Hearings before the Subcommittee on US Security Agreements and Commitments Abroad of the Committee on Foreign Relations, US Senate, 91st Congress, Vol. 1, parts 1–4, and Vol. 2, parts 7–9.

House Foreign Affairs Committee:

The Continuing Near East Crisis, Background information prepared for the Subcommittee on the Near East of the Committee on Foreign Affairs, House of Representatives, 91st Congress, 1st Session, 10 January 1969.

Report of the Special Study Mission to South and Southeast Asia, By Hon. Robert Taft, Jr, Ohio, Committee on Foreign Affairs, House of Representatives, 90th Congress, 1st Session, 5 May 1969.

US Overseas Loans and Grants and Assistance from International Organizations, Obligations and Loan Authorizations, 1 July 1945–30 June 1966, 1 July 1945–30 June 1967, and 1 July 1945–30 June 1968, Special reports prepared for the House Foreign Affairs Committee by AID.

Other:

The Battle Act Report, 1966, Mutual Defense Assistance Control Act of 1951, Nineteenth Report to Congress, Department of State, January 1967.

Report to the President of the United States from the Committee to Strengthen the Security of the Free World – The Scope and Distribution of US Military and Economic Assistance Programs (Clay Committee), 20 March 1963.

US Foreign Assistance in the 1970s: A New Approach, Report to the President from the Task Force on International Development, Washington, 1970.

United States Foreign Policy for the 1970s, A New Strategy for Peace, A report by President Richard Nixon to the Congress, 18 February 1970.

Index

342 *Index*

Dominican Republic, military
coups, 70, 263; National
Guard tanks, 264; domestic
defence production, 282,
283–4
Douglas-Home, Sir Alec, and
arms for S. Africa, 120, 121
Draper Report (Military
Assistance Program), 55,
56 n; and Battle Act, 65; and
civic action, 69; supplemented
by transfer of weapons, 72,
76; US anti-submarine
programme, 60, 215, 271
Dutch, the, and Indonesia, 175–7

East Africa, 1964 mutinies, 233
Ecuador, 259; army/air force
conflict, 263; military coups,
263; purchase of sophisticated
weapons, 278–9
Edwards, Sir George, 111
Egypt, 92; industrial and
technical resources, 40; arms
agreement with
Czechoslovakia, 51, 90,
104, 135, 211–12; Suez crisis,
66, 90, 104–5, 203, 211–12;
Aswan Dam negotiations, 66;
US freezes her dollar assets,
66; USSR economic
investment, 78; arms supply,
92, 98, 211–12, 214, 219;
military advisers, 93; strained
relations, 213–14; nationalism,
89, 203, 210; UK arms supply,
101, 104, 211; alliance and
occupation, 203; policy
towards Jordan, 104;
Suez–Sinai conflict, 135, 217;

and Poland, 176; pattern of
arms supply, 201, 209;
armed forces and
independence, 203; Waf'd
government, 210; circumvents
arms ban, 210–11; US policy
(military assistance), 211, 213,
215; domestic defence
industry, 213–14, 282, 283,
285–8 *passim*, 291, 293;
post-June War, 216–17;
USSR Treaty of Friendship
(1971), 217–18; expulsion of
her personnel, 219–20, 229;
aid for Morocco, 225; for
Africa, 239; role of foreign
scientists, 290–91; over-
ambitious projects, 290–91
Egyptian Communist Party, 213
Eisenhower administration, 62;
Doctrine on Middle East
policy, 66–7, 208; terms, 212
ELF (Eritrean Liberation
Front), 99
ENDC (Eighteen-Nation
Disarmament Committee),
303, 304
Eritrea, Eritrean Liberation
Front (ELF), 99; US
communications base, 245
Ethiopia, 230, 239; US military
assistance, 67, 68, 235, 244,
245; UK, 245; Chinese aid
to revolutionary
movements, 143; attempted
coup (1960), 234; receipt of
major weapons, 235, 244;
border clashes, 242, 244;
sources of aid, 244–5;
Italian invasion, 244–5